MIND AND IDEOLOGY

MIND AND IDEOLOGY

Sumner MacLean

GYAN PUBLISHING HOUSE
NEW DELHI-110002

Printed in India

Cataloging in Publication Data
MacLean, Sumner, 1932-
Mind and Ideology: The Brain and its Cultural Shaping /
Sumner MacLean
First Edition

New Delhi: Gyan Publishing House, 2009
376 p.
Includes bibliography and index (p. 357-375)

ISBN: 81-212-0969-2

LC Class. B823.3
Dewey 320.5 19
Ideology-History
Religion and Politics
Totalitarianism-History
Philosophical Anthropology-History
Psychological Anthropology

CONTENTS

FOREWORD

This book is intended for those who seek to understand the world we live in. Many disciplines were drawn upon to provide, in a single volume, an appreciation of aspects of man's psychology and the circumstance that lead to extraordinary political organization and, often, to terrorism.

The facts and views are very concisely presented. The reader or the instructor is thus able to form his own interpretation or explanation of events. The book reflects many years of study and some active personal experience.

An extensive selected bibliography is supplied to guide the reader to important works. An index facilitates reference and research. It is a book that may be used to supplement many different academic courses, but it is a book for the general concerned reader.

The author has enjoyed the search that led to the present work and hopes that the reader may find it meets a need.

1

THE NATURE OF MAN

Can man know mankind? Does it require the perspective of a more omniscient being to adequately see the nature of man and his history? Although our individual and collective perception may be flawed, we must still make the effort to objectively assess ourselves. This will require rising above our conditioning.

There is wide variability in individual worldviews. What constitutes reality is a matter of personal psychology. Each person sees that world differently. Great effort (and much blood) has been expended to try and have all men see the world in the same way. Let us here try to do the impossible- to keep an open mind.

Ideology is mentally necessary. With little success or agreement, philosophers have tried to explain the place of man in the universe. Psychology emerged from philosophy with scientific pretensions, but psychologists have not been much more successful than the philosophers. Historians have shown us the wide extremes to which men have adapted. For their adaptations, they have developed mythical explanations. These explanations take the form of general symbols structured to explain reality and to guide action, of ideology.

In studying remote enclaves, ethnologists have shown the variety of worldviews and cultures that exist among men. Physiologists have begun to show us how man's mental structure differs from that of other primates, lending support to the notion that human mental structure is especially constructed to foster ideology.

Worldviews cycle with time. In five thousand years, Chinese views of man and the government he needs have alternated about these basic issues: was man good or evil, selfish or altruistic; was there a universe of change or of stasis; was there teleological progress or circularity; was truth transcendent or was it immanent; did reality reside in the mystical or in the physical; should one follow a leader or follow a ruling principle? The social prescription for man would change with the assumptions, and the assumptions changed with the circumstances.

How much is constant in human nature? "Human nature" has been equated with a "psychic unity of mankind". Is this human nature universal, typical, or only frequent? Is it constant or changing? Does "nature" refer to limbics, or to more abstract attitudes? Looking at the extremes to which particular cultures, such as the Incas and the Aztecs, have pushed human nature, what constitutes "human nature" is shown to be a very broad category ?

Concentration camp experience: Bettleheim (1943) has shown that, after three years, the camp becomes the universe and the inmates begin to identify with the guards. This illustrates both the tolerance of humans for extreme situations and the ability of circumstantial factors to override or determine what might be considered "normal" in human nature.

Idols of the Mind: "Four species of human idols beset the human mind, to which we have assigned names, calling the first, the idols of the tribe; the second, the idols of the den; the third, idols of the market; the fourth, idols of the theater. The idols of the tribe are inherent in human nature. All the perceptions, both of the senses and of the mind, bear reference to man and not to the universe." Francis Bacon, *Novum Organum*, 1620. Each individual, in his den, has his personal imaginings. Today, group thinking reflects the momentary values of the marketplace. Bacon noted that the same word meant different things to different men in their dealings. Constructed ideologies convey a theatrical reality with symbols that are both evocative and vague.

There is "objective reality"; a "symbolic world" presented by the media; and a "subjective" reality as we interpret the world about us. As we sit for long hours before a television screen absorbing highly processed views, the "symbolic world" may become more real to us than any other.

Perception is hypothesis driven (Postman, 1948). An individual, shown ambiguous stimuli, will pose answers according to the imagination resulting from his mental circuitry. Religious myths are examples of such solutions.

Neocortical organization and related functions are influenced by both genetics and experience. Genetic influence is most evident in the prenatal stage and experience is most influential while the organism is postnatally developing. Individual differences in human brain volume show strong genetic influence (P. M. Thompson et al. 2001, Posthuma 2003, Wilke 2003).

Maguire (2000, 2003) found that hippocampal volume increased with time spent as a taxi driver. Contrariwise, those raised in impoverished environments have smaller brains. Genetic constraints and plasticity both exist (Rutter 1999, Pfefferbaum 2004). Plasticity is pronounced until sexual maturity (Wexler, 2006). It is the frontal lobes that are most particularly subject to environmental modification, and these are concerned especially with planning, inhibition and language acquisition. Later, the adolescent will start modifying his environment, rather than being exclusively molded by it.

Differences between men and women in attitude and behavior are influenced by evolutionary history, cultural norms, and individual experience. Speculation, and examination of present day hunter-gatherers suggest that large animal hunting and farther ranging have been male occupations, whereas females do fine handwork and gathering closer to home. Individual experience does effect changes within the brain (Greenough, Black & Wallace, 1987; Quinn, PC, 2006). Such changes are effected by genes and some such genes should be inheritable. Cultural norms appear to be, in part, a response to biological requirements.

Between the sexes, there are certain structural differences within the brain. Brain circuitry enables males to test better at mental spatial rotation, throwing, and mathematical reasoning. Females have better finger dexterity, better verbal memory, and can better locate objects within an array despite interference (Stroop test). Males are very evident at the higher end of mathematical aptitude. Sex hormone levels continually influence behavior and early exposure to sex hormones has a permanent effect on behavior (Kimura, 2004).

In intelligence, men have a three to five point advantage over women in IQ, according to a meta analysis by Irwing & Lynn (2005). A sample of about five hundred is required to detect such a small difference. A five point difference would suggest that three times as many men as women have IQs over 145 and that five times as many men have IQs over 155. However, only about twice as many men test at the level of around 130, and this level is deemed very adequate. Practically, this small difference is thought to be important only in high-end research.

The associative areas in man's brain have grown through past eras. The general growth of the neocortex during the latter Pleistocene was concurrent with the development of social living (d'Aquili, 1972).

Social living may be the determining factor in the development of higher cortical functions. The neocortex volume varies with species sociability. Recent research has identified "mirror neurons" in different species that fire when observing an action performed by others and also when the observer performs the action. There is speculation that these neurons are related to communication and social living.

We are approaching a more physiological description of "mind". Imaging techniques, such as positive emission tomography, magnetic resonance and voxel-based morphometry, have enabled researchers to localize feelings like music appreciation, etc. Gerhard Roth has used these techniques to claim a more important role for the limbic system in moral decisions. Through statistical averaging, the typical patterns in and among individuals can be determined.

Primates show the understanding of emotional situations, but have difficulty forming abstractions. The intelligence of communication is inversely proportional to the determinacy of the signal, and the signals of the lower primates seem to be more programmed, rather than being thought out. What is currently called the "Theory of Mind" refers to the ability to infer the intentions, beliefs and emotions of others. Certainly, primates and even squirrels have this and even exhibit what is called "tactical deception", acting to deceive others.

Association of ideas and abstraction take place in the inferior parietal lobule on the dominant side. It is an association of association areas, permitting transfer of information independently of the limbic system. The ape has a less developed parietal lobule, so it is only man who is known to have such extensive equipment for *association and abstraction-the symbolic basis necessary to ideology*.

There is a "causal operator" that allows man to imagine a "cause" where none can be logically inferred from the senses. This allows man to form ideologies that contradict the perceptions of his physical senses. D'Aquili and Newberg (1998) suggest that the inferior parietal lobule and the anterior convexity of the frontal lobes on the dominant side supply the causal explanation for realities perceived by the senses. One may thus claim a physiological basis for myths and religious explanations. "God", for example, can be postulated as a cause for everything.

A simple and closed system is needed. Man must try to make sense of his world, and he will do so with whatever explanations he can develop or imagine. Depending on his experience and sophistication, the explanations he uses may range from animism to science. In the religious domain, the "causal operator" will supply anthropomorphic beings because they are easy to imagine and manipulate, corresponding to the organization of power in his society. Thus do we get two-legged gods.

Left and right brain functions differ. In general, the left brain is associated with verbal and logical reasoning, while the right brain seems more concerned with overall emotional and artistic perceptions. It has been argued, for example, that much of the Nazi appeal was directed toward the right brain of Germans. Experiments have now established that the right brain dominates in the response to symbols.

The cognitive imperative welcomes fundamentalism: Man yearns for a simple and closed intellectual system that will explain the world and offer him the hope of being able to cope with it. This aspect of human nature is a fundamental factor in ideologies. It is also fundamental in man's attempts to explain his own nature. Fundamentalism offers simple and exclusive binary truths to respond to this human need and responds to the cognitive imperative.

If man does not order and classify information to make sense of his world, he suffers great anxiety. Thus, he is motivated to understand the world and his place in it. This desire to introduce order is part of what may be called the "cognitive imperative". Through the "causal operator", if an explanation is not proffered, man will imagine it.

If the "causal operator" relates objects irrationally, it is called "magic". Man is aware that he will die. This is a source of existential anxiety and the subject of demand and mythic attempts at explanation and consolation. Western religions postulate the intervention of personalized movers (gods) who are often called upon to perform magic to assuage such anxieties. A political leader can appear to serve this function of a god and his ideology can offer the mythical and magical explanations seeking to relieve angst and satisfy other needs.

Men often grow fond of what is familiar. Habit, custom and affect are thus linked in the human psyche. Combined with these factors, man wants to classify and introduce order. Myth, ritual and ideology in general can thus be seen as responding to the biological and psychological needs of man. "Mind" may attempt to order external reality in terms of a culturally imposed symbol system that sets the framework. The real situation will be described so as to fit the ideology.

Personality is also the organization of needs: Personality is primarily evidenced by the organization of needs, drives, wishes and emotional impulses. Needs and drives could be fundamental, but it is difficult to adequately identify them or to rank them in importance. Can psychic needs be ranked in order of importance? Could society be reorganized according to such ranking? Can such order be imposed on an individual? Totalitarian systems seem to act as though man and society can be so molded, creating a "new man".

Eating comes before principles. Abraham Maslow speculated concerning the "why" of behavior and suggested that lower needs (physical, safety, sex, and esteem) had to be satisfied before people's basically good nature would allow them to behave as middle-class liberals told them they should.

Behaviorists see plastic men. Does human psychology favor a closed system? Behaviorist psychology sees human machines operating to maximize "adjustment", "adaptation", and "conformity". Such criteria are used to evaluate public school students. Montesquieu observed that a person could easily assume the nature that society assigns to him. Would this represent deformation or elasticity? Are we all "plastic men"?

Goals require desire, so those who set goals want to control desires. The stimuli that cause desire are most important to those who would build a "new man". If environment determines desire, one could thereby justify the closed society, censorship, and other techniques that would tend to control the total person. Catalogs, television and advertising display a different, tempting, and often unreal world to those living in a less fortunate society. Closing out such uncontrolled influences is better for order.

Idols are symbols arranged to form concepts in minds. "The idols of the den are those of each individual, for everybody (in addition to the errors common to the race of man) has his own den or cavern which intercepts and corrupts the light of nature, either from his disposition, or from his education and intercourse with others... so that the spirit of man is variable, confused, and, as it were, actuated by chance... man searches for knowledge in lesser worlds, and not in the greater or common world," said Francis Bacon.

Expansion disturbs order and may make fitting in new items problematic. New items are accepted only when they can be fitted within an ordered worldview. Curiosity causes us to seek variety, but, to reduce mental tension, we also seek order. Censorship and a structured society would therefore appear psychologically desirable in balancing human desires of variety and of order. However, accepting a new ideology as a complete package will meet the need for an ordered worldview- and save much mental effort.

Behaviorism is the environmental association of ideas. How much do habit and environment form cognition? Does "mind" essentially result from repeated exposure to sequences of simple elements? Association of ideas would then become the main explanation of man's mental processes. Such repetition and joining of ideas and events can become fixed as "*engrams*" and integrated. Behaviorism would then explain man's psychology. Free will would not thus be recognized. This would also mean that man is formed by his environment (perspectivism).

"Free will": how much does the universal order constrain man and what does "freedom" mean? Man is constrained (1) by the physical structure of his individual brain (2) by his upbringing (3) by his present environment- social, financial, physical, and cultural. Within such constraints, freedom of action and thought is usually quite limited and much would seem "predestined". If one wants to act and has the unconstrained power to act, then he can exercise free will. In the real world, most people do not exercise much "free will".

Fantasy, myth and ritual are similar constructions. In trying to make sense of things, words and symbols may be loosely joined to seek explanations or causes. The resulting mental integrations need have no real connection to logic or to facts. Wild constructions might be called fantasies. With repetition, the more restrained developments can become myth and ritual.

Epistemologically, does man have a "mind" at all? Is there an essential difference between mind and body, or is it all a matter of neuron connections? Can the principles of physical science be applied to the immaterial? Is psychology, viewed as a subset of philosophy, an appropriate organon? Are psychological schema so flexible as to yield contrary results when applied to the same data? Such epistemological caveats must inform us as we gingerly deal with the matter of "mind".

Patterns of experience influence neocortical connections. Thus, life experience is reflected in the structure of the brain. The connection patterns are changed, some being activated and others becoming inert. The emotional experiences of the child influence how he sees the world as an adult, as do his other life experiences and the reactions he observes in others around him.

The neural networks within the brain are so diffuse that deterministic models of "mind" become problematic. When a schizophrenic "hears" voices that are not there, he is getting physical signals from within his brain, rather than through his ears. It is arguable that reality for each person is determined by the connection of cells within his brain. Long before we knew anything about neurons, Lu Hsiang-shan (d. 1193) said: "the universe is my mind and my mind is the universe".

Man's social capacity increases his power. As an animal, man has biologically determined needs for food, for sex, and, perhaps, for aggression. With his advanced cerebral cortex, he has a neurological need for more stimulation and response (Berelson, 1964). As with other animals, the social instinct enables him to extend his capacities. The extended capacity of social man also helps to extend his genes.

Can the limbic predator become the social man? Whereas once man had to respond to predators and to the physical world, today his interactions are largely social. Successful social adjustment will thus be genetically favored, but at what rate? And, will that rate be sufficient to overcome the increasing technological capacity for destruction, considering his atavistic aggression?

Man is both a subjective individual and a group member. Westerners pretend that the mind of man can be objectively analyzed. East Indians, on the other hand, tend to see mental processes as hopelessly subjective. The uniqueness of each individual makes it difficult to speak of the nature of man in general. There may be a duality of opposites within each person, the expressed and the repressed. There is also the dual identity of man as an isolated individual and man as a member of a communicating species. What, then, is implied when we speak of man's nature?

Man is inconsistent and changeable. There is great inconsistency in man, even within the same individual. Love and hate, for example, can co-exist within the same person. So, also, can altruism and selfishness, firmness and vacillation, the animal and the transcendental, the conscious and the unconscious co-exist. The same man will want the comfort of routine and wish for the stimulation of variety. Can these inconsistent dualities alternately be manifest?

Social moods of carnival and atonement may alternate. When one psychic need has been satisfied with a particular social approach, some competing need has been repressed. That repressed need will be satisfied by the succeeding dominant social philosophy. The desire to exercise freedom, for example, may be supplanted by the desire for social security. Values among succeeding generations of university students seem to come in and out of fashion in this manner.

Psychic ambivalence is manifest through time. The psychic nature of man is inconsistent. His desires often conflict. They change with his mood and with the times. People desire both spontaneity and order, they want rules and they want freedom, they want order and they want fantasy. This mind of man that we seek to describe is an unruly thing.

Some psychological categories also show the dualities of human nature: the hysteric wants constant change, but likes security and stability; the compulsive is said to seek order while being fascinated by movement; the schizoid seeks to isolate himself and yet desires intimacy; the depressive wants both unity and transcendence.

The utopian ideal must change with the times. How, then, could one design a utopia best suited to the nature of man, when there is so much change, both within the individual and in his circumstances? Perhaps a utopia should not be static, but should give alternate expression to dominant and repressed aspects of the personality.

Man wants to realize his different selves. Huizinga saw man as having three essential aspects: *homo faber*, the artisan or maker of things; *homo ludens*, the playful creature; and *homo sapiens*, the thinking being. The same person took on these different aspects at different times. There is also the desire for "self- realization". Some claim that the latter is important in the desire for religion.

Can a "new man" be fashioned? Does being "good" consist in doing what one ought to do, or, within limits, what one wants to do? The bipolar nature of man admits of both good and evil, in varying degrees at different times. Whether externally coerced or with internalized standards, is he to conform to the "new man" or to his own nature? Modern totalitarians are more concerned with changing human nature than with changing the external world. Experience, however, indicates that the nature of man has not changed. This clash of ideology with experience portends tension for our world.

Is man still limbic? Through time, man's view of himself has been reflected in primitive legends, in myths, in theological dogma, in systematic philosophy and in efforts at scientific psychology. Has man changed? Historical writings available to us do not reflect it. Man's motivations rest, in part, on limbic response. This uncomfortable reality must be borne in mind when we consider ideologies and collective political organisms. Genetically, we are probably constituted for a hunter-gatherer type of life, yet we know we must adapt to civilized social life.

If men were hunter-gatherers for several million years, then present-day humans could be the result of natural selection for hunter-gatherer responses. More widely appreciated is the approach of behavioral primatology that compares the brain function genes of non-human primates with the human.

Various feelings function as motivations for action. Among them are fear and sentiments of angst, insecurity, agitation, anomie, alienation, isolation, dependency, need for affect, etc. Aggression and passion are also feelings. Of course, people can manifest these feelings in different degrees at different times. People also want to have a sense of purpose, of importance and identity, and a sense of community. A certain amount of altruism is also part of man. The imaginary world of ideology must accommodate these feelings and needs.

The nature vs. nurture controversy continues. Whatever the nature of man, how much of that nature is inherited? Ferocious ideological controversy breaks out at this point, for we have broached the "nature vs. nurture" question. Immense ideological structures have been erected on the dogmatic assertion that man is perfectible through conditioning. The dogma that the nature of man is determined by his environment is fiercely adhered to by many who call themselves liberals, and by totalitarians-who would make a "new man" to populate their new social orders. Conservatives, generally, do not cherish the illusion that man is perfectible, no matter what the environment.

Science has not yet come to the rescue in the nature vs. nurture argument. In 1935, Shuttleworth attributed 75% of intelligence to heredity. Work done with identical (monozygotic) human twins who were reared apart indicates that gestures and, perhaps, occupational aptitudes, are inherited. In early tests, the intelligence quotients of such twins showed a 0.78 correlation, those reared together showing a 0.85 correlation. The correlation with parents and with siblings is around 0.55. More recent studies continue to show that over fifty percent of intelligence is due to genetics, some studies showing as high as seventy five percent (Segal, 1999).

What is intelligence? Gardner thought we should differently quantify logical-mathematical, linguistic, spatial, musical, personal and sport-type intelligences. Some say that intelligence should be measured by the ability to solve new and different problems. This is also called "Fluid intelligence". Cattell's *Culture Fair* test asks one to pick out an incongruent picture among four, and is often used to measure such problem solving ability. Colon et al. relate various measures of intelligence to gray matter volume and find them all correlated (*Neuroimage* 31:1359 2006).

Man's brain and his intelligence probably evolved in response to his environment. (Some argue that embryonic development recapitulates this evolution). During the Pleistocene era, evolutionary development is thought to have caused those parts of the brain used for solving specialized problems to become larger. Thus, much of the large whale brain is used for sonar, etc. Such specialized development could suggest a determining role for the anterior cingulated cortex and other frontal areas of the brain in human problem solving (fluid intelligence).

Environment can alter inherited mental tendencies. In the twenty years separating J. P. Rushton (1984) and J. J. Hudziac (2004), researchers have remained fairly constant in estimating the genetic effect at something over fifty percent and the specific environmental effect as somewhat less. R. J. Rose found heritable variance in the mental characteristics of: neuroticism, psychosis, extraversion, somatic complaints, inadequacy and cynicism. The heritability was higher in females. This suggests that interaction with the environment, greater in males, can override genetic predisposition.

Heredity appears to influence many mental characteristics other than intelligence, too. Rose found shared environmental factors in the measures of extraversion, intellectual interests and religious orthodoxy. Rushton found altruism, empathy, and nurturance as about 50% genetic. Loehlin reported similar results in 1992. Hudziak found obsessive-compulsive behavior in twelve year-olds to be 55% genetic and 45% due to environmental factors specific to the individual. The group influence, as we shall see later, is a powerful environmental factor.

Genes determine much of man's physiology and psychology. Growth and gray matter disappearance in the brain respond to a genetically determined timetable. Genes have been identified that regulate brain size during development (Evans et al 2004). It has been suggested that social complexity especially influences hippocampal development (Dunbar, 1992; Byrne, 2000).

Environment may influence gene *functioning* within a human. Some genes (that code for the production of proteins within an individual) can be switched on and off according to environmental conditions. For example, artificially closing a mouse's eye reduces the amount of brain-derived neurotropic factor gene within the brain. Olfactory experience can reportedly change the activation of NMDA receptor genes (Tang, 1999; Philpot 2005).

Animal breeders earn their living by relying on genetics. Many ideologists and social scientists, however, insist that the human animal is determined by his environment, rather than by genetics. Some psychologists are now claiming that half of human *behavior* is genetically determined. (May we, without offending anyone, assert that various breeds of dogs have distinctive temperaments?) (Scott & Fuller, 1965; Ostrander 2000; Mellersch 2000; Gosling 2001).

"Genotype" refers to the set of genes inherited, the capacity and tendency we have to begin with. "Phenotype" shows the reaction of the genotype with environment. The current consensus is that human intelligence and temperament are influenced both by heredity and by environment. There is no scientific agreement on the relative influence of each, although much evidence puts the hereditary influence at over 50 percent.

Animal experiments show that a crowded, stressful prenatal environment will result in female offspring with higher male hormone levels, concomitantly with males showing retarded maturity. Point mutations in genes have been identified that affect anxiety and aggression.

Meisenberg (2003) suggests in a review that 14% of the variation in IQ is due to race and that latitude is significantly correlated with intelligence. Since personality is, to a degree, inherited, this could explain a racial aspect to character. Experiments with identical twins reared apart show intelligence, gestures, and occupational aptitudes to be influenced by heredity. R. B. Cattell (1965) claims group-dependence, shyness-boldness, ego strength and dominance/submission to be similarly influenced by heredity.

Much research ignores heredity and seeks to claim that there is a common and uniform human nature, together with a set of universal problems shared by all. Differences in behavior are thus claimed as due to differences in the social, cultural and economic environment.

Economic factors are important in determining personality. This seems to be supported by the observation that occupational groups, such as farmers or police, have more in common with their foreign counterparts than they do with other classes in their own countries.

Genetic change can be rapid. If we postulate that a given trait is inheritable and if we control the population, with five generations of selection, a characteristic originally present in only five percent of the population can be made to predominate among 95 % of the population. Ten generations could produce a thousand fold relative increase in the characteristic.

The gross structure of the brain is determined by evolutionary inheritance and the plastic connections within are importantly established by individual experience. A six-month-old child is already forming and discriminating among categories (Quinn, 2006). There are sensitive and critical periods in the development of brain and behavior (Knudsen E, 2004). For example, the capacity to form strong social relationships and exhibit typical responses to stress require early positive interactions with a primary care giver.

The plastic circuitries are initially only weakly activated. Repeated activation can make them stronger. Cell adhesion molecules can cross link potentiated synapses and make them very resistant and permanent (Tanaka, 2003). The duration of plasticity basically depends on the function of the individual circuit. The amygdala, the molecular layer of the cerebral cortex and the CA1 of the hippocampus maintain plasticity throughout life.

Can ideology overpower the id? Some postulate the limbic (reptilian) system as the base of man's behavior. This would leave little place for values and ideology. We must consider the parts of man's brain that make him more susceptible than other primates to ideology and that allow society to more pattern his conduct. Golde notes that the human brain lets man perceive himself, envision the future, foresee alternative courses of action, and share meanings with others. She asserts the existence of an unconscious created by cultural prohibitions. The foregoing argues for non-limbic motivation and well describes what we mean by "human".

Belief and Ideology

Ideology starts with the representation of specific things by symbols. A thing thus gets abstracted to a symbolized idea. Such symbols can then be easily rearranged in the mind to give an imaginary representation of reality.

A constructed ideology usually: (1) offers a general explanatory theory about human history and development (2) pronounces an abstract and generalized set of goals (3) sees a struggle to obtains these goals (4) seeks to recruit and obtain commitment from the mass (5) establishes an inner leadership group.

A belief system becomes an ideology when it involves an action-oriented set of ideas in the social sphere, e.g. in political action. Ritual, drill, indoctrination and simply absorbing the prevalent worldview can all help to create a belief system within the individual.

An ideologue operates from a single frame of reference-the ideology. He does not form his ideas one at a time from different sources and integrate them to form a personal view. He gets his conscious views as a set from authority. A political activist is not necessarily an ideologue.

Attitude and personality are related concepts. If personality is defined by a "generalized tendency of response", then it is close to what we mean when we say "attitude". Cattell and others claim a cross-culturally valid personality description based on factors of (1) extroversion; (2) agreeableness; (3) conscientiousness; (4) emotional stability; and (5) cultural sensitivity. Concepts of self, a basic view of the world as friendly or hostile, and attitudes towards authority have been advanced as other fundamental descriptors of personality.

Key attitudes may sort out personality types. Identifying dualities or conflicts provides us with a conceptual category between "deep" personality and values. Such dichotomies include: (1) is everyone considered as a brother or as a stranger; (2) are some to receive favored treatment or are all to be treated the same; (3) is one born or appointed to status, or must he earn it; (4) is one self- assertive or unassertive; (5) idealist or realist; (6) is there tight or loose control of impulses; (7) inner-directedness or other-directedness? Such words tend to refer to socially imposed systems and attitudes. Indeed, the word "attitude" implies that there be a culture.

Values and attitudes provide indications of personality structure and probable ideological preference. Gordon (1960) sought to measure interpersonal values of support, recognition, conformity, independence, benevolence and leadership. Allport (1951) classified the dominant value set of an individual as knowledge-oriented, or practical, as aesthetic, social, power-oriented or as religious (seeking unity with the universe). "Personality" is today thought to include traits, motives and values.

Would one prefer to start with a blank page or a complete manual of life? The question poses a false dilemma, for neither is possible. One cannot start with a blank page, for he has the limbic development history of his species, his genetic predispositions, the orientation he has received from his parents, school and social milieu, as well as the calculated indoctrination directed toward him by various special interest groups. Similar biases, plus aspects of self-interest, would alter the actions of one who claimed to be following a totally specified scripture or manual for life

Summary: We have seen that the individual is changeable and has conflicting desires. Both heredity and environment are important in forming character. Existing behavioral theories seem to support the model of a closed mind. Psychological science offers strong arguments for the importance of behaviorism, seeing the early establishment of habitual connections through reward and punishment as determining human behavior.

Perception is molded by unconscious beliefs. The belief system is not really a conscious thing. Much of our thinking and our perception rest on the belief system that we have without being aware that we have it (Berelson). When we become aware of a belief, it is no longer a part of our primary, unquestioned, belief set. If we are unaware of it being a belief, we probably call it "reality".

Gerhard Roth has pointed out that the amygdala is fully formed by the age of thirteen, although cortical development continues. This implies that visceral attitudes and beliefs, especially those related to fear, can be set early. Thus, we may have decided on many actions long before we become aware of our decisions.

Core belief: is the world friendly or hostile? In his *Open and Closed Mind*, the psychologist Milton Rokeach postulates two primitive factors: a basic core of identity and a view of the world as friendly or hostile. An individual assumes that everyone else shares the same core belief and outlook. This core view is said to be formed before the age of three. Is there fear, or basic trust and love? For Rokeach, this is the central, primitive, core of belief.

The terms "belief", "attitude" and "value" are ill-defined. An "attitude" may be a predisposition to consistently classify things and respond to them. Attitudes can be held with different intensities, and determine our reactions. Some attitudes may be unconscious or ambivalent. "Central values" might refer to role expectations- what the culture expects of us.

Beliefs are assumptions absorbed from parents and the surrounding culture. Views of self and of reality are core

beliefs that we do not even recognize as beliefs. Imbuing children with the traditional worldview helps the stability of the culture. The individual's understanding of "reality" is thus in large part inter-subjectively derived.

A recent attempt at holistic personality assessment (the "Belief and Value Inventory") considers the following scales: (1) Negative Life Events (2) Naïve Determinism (3) Societal Closure (4) Authoritarian Introjects (5) Religious Traditionalism (6) Need for Control (7) Emotional Attunement (8) Self Access (9) Separation/Individuation (10) Gender Stereotypes (Shealy, 2005). This inventory would seem to have the authoritarian personality (q.v.) in mind.

Challenging belief threatens the individual's life. The underlying assumptions in the foregoing inventory are that belief is formed from all the scales measured, and that belief is integral to the identity and psychic life of the individual, as well as to his worldview and consequent actions. Thus, a perceived threat to that belief system will be a threat to the "life" of the individual and he will wish to destroy that threat.

A child brought up to feel insecure will be more likely to be comfortable with the reassurance of a closed belief system. The insecure may respond to anxiety and frustration with an aggressive reaction through violence and projection. The ideology may articulate a target for the frustrated. This may be the genesis of the authoritarian and fundamentalist personalities.

The culture itself may be responsible for prejudice. Prejudice and violence towards out-groups may accompany a closed belief system. These are emphasized in the Zoroastrian engendered religions: Judaism, Islam, and, to a lesser degree, Christianity.

Values tend to be binary, black and white criteria. They tell us whether a situation is good or bad, whereas attitudes guide our reaction to the situation. Children continually hear evaluations, and when these are internalized, conform. Values are collectively shared preferences, partly coerced, which are linked to a worldview. As attitudes, such values orient actions.

The next layer of belief, according to Rokeach, involves one's view of authority and how to utilize authorities. Still further removed are the beliefs that we derive from authority. Lastly, there are inconsequential beliefs. From such a model of the belief system it would appear that peripheral beliefs are relatively independent of the personality structure, whereas core beliefs are integral to that structure.

There is a bias toward belief. Human cognition, say Nisbett and Ross (1980), evidences a bias towards belief. We tend to see (when told) what is not there, to remember only supporting instances and to give more credence to apparent personal experience than to statistics. Once they are formed, we hold tightly to these beliefs even in the face of preponderant conflicting evidence.

Superstition, worship and intolerance are endemic. The interest in horoscopes and occultism shown by the public would indicate that superstition is endemic. People would thus appear naturally receptive to the prescriptions of religious and political medicine men. This suggests the presence of a strong vector of belief or gullibility.

The desire to submit is endemic. Is there a natural desire to worship, to believe in and be subordinate to the object worshiped, to obey and to conform to that object? Is this a projection of personal responsibility? If there be such a will, would it not imply the desire to have unanimity of public opinion and the desire to be isolated from discordant views? Those imbued with the idea that "my god is a jealous god" will likely be intolerant. Perhaps such submission and intolerance go hand in hand.

Stereotypes are psychologically necessary. People need to quickly assess a situation and predict outcomes. For efficiency, it is necessary to use established internal patterns to effect this assessment. The brain is constructed to do this. There is thus a necessary and natural place for such beliefs as prejudice, stereotyping, binary thinking and the acceptance of canned attitudes and beliefs. Routine, ritual and drill establish attitudes because consistent behavior can establish a pattern and thus an attitude.

A belief system must combine the requirements of reality, the demands of the social environment and the needs of one's internal psychology. For a man to act quite rationally, he must have an open belief system. Yet, men do not have open belief systems. Kant noted that the *practical reason* guiding human behavior was not the *pure reason* of mathematics. Behaviorism sees the mind as a closed system, determined by external rewards and punishments. The internal motivations assumed by many psychologists also presume a closed model of the mind.

Religion operates to give emotional satisfaction. It need only be rational enough to appear plausible to its adherents. It is therefore not limited by logic and proof and may address questions to which science can offer no explanation or consolation. Political ideology can be close to religion in this, as social and political principles are not easily measured. The disconcerting conclusion is that man is not totally rational.

Socialization and the Group

Man exhibits two fundamental aspects: as an individual and as a member of a group. The individual ego of the baby has no limits. Worldview, reality, and norms are later absorbed from the group, consciously and unconsciously.

Social learning, behavioral innovation and tool use correlated (0.24) with relative and absolute "executive brain volume" (Reader and Laland, 2002). Computed on the basis of (cortical volume + striatal volume/ brainstem volume), relative brain sizes were therby adjusted for overall primate size. In primates and carnivores, the neocortex size is positively correlated with social group size. Social learning, however, was not correlated with group size.

Socialization is getting the knowledge, skills, awareness, habits and attitudes necessary to function in the society and its culture. Culture is a mental thing common to the community. Ideology, history, myth and manners are all part of it. Actions pursuant to it create physical realities. Culture arises from adapting to the environment, from the urge for social living, and from incorporating myth and story telling. We develop attachments to familiar persons and things and have a need for positive affect (Goldschmidt, 1959). Such factors help to motivate social living and cultural accommodation.

"Community" implies a common psychic state. If a common psychic state exists among the members of a group, we might call the group a "community". Initiation and conditioning, together with the need to conform and to believe, tend to make the individual think and feel along with his group. Man exhibits a tendency to form groups. This may be both instinctual and practical.

Hostility to out-groups (xenophobia) usually accompanies the tendency to form groups. This reaction is found even when teams are formed for parlor games. In primitive (and also in not so primitive) societies, people often split into two opposing groups or halves, called *moieties*. The culture then develops ritual mechanisms for peacefully accommodating these moieties. Since the same thing happened with the Blues and the Greens in ancient Rome who cheered different teams in the Coliseum, this might be an example of *homo ludens*, playful man.

Family, community, school and peers transmit the culture and mold the individual. The relative importance of a collectivity (often the extended family) has been a constant characteristic of the Chinese worldview. Western culture puts more emphasis on the individual. In both approaches, the society is of overweening importance. Values, belief systems, even the sense of what is real, are in part derived from others. How much of man's nature is fixed and how much can be changed by others and by the environment? We are finding out more about this.

The child always absorbs the worldview of the culture. The worldview of tradition and culture is usually functional. One living totally within a culture is not aware that other cultures or views of reality exist. With isolation and censorship, totalitarian churches and governments try to assure such unawareness. Our semantic memory makes reality. Personal reality involves the linkage of words and phrases in our mind-in our semantic memory. These linkages are created more implicitly by experience than by conscious indoctrination.

Schools adjust the worldview. A worldview can be unconsciously absorbed, taught, adopted, or adapted. The myths, rituals and school system use words, pictures and symbols to tell the individual what consensual reality is and how to react to it. For those who would instill superstition or make a "new man", the struggle to control early schooling is fierce. The more bizarre the ideology, the greater is the need to instill the connections early in the unformed semantic memories of the young. (Recall the phrase often attributed to the Jesuits: "give me a child until the age of seven, and I will have him for life").

The "ideological state apparatus" refers to the techniques by which the state controls the beliefs and attitudes of the people. Knowledge of arithmetic and gravity can be true or false, but who can prove truth about the religious and social life of man? People who would dominate the society would control the myths of the society and much else that forms the semantic memories. Ideology uses language to integrate the psychic apparatus of the individual with the organization of society. Thus, the ruling party would have books, priests, and schoolteachers under its control. On his death-bed, Confucius is reported to have said "the secret is: control the language!"

One need not consciously foster or receive the "ideological state apparatus". The individual living in a society will naturally absorb most of the official explanations. Satisfied or fearful conservatives will predictably stick with the old ideology. The less fortunate may even consider themselves better off, if persuaded by media and leaders. Consent may be engineered, but it also comes naturally as one seeks to conform to society.

Is there a group personality? Different environments are associated with different specific worldviews, core beliefs, etc. The group is an important aspect of the environment. Does culture reflect a collective mind? Is the individual personality largely the product of the culture, or is there continual interaction? When men develop in a group, anywhere, common aspects of classification or of behavior always occur (Murdock, 1965).

Since behavior and institutions vary from culture to culture, the key is how basic drives are handled, says Kluckhohn (1953) and whether such behavior is reinforced. This presents the trained and conditioned human.

Does a common worldview define human nature? For Redfield, commonalty of worldview establishes "human nature". For him, worldview consists in recognizing self and others, their commonalty and distinctiveness. Efforts have been made to trace the physical changes in the human brain as this awareness develops. If the ideological state apparatus gives us our worldview, then it would also do much to form Redfield's "human nature.

When man is perceived as something apart from nature, then it is easier to think of teleological "progress" and change, says Redfield. Does one change the world or seek to preserve it? (One could here think of the effect of Western religions and their modern secular counterparts (e.g. Nazism and Marxist-Leninism) and the problems of the "greens" (environmentalists), as contrasted with Confucians and Taoists. Does one see "time's arrow or time's round"?

Religion, language, ethnicity, values, worldview, economics, etc. may, over time, form a "civilization". Civilizations included the: Mesopotamian, Egyptian, Cretan, Mediterranean Classical, Byzantine, Middle American (Aztecs) and Andean (Incas). Today, one may posit Confucian (Sinic), Japanese, Indian (Hindu) Islamic, Western and Eastern Orthodox civilizations, always remembering that there is great diversity within such groupings.

Plasticity makes drive reduction possible. Plastic man is putty for the ideologists. Speech and symbolic reasoning capabilities, coupled with an imperative for social living, make men especially flexible and receptive. There are many forms of responses to basic urges, of drive reduction. Man's sense of reality is derived with others and he is vulnerable to ideology.

Man can and does adapt to a wide range of real and imaginary social organization. Manipulators easily redirect his drives.

Conformity, tolerance and mass delusions dissolve the individual. Many individuals are quite willing to give up their own views and to fanatically adopt the views of the group, should conformity seem to require it. This is a surrender of individual identity to that of the group. Tribal cohesion, religious unanimity, social and economic interdependence, all boost the argument that man depends on others for his perception of what is real and worthy. If the sense of reality is in part inter-subjectively derived, are not mass delusions likely? Could the sameness of televised messages and the isolation of individuals absorbing them not create mass delusions?

Intolerance is natural. Man finds comfort in his worldview. He does not want the tension of disagreements or challenges to that worldview. Man therefore finds tribal cohesion and unanimity of religious opinion psychologically protective and comfortable. It is his nature to demand tolerance for his own views and deny tolerance to the conflicting views of others.

The id, ego and superego are the battle ground between self and society. Although a man may get his perception of reality and the "oughts" of life from others, there remains an inevitable tension between those norms and his personal wishes for himself. Freudian terminology provides some useful names for aspects of this tension. The "ego" is said to govern relations between the self and the outer world, as well as between the self and the deeper layers of personality. The "id" is the name given to the source of instinctual or libidinal energy. The "superego" is the internalization of the perceived normative values of society. More simply: "superego" is the conscience that society gives us, the "id" is the monster deep within us, and the "ego" is our conscious desire. There is agreement as to what these Freudian terms are supposed to signify, but no agreement that the terms represent anything real.

Key cultural institutions (church, government, public broadcasting networks, etc.) serve to mask, control and

channel conflicts. If the nature of man is deemed selfish, aggressive, competitive and playful, then the key institutions of the culture may provide rules that mask, dampen and channel these tendencies. They must also treat gross human folly seriously and pretend that it is not all a game. (The *wu wei* of the Taoist is anathema to the driven ideologue).

Roles respond to the affect and mirror of others. How others regard us and how we regard ourselves produces a sense of identity. The opinion of others focuses on one's role in society. Role identification may be another way in which the external culture is incorporated into the individual personality. As one Italian told me "I feel as though I have jumped out on a stage before a big audience and that I now must perform".

We need affect. Although it can do much to influence the sense of reality, ideology can do little to supply the basic need for affect, for human affection. In traditional China, the extended family supplied place, purpose, support and affect. Service to the lord served a similar function in Tokugawa Japan. The fellowship of a church group might partially fulfill this need. If the institutions of the society do not meet the physical and psychic needs of the individual, then the society is unstable and mass movements or revolutions are more likely. This might have been among the motivations for the mystery religious cults in the Hellenistic era.

To what degree will the psyche conform to the culture? If, as Redfield suggests, the worldview determines human nature, then human nature can differ in different cultures. For example, the projective systems, worldview and ideological state apparati of the Far East emphasize the collectivity, whereas the Western emphasis is on the individual. Behavior will consequently differ, even if the human psychology remains constant.

How pliable is man? Man has a special susceptibility to words and ideologies. What, then, are the limits to which man's nature can be stretched? What are the limits when the society does not employ massive physical coercion? Excluding celibate societies and those that have not survived for several generations, we can consider socialist societies like the Guarani under the Jesuits, or those of the Incas and the Aztecs. Although harsh, they flourished.

Perhaps ideology can even overcome some primary drives. Greenough (1983) reports that, among Bengali peasants, the religious value of dependency is so inculcated that people actually starve rather than take aggressive action to secure food. If his observations were well taken, this suggests that cultural influence may overcome a primary drive. We have also seen that inmates can incorporate the structure of concentration camps into their personal identities.

Man can be altruistically transcendent. Ortega y Gasset saw man not as a thing but as a drama, it being for each man to find his own authentic self and mission. Man had the possibility for transcendence, for rising above physical and conventional constraints. Some sociobiologists claim that altruism, a form of transcendence, is preserved in the genes through a history of sacrifice for family units.

Altruism could be genetically favored. If the behavior benefited family members, if there were reciprocity among non-kin, or if there were natural selection among groups. The cooperative behavior among bees, William Hamilton suggested, might be explained by the fact that sister bees shared three fourths of their genes. Specialization in such a cooperating group could justify sterile castes. The investment of parents in their children is also a behavior that favors the survival of one's genes.

Altruism can externalize the self. Can altruistic behavior be sustained? Can the concept of "self" be transferred to or merged with the collectivity? The superego (conscience) can be externalized to a leader, and the ego greatly diminished, but what of the id? Can that "self" be separated from the "body"?

In the West, ideology can produce an initial enthusiasm for war, but this soon degenerates into individual and small group survival. For the Japanese psyche a different result may obtain. During the War, it seemed that many Japanese soldiers were eager to sacrifice their bodies because they so completely identified themselves with their family and with the collectivity in the person of the Emperor (Leighton and Opler, 1946). However, the anthropologist Ohnuki-Tierney (2006) consults the diaries of Kamikase pilots to present a totally contrary view.

There is a group superego, an externally derived conscience. Boyhood gangs and military organizations strive to achieve a group superego and succeed. Man in a group becomes the sort of person that the group expects. In the process, he can lose much of his original nature.

Weak people externalize the superego. The weak ego seeks conventional and authoritarian attitudes. Fear of parents and consequent reliance on them for standards of behavior represents a special case of the externalization of the superego and weakness of personal ego. The individual with a weak personal ego does not develop the personal standards normally expected of a mature adult. Others (priest, superior, a celebrity and/or a group) have formed one's attitudes and values. Having a group superego is psychologically useful.

Responsibility can be projected on scapegoats. Resolution of psychological tension within the individual is of fundamental importance. Responsibility for that which is bad is shifted from the individual, even away from the group, and onto a scapegoat. The ideal scapegoat is a foreign devil or a minority group within the community.

With projection, one's own faults become the faults of distant, and often imaginary, enemies. Unresolved internal anxieties are transferred or projected. The individual escapes responsibility for having personal standards by accepting the standards of the group. He escapes guilt by projecting guilt feelings onto the Devil, someone else or an imagined enemy outside the group. In the projection process, one may imagine threats in the political world.

Negative projections are chosen among the more distant objects; for favorable projections, closer objects, such as the leader or the group, are selected. The group can be cruel and can kill. But the group psyche has been useful. Cooperation in the face of a threat enhances survival.

2

MYTH

Myth offers imaginary explanations and ritual installs them. Both are invoked by religion to present meaning, coherence and transcendence. When man feels threatened by matters beyond his comprehension or control, magic is invoked. If connected with ritual, myth may appear imbued with magical potency. The viewer steps out of his normal station and shares the group identity. He can feel he is sharing in the collective *mana*. Ritual symbolically reinforces group feeling, the structure of society and hierarchy. Rituals form a major part of military training.

Shared myths serve to channel both thinking and emotional response through observation, participation and repetition, myth and ritual. For Bettleheim, myth augments the power of an awesome superego. Myth and ritual express and codify belief. The culture of a society reflects the norms and morality of the society. Repetition of myth serves to reinforce the culture. Repeating stories with ideals promotes values. The illusion of having common goals and the hope of wish fulfillment also give myth and religion a place in the service of the culture.

Illusion is necessary. The "social imaginary" of collective dreams and folk heroes was recognized by Plato in his *Allegory of the Cave*, claims Pierre Ansart. Weber's *Protestant Ethic* is cited as a demonstration of how an imaginary religious structure could influence social and economic life. As selfish human animals we seek instant gratification. What will persuade us to deny our wishes and to behave with altruism, if there is no incentive of illusion? But, if we believe our own ideology, where is reality?

Myth is perceived truth and wish-fulfillment. Myth is often used to smooth over inconsistencies. If people define their world in terms of opposites, then myths may be seen as the resolution of contradictions. It is typically simplistic and/or mystical. The symbolic mixture appeals to emotion, and to the right brain, rather than to logic. For the Greeks, myth and poetry expressed collectively perceived truths that were more important than historical truth. Myth may represent "collective desire personified". Myths also provide for the imaginary fulfillment of wishes that cannot otherwise be satisfied. Myth can tell us much about the real values of a community.

Zoroaster's teleological route leads to the Kingdom of God. Jewish tradition offers the myth that history represents the progressive fulfillment of the Chosen People. Such "salvation history" goes by various names: eschatology, *heilsgeschichte*, teleology etc., this is "Time's arrow" leading to the Kingdom of God on Earth or in Heaven. The Eastern view is different, seeing history as repeating in the long cycles of "Time's round".

Myths portray the cultural hero. Campbell, in his *Hero of a Thousand Faces* (1968) summarizes the pattern. In brief, the hero is called, meets an initial obstacle to his mission, enters a threatening world populated with helping and hindering forces, engages in an ordeal and returns with a boon for his people. Within this basic framework, a variety of symbols can be inserted and the desired message created.

Perhaps the Christian myths were not deliberately invented, but developed naturally from the popular wishes of the then prevalent mystery religions and the hopes for a Messiah. State religions in the ancient world did not promise salvation or rescue from death, as did the Christian myth. The Christian success may be evidence that the illusion of wish-fulfillment is psychologically very important.

Myths explain how things came to be. Among primitives, myths serve primarily to explain natural phenomena. At later stages of civilization, myths reflect cultural traditions and versions of historical events. Always, they purport to explain how the present came to be. "How" merges with "why" and ideology slips into historical etiology. Myths often serve to harmonize the real and the ideal or to explain conflicts that exist in the society. Myths are frequently invoked to explain contradictions, inconsistencies, or impossibilities in the usual explanation of things.

One prefers the strength of conviction to the tension of doubt. The brain is built to imagine explanations where none exist. Complete materialism offers no consolation of belief. Thus, by starving the mystical sense, materialism may actually foster superstition and myth.

The immaterial and the infinite are domains of choice for the purveyors of myth. Since myth and symbol are means through which men objectify the world in their minds, manipulating these is a dangerous business. Fortunately, most purveyors of myth are interested in preserving the status quo.

New conditions bring new myths and new gods: Myth and religion substitute for philosophy among simple folk. Thus, new world conditions and new values cause new myths and new religious expressions. The rise of the god Dionysus in Greece has been said to reflect a change of ideals wherein people sought to lose themselves in the stream of life and in hope for a life hereafter, rather than to continue as responsible and anxious individuals in times of change.

Ideology, as integrated myth, can be a means of achieving social solidarity. It can then serve to guide the mass it formed. Thus, the ruling class may use myth to manipulate and control the masses. Myths of heroes can articulate social ideals. Popular films, as mythopoetic expression, can reveal collective fears and fantasies, and can partially assuage neuroses.

The establishment requires and produces myths of legitimation. Those in power seek to control their own images and then use the image system to reinforce their own legitimacy. Hate and adoration potentiate collective illusion, notes Ansart. Can we do without illusion? Can we do without devils to hate? For Sorel, providing society with an appropriate myth was a most important function of the ruling class. He described myth as a set of symbols and images capable of calling up sentiment and of moving people to action.

Nazism became a civil religion. Hitler said that the worth of a religion depended upon whether an obviously better alternative was available. The Catholic Goebbels, in his diaries, said "National Socialism is my religion". In Nazi Germany, Hitler's statements formed the changing scripture of the society. It was his wish that a well planned Nazi liturgy should be implemented, so that ritual could compensate for subsequent variations in the quality of leadership. Political acts under the Nazis took the form of new myths and cults. Myth was created to supply history and purpose.

Can mythopoetics be independent of the zeitgeist? Can leaders do other than move in the direction indicated by public opinion? Given television, how rapidly can that national psyche be molded? Plato felt that society needed controlled myth. To foster unity, Augustus tried to revive the traditional religion of the Roman Empire and commissioned Virgil to create the *Aeneid*. This was part of Augustus' attempt to create a religion of the state. Today, and historically, bards and folksingers recount myths and legends of the culture.

As originators of myth, poets are effective. Poetic expression is one of the fundamental forms of communication among educated Chinese. The Spanish Fascist, Primo de Rivera, claimed: "people have never been moved by anyone except poets". Santayana argued that religion should be viewed as a form of poetry.

Wagner and the poet Stefan George provided mythology for the German youth movement of the early 1800's. This was a precursor, and ultimately a component, of Nazism. In the Quebec of the 1960's, poets, singers, and politicians took on the role of social prophets, replacing Churchmen and their chosen lay leaders.

Intellectuals are prone to self-delusion: Santayana believed the ideas of passion to be more vivid than those of memory. He also observed that the authors of doctrines were often misled by their own creations. It is the intellectual, rather than the practical man, who can more easily be swayed by words.

Salvation, martyrs, and myth construction: Salvation may psychologically (Ostow in Halperin, 1983) be a reunion with lost parents, accomplished by sacrifice. Martyrs are useful as role models of sacrifice in a myth to promote group cohesion. Myths telling of a common origin and crisis also further solidarity. "Salvation" may also be relief from oppression. (Thus, the image of Christ crucified has a liberating message to the oppressed of South America).

W. R. Halliday's *The Pagan Background of Early Christianity* provides some examples of the construction of important Christian mythology. The Christian clergy have always sought to co-opt and adapt pagan deities and celebrations, making them appear Christian. Christmas itself is the pagan Festival of Lights. Easter was the Hilaria and the celebration of the goddess of spring, Eoster, etc. Toynbee lists more than eighty similarities between the Jesus story and various Hellenic predecessors. In essence, existing beliefs are adapted to the new ideology.

A limited myth with a special purpose may often be accepted for its symbolic usefulness, apart from any considerations of belief. The superhuman hero whose mother is human but whose father is reputed to be a god is frequently encountered (e.g. the Egyptian pharaohs, Alexander, Augustus, Jesus, etc.). Such stories were common and gave an element of legitimacy to the new leader. Today, the story is more likely to involve the new leader being a disciple of a venerated hero.

The Spanish occupiers were resented by the Indian population of Mexico. The Spanish then had the Virgin of Guadalupe make her appearance in the guise of an Indian goddess "discovered" by an Indian peasant on a hill formerly dedicated to a goddess of the old religion. This quickly became an alternate national symbol of Mexico, unifying the existing worship of the old religion with the new religion of the conquerors.

Ancient Sumeria worshipped a compassionate mother-goddess, Ninkhursag, who grieved for the unhappiness of men and interceded for them with less compassionate deities. The important competitors to the Christian gods in the early days were in the Earth-Mother tradition, such as Isis, Rhea-Cybele, Gaea, Demeter, etc. The basis for Mariolatry is evident.

Bishop Cyril was anxious to convert Ephesus in 431 A.D. He therefore credited Mary with most of the virtues of the Ephesians' favorite goddess, Diana. The local city council then declared Mary to be the mother of God. In the next century, the August 13 festivals of the goddesses Isis and Artemis were taken over, for this date was announced to be the "Feast of the Assumption of the Virgin into Heaven".

In the Middle Ages, a Gospel of Mary developed, perhaps in response to the adoration of noble women that was taking place in southern France. In 1854, the Church promulgated the doctrine of the "Immaculate Conception". Marina Warner (1976) suggests that the "virgin birth" was necessary to support a claim for Christ's divinity. Also, Christianity associated sex and sin and death. Thus she suggests the "virgin birth" and the "assumption" link the conquest of lust with eternal life. This would offer a symbolic salvation

The Nicean Creed rejected the Mother-Goddess concept in favor of a father image. The Christian set of saints and gods then lacked a female component. In Patristic thought, Mary was the figure of the Church. Jung notes that this approach leaves out the magic fourth element, feminine or evil. Jung also speculates that the recent elevation of Mary marks an increase in feminine erotic mysticism in the collective psyche. (One should careful with such psychoanalytic interpretations).

Myth is usually specific to the nation: The symbolism of language (and thus national etymology) is an important determinant of myth. Myth tends to be specific to the nation and its language. Bardic poetry and folk songs belong to particular cultures. Myth everywhere reinforces the community. With the salvation religions (Judaism, Christianity, Islam and possibly

Marxism) myth is used for recruiting to the community.

Much Western mythology is based on the Oedipus theme, where the son takes the place of the father. In Iran, there is a myth that talks about a severe father killing his son. In the 1980's, a totalitarian theocracy arose in Iran, focused in the hands of a patriarchal father figure. As long as the Shah was considered the father, no one could speak against him. When the image of the Ayatollah Khomeini replaced the image of the Shah, it then became possible to shout: "death to the Shah". Khomeini became the new father.

Receptivity to myths may differ with the nation. Nietzsche saw the German spirit as "obscurationist, enthusiastic, and atavistic", and thus naturally hostile to the ideas of the Enlightenment. To Hans Kohn, the Third Reich was a concoction of the myths that had defeated the Enlightenment in Germany.

Myth is used to control the common folk: Six priests testified that Pope Boniface VIII (1300) had stated that all supposedly divine laws were inventions of men to keep the common people behaving through fear of hell; that it was "fatuous" to believe that a virgin had borne a child, or that God had become man, or that there was a future life. "So I believe and so I hold, as does every educated man. The common people hold otherwise. We must speak as the common folk do, and think and believe with the few". (Reported by Durant, quoting H. Milman's *History of Latin Christianity* v. 6, p. 494).

The rootless are susceptible to myth. Children, the moldable future, are particular targets of myth. Plato thought that nursery tales should be controlled, with especial attention paid to assure that evil was presented as something alien. The immigrants to America had only the ideology of the American Dream to bind them together. Feeling remote from their roots and from any sense of protection, people today will want to accept a myth that will make them feel a protected part of society.

As the object of myth, the authoritarian personality adopts cliché and slogans as though they were his own . By accepting views from authority, one evades personally integrating such views and thus one can be more comfortable with inconsistencies. Totalitarian myth is rather special in that the force of the state is used to try to bring reality into apparent conformity with the myth. Do national myths and liturgies enable people to worship themselves?

"We apply to nature the anticipation of nature. Anticipations are sufficiently powerful in producing unanimity, for if all men were to become uniformly mad, they might agree tolerably well with each other" said Francis Bacon.

Myth is psychologically useful: Man seeks myths to put order into his views of the world, thereby reducing his mental tension. Myths must first enable a person to find his place in the world. Once accepted, myths serve to enhance the solidarity and order of society, fostering a sense of community.

Public actions are always done within the established systems of myth and symbols of the civil religion. A myth that shows historical continuity can make change seem less disquieting. The Nazi myths were designed to show continuity, to provide a useful worldview, and to foster a feeling of solidarity. Myths can establish ideals of leader conduct. As people need goals to strive for, so, too, do they need heroes to emulate. Today, entertainers and athletes seem to have replaced the saint as heroes to emulate.

Historicism, itself a myth, claims that there are large movements of history, controlled by laws which apply to societies as a whole. It claims that knowledge of such laws enables one to predict future events. American imperialists spoke of a "manifest destiny" which motivated and justified their actions. This "Manifest Destiny" combined ideas of the will of Providence of spreading American "democracy". Others were serving God by "taking up the White Man's burden".

Advertising is mythopoetic. In our society, popular songs seem to serve the mythopoetic function well. Parable and myth can reach the common people. Does advertising replace myth? Instead of groups and societies, do we have markets? Have shared community values been changed to demographics, as some suggest? The consumer society and its myths emphasize productivity, abundance and life. Hanna Arendt called these "laborer's values".

Myth, belief, and social reality: If people act as if myths were true, then myths have a certain reality. The beliefs that form myths can be supported by rites. Interrelated rites form institutions, in Durkheim's view. Society is thus seen as a normative structure created by myths and rites, an ideological community without acknowledged premises

Core beliefs are not ideas. We live within such beliefs as reality and are thus usually not aware of them. There is also a difference between the faiths men profess and those that control their conduct.

Myths tell and explain the beliefs of the society and serve to provide a common worldview. When myth is combined with ritual, emotions are concentrated. A sense of magic communion is then conveyed and ingrained. Feelings of solidarity within the society are thus enhanced. The dependence of mythopoetic expression on language tends to the creation of myths particular to a nation. Those who would mold society must also seek to create and mold its myths. They do.

3

NATIONAL CHARACTER

Is there such a thing as national character? If so, how could we discover it? Literature is a product of an elite. The response to popular music is strongly influenced by marketing. How well do such cultural products express any national psyche? Can the deeper levels of personality be assessed (as with the Rorschach) or must we content ourselves with observing the socially evidenced personality?-

One-third of the population shows the national character. In evaluating two American Indian communities, Wallace found (1961) that about one third of the population within each community shared a common set of Rorschach results. Guthrie and Bennett (1971) found the expected personality trait set of an individual somewhat culture- specific. Thus, one might expect part (perhaps a third) of a population to display the "national character".

National character is reflected in ideals and myths. Duijker and Frijda (1960) and also Peabody (1985) surveyed national differences, and suggest the following descriptors: the distribution of personality types; national elites; the hierarchy of values; self-concepts; differences between norms and practice; and norms of etiquette. Of course, myths are also important in setting ideals. Since manifestations of what is called the "national character" can change rapidly, the dominant philosophies of each period are also descriptive of that character.

An individual has superimposed "characters": (1) his own temperament or personality, (2) a social personality or persona, (3) a worldview and (4) the outlook of his group or social class (5) the imposed ideology of his religion and of the civil religion.

Is there as much variation within a culture as there is between cultures? Is the essence of culture the accommodation of diversity, as Kluckhohn suggests? Recall that even in isolated Indian communities, the modal Rorschach was found only among about a third of the populations. If we claim that there is a basic personality structure associated with a culture, then many psychologists would insist that such a personality structure arises from some commonalty in the treatment of the young.

Genetic, individual and shared environmental influences: Current scientific efforts to assess the genetic influence on behavior distinguish between genetic, individual environmental and shared environmental influences. Shared environmental influence is stronger among males and has been reported at 16%-25% (Borkenau 2001, Hudziak 2004, Rhee 2002).

Franz Boas' cultural relativism requires the understanding of how and why a culture functions before passing judgment on it. Since relatively few people understand even their own culture that well, people should, but rarely do, reserve judgment on other cultures.

Ostensible "national character" can change rapidly with external circumstances and with the observer. Almond and Verba (1963) found 93% of Germans expressing generalized mistrust in 1948, but only 59% as doing so in 1959. This raises questions about the widely accepted claims that basic attitudes of trust or mistrust are formed before one is three years old.

National character can be partially described by five factors. If one considers personality types, then McCrae's (2002) five factors (decreases in Neuroticism, Extraversion, and Openness and increases in Agreeableness and Conscientiousness) from adolescence to adulthood-appear to be universal. But the scores on the various factors show regional patterns.

Dimensions for measuring national character exist. Hofstede suggests five dimensions for measuring national cultural differences (1) how great the underclass perceives social distances to be (2) individualism vs. collectivism (3) competitiveness vs. passivity (4) tolerance for ambiguity, for the unknown (5) long term vs. short-term view. Other possible dimensions: (6) whether particular circumstances or a universal code are decisive and (7) male/female role differences. In the current literature, the relative importance of the individual vs. the group is receiving the greatest emphasis.

National character is also reflected in conventions. The ostensible social personality may even be a conditioned reaction formation, where the individual acts contrary to his natural inclinations. Here, the culture is controlling and the culture may be determined by the environment.

If the environment reciprocally shapes the culture, individuals become as elements in a regenerative feedback system and the system as a whole would then determine the response characteristics. Such arguments favor the idea that national character exists. When ideology supervenes, the individual becomes relatively unimportant. There follow some thumbnail sketches of outlooks that have evolved or that are evolving in different national environments.

Religious Ideology and National Character

Protestant Ethic and Catholic Corporatism. "The Protestant Ethic" has been advanced as the great ideology informing the capitalist development of the West. This is often contrasted with the fixed occupational and class structures of what is called "Catholic Corporatism". In theory, the Protestant Ethic evinces: (1) work as a calling; (2) achievement and motivation; (3) worldly asceticism; (4) individuality rather than brotherhood; (5) practicality and empiricism over rationality and dogma; (6) inner-directedness rather than other-directedness; and (7) individual responsibility and freedom to act.

Has capitalism become the Protestant religion? With television and advertising, have self-centeredness, hedonism and the transitory replaced the ideals of the Protestant Ethic? (Peabody, 1985).

African character may be multiple. The gods, as Swanson (1964) has shown us, are a projection of the existing social order. Thus, a loosely organized society will have many gods and will tend to blame witches for things that go wrong. Witchcraft seems to be a core belief in Africa where the fundamental ethos is tribal and pluralistic (MacGaffey, 1981). Some claim that the colonial influence has affected Africa to such an extent that an educated African will use one ideology in dealing with the outside world and another in dealing with Africans. In general, such dualities and tribalism make it appear that conditions in black Africa are not yet appropriate for sweeping ideologies of the Western variety.

Japan

The Japanese show a conflict between the inner and the outer person. There are, says Bellah (1957), two basic concepts of the divine in Japan: the "nurturing god" and the "inner essence of reality". Preindustrial Japan was said to have political values superior to economic values. The political values emphasized performance; extolled collective goals over productivity; had loyalty as the primary virtue and selfishness as the cardinal sin; considered power more important than wealth and saw controlling as more important than doing. Good nurture required filial piety and loyalty to the leader. Later, such loyalty was to be expressed by military-like performance in all areas of activity. Goal attainment took precedence over integrative values. There developed a unity of religion and politics. Parties were despised and power was rationalized.

The economic values of post-war Japan are characterized by a rationalization of means and a universal search for adaptation. Cramped for space, rice and recognition, the Japanese evolved a moral order that facilitates adaptation to these conditions. One seeks to dissolve selfishness in unifying with the essence of beauty in the universe. Here one may express the compensating values of harmony, compromise and passivity.

There is now a search in Japan for values that might supplement economic self interest. The head of a government sponsored institute suggested "reverence for nature", "service to others" and "equality", while another leader recently suggested "harmony" and "paternalism" as supplements to economic criteria. These represent a reprise of Confucian values. The attempt of an individual to live with both world views must produce much psychological tension.

China is characterized by dependency. With a different physical, economic and political environment, the Chinese emphasized familial, rather than organizational, dependency. In the traditional Chinese world, says Hsu (1961), the individual had a secure position oriented to mutual dependence within the clan. There was no internal drive for change. The world of the individual was compartmentalized and principles depended on local circumstances. As early as 270 B.C. Hsún-tzu articulated the function of the ruler as providing a place for everyone and recommended that everyone perform well in his place.

In three thousand years, the Chinese have experienced changing sets of ideals, including those resulting from Taoism and Buddhism. Among the basic alternatives questioned: loyalty to a personal leader vs. to a ruling principle; transcendence vs. immanence; the mystical vs. the physical; stasis vs. change; the teleological vs. the circular, selfishness vs. altruism; unity vs. plurality; and thought vs. force.

Chinese philosophical precepts developed with time. Material force was reality, but it should be balanced by love for humanity *(jen)* and controlled by principle (*li*) to achieve harmony *(xie)*. The dominance of the collectivity, and hence the importance of harmony, called for a response that differed from the earlier familial orientation.)

Chinese dependency vs. Western self-reliance and individualism. Hsu contrasts Chinese social dependency with Western individual striving for self-reliance. Alone, without a spirit of dependency, Western man can never achieve enough security. If the Western individualist must challenge standards imposed by others, this makes for constant change. Western man must then continually seek some ideology to give him bearings in an uncertain world. For Hsu, the Chinese system of values avoids these problems.

The Tao and Confucianism have been major influences shaping the Chinese character. Buddhism and the Tao stem from Indian roots. Thus, Chinese philosophy has been likened to a "Three Legged Stool". The work of Bauer (1977) offers a study of Chinese utopias. He interprets these as evidencing a longing to escape from drudgery into happiness. Shamanic journeys and idealized village life are featured in the utopias. The ruling classes introduced strong principles of social and moral order and these have been so internalized that Bauer views freedom as contrary to the Chinese character.

Chinese philosophy is more perceptual than speculative. Anthropomorphism and spirits gave way to a universal ideal, *tien,* around 1100 B.C. If the ruler were able and virtuous, he would have the right to rule. With Confucius (500 B.C.) the "superior man" would replace the "son of the ruler". Mencius (340 B.C.) expounded on the basis of man being essentially good, but Hsun Tzu (270 B.C.) saw man as essentially evil and therefore needing guides and strict laws. The natural order was to be realized through dedication, altruism, honesty and harmony.

The Taoist school (c. 550 B.C.) emphasized passive accommodation to the natural order. With Chung Tzu (330 B.C.) the particular atoms changed according to their own laws and all was flux, but this flux was evidenced in great, repeating cycles according to the interaction of the forces of Yin and Yang.

The Legalists put a temporary end to social flux in 213 B.C., suppressing thought and burning books. For the Legalists, men were bad and needed forceful guidance. The emperors Shih Huang-ti (230 B.C.) and Wu Ti (100 B.C.) implemented socialist reforms with legalist rigor.

Confucianism, then incorporating the idea of constant change, became the state religion in 136 B.C. Man had a bipolar nature of greed and love said Tung Chungshu and everything in the universe influenced everything else. In 75 A.D., Wang Ch'ung was claiming the insignificance of man and the epistemological exclusivity of physical evidence. Was reality singular and transcendent, or plural and immanent?

Meditation will allow harmony to overcome illusion. With the influence of Indian Buddhism, the phenomenal world was viewed as the temporary product of elemental forces and thus empty. The interaction of forces and phenomena resulted in a universal harmony that could be perceived through meditation. This Middle Path offered China its own Trinity-type resolution.

Love was mixed with neo-Confucian realism. By 1050, Neo Confucianism was claiming *ying* and *yang* to be governed by a single ultimate principle. The exercise of *jen* (love, human compassion) was the way to achieve unity with the universe, but force made a thing concrete. Was man of one mind or two and was he good or evil?

For Lu Chuyuan (1160) there was but one mind and within it one could discover all things. Wang Yang-ming (c.1500) led an idealist movement as a strong reaction against Neo-Confucian rationalism. Through *jen* (love), man was to become one with the universe. Toward the universe, love is reproduction. Toward society, love is respect and altruism. The collective mind is within man and one may discover and extend this consciousness. The collective consciousness can only be realized through deeds.

The history of China suggests a people who have always had to be concerned with survival. From this has emerged a focus on practicality. There is also a strong sense of veneration and duty towards parents and ancestors. From this, obligations to the family will always have priority. The need for group survival has put emphasis on the collectivity, obedience to authority, harmony and compromise as essential values. Much popular opinion holds that Han practicality, Legalism and force have overridden Confucian concepts. This view claims that amoral material pragmatism now rules in China.

Confucianism, Taoism, Legalism and Marxism were the four vectors Alain Peyrefitte (1977) saw in Chinese thought: Truth is to be found in the concrete, rather than in the abstract. Confucianism honors harmony, tradition and the "superior man".

Both the "superior man" of Confucius and the "New man" of Mao honor courtesy, harmony, justice, integrity, self-control, reliability, loyalty, and faithful performance of duty. Taoism avoids the binary Manichaeism of the West and counsels a winding path, together with quietism and a refusal of power.

Chinese legalism eliminated individualism. Legalism has been a factor in China for more than two thousand years. The idea is that laws and regulations are supreme. The individual is therein considered incapable of charting his own course. Secret police and terror are believed necessary to the training of citizens and to the maintenance of public order.

Charles Moore notes twenty-one distinctive features of the Chinese outlook in his *The Chinese Mind* (1966). For the educated Chinese, philosophy takes the place of religion. The central problem for the leading class is how to be a sage and how to act as a good ruler. Humans are said to come first and ethical humanism receives emphasis. One strives for harmony and individual rights are entirely secondary to duty, and non-existent if they pose a threat to the state. There is also "*both / and*" as a possible response, rather than the Western "*either / or*".

In the 1980's, the Chinese government began to extol the importance of Confucianism. In the 1990's, there was also an emphasis on Chinese nationalism that included overseas Chinese. It was thus an appeal to an ethnic civilization.

The urban middle class in China now enjoys some capitalism, (a prosperity without political opportunity), and the peasants are once again able to farm their own land. The social contract still requires absolute submission to the Party. Fluctuations in policy are to be expected, for continual change is part of their worldview.

Most interestingly, for two generations, the ideology of Mao was exclusively indoctrinated in everyone as the only religion. Now, that has become a void, largely supplanted by selfish capitalism. The Communist Party realizes this and appears to be encouraging the native religions of Taoism and Buddhism as sources of ethical principle, in addition to the ever present Confucianism.

Asian values are different, but are changing. The ethnic Chinese leaders of Singapore lauded the "Asian" virtues of order, discipline, family loyalty, hard work and restraint, contrasting these with the self-indulgent, lazy, individualistic, ill-educated and individualistic West says Mabubani (1994). It is said that the "Asian Tiger" economies attribute their success and growing power precisely to their cultural differences from the West.

Questions concerning the concept of "East Asian values" being different have been raised by the Pew Global attitudes survey, and the East Asian Barometer Project, Freedom House publications, as well as by Dalton & Ong (2003). There is a generation gap evident and it may be that publicly expressed values and those privately held by individuals are at variance. There is also wide variability within the East Asian nations and the effects of economic development are not uniform. India, especially, seems apart from the Chinese values and attitudes. (http://pewglobal.org/reports;http://www.worldvaluessurvey.org/Upload/104_asian_values_hypothesis.pdf.
http://www.freedomhouse.org/ research/index.htm

Traditional Indian values include the pre-Aryan concept of moksa, (the goal of being released from the cycle of rebirths), and, to some degree, *ahimsa* (not harming). Other primary values include: *dharma* (religious or ethical virtue or law); *artha* (political power or wealth); and *kama* (pleasure). These values find religious/philosophical expression in four major views (*darsana*) and in many related groupings. Adherence to the caste system is also a traditional Indian value that becomes more controversial as globalization and economic development effect changes.

Hindu philosophy is very pluralist and very personal. It assumes that the ultimate truth is to be found within the individual. Such truth is believed to be permanent and universal. It is to be found by stripping away all the impermanent impressions of reality through meditation. Subjective knowledge of the self is more important than objective knowledge of the world. Intuition, rather than logic, is the only means of perceiving this truth. One who has discovered such truth is to be revered as a distinguished authority. The ultimate goal of this subjective spiritual search is *moksha* (or *nirvana*), a release from the cycle of rebirths.

The Hindu worldview assumes that there are four stages of life: that of student; that of householder; that of retirement, homage and benevolence; and that of contemplation and complete renunciation. The practical message of Hindu philosophy is to reduce desire and sensitivity. Globalization has brought a prosperous burgeoning to the middle classes. It remains to be seen what resolution the consumer society will have with traditional Hindu values.

The caste system conditions the application of many philosophical principles. Pandian (2007) describes the system as involving Brahmins, the superior and priestly order; the *jati* or mid classes; and the untouchables. The *jati* include the *Kshatriya* (those with the greatest economic and/or political power), the *Vaisiya* (affluent, but without power; and the *shudra* (artisans and laborers). The belief in *karma* (the idea that one is reborn in the status that his prior life merits) serves to justify the caste system. Similarly, *karma* may be seen as dampening millenarian zeal and encouraging a more fatalistic acceptance.

America

Many American attitudes seem to have been consistent since De Tocqueville. The American economic environment at the founding of the republic was one of plenty. Land was easily available and manpower was scarce. Socially, there was fluidity and opportunity. Isolation permitted resistance to Britain. The lawyer, rather than the priest, was the spokesman of the community. In general, the idea that value can be measured with dollars seems to be an unexamined assumption in American discourse.

The American Revolution emphatically established certain differences from England. The English common law, new theories about natural rights and the worldview of the

Enlightenment informed the American Revolutionary outlook. A nobility, a state religion and a powerful legislature were specifically rejected. The fiction of that era, a "social contract", was also postulated and the idea of a supreme organic law embodied in a constitution was realized. Pluralism and the separation of powers were also deemed to favor the ideals of "life, liberty and the pursuit of happiness. The "pursuit of happiness" appears to have been a euphemism of the time for commercial "free enterprise".

There have been constant themes of military-commercial expansion, religious involvement in politics, and exaggerated consumerism. The first settlement in America was launched as a religious-military-commercial venture. Throughout its history, America has used military violence to further its expansion.

The first permanent settlement, in Massachusetts, was of Pilgrims who sought to establish an ecclesiastical state. The Salem witch trials were the most famous fruit of their effort. In the decades before the American Revolution, the variety of imported goods increased by four thousand percent, and *consumerism* competed with Puritanism.

Evangelical movements or "parachurches" that cross doctrinal boundaries have been a common feature. C.J. Finney (1792-1875) described his successes in *Lectures on the Revivalism of Religion* (1835). He advocated long meetings to induce fatigue, long hypnotizing prayers, sermons alternately inducing fear and hope, and personal harangues. His techniques included the use of advance men and collaboration with local pastors. D.L. Moody (1837-1899) used Finney's techniques and induced local businessmen and ministers to financially support his revivals. Billy Sunday (1862-1935) was an entertainer who had a large and efficient revivalist business. He became acquainted with leading businessmen and politicians. Megachurches and drive-in churches highlight the fact that religion is viewed as a consumer marketing phenomenon.

Is there an American "economic man"? Declaring independence, the Colonists called for "life, liberty and the pursuit of happiness". The ideological justifications of the American founders have also to be considered in terms of economics. Their "happiness" may be construed in the sense of Hobbesian "felicity"- the unimpeded enjoyment of one consumer item after another. The paramilitary pre-Revolutionary Sons of Liberty were principally artisans and mechanics who saw profit in free trade and the curtailment of English imports. (Cohen 2003, Kendrick 1982, Breen 2004). Since their first encounters with the Barbary pirates, Americans have been engaged in wars of commercial purpose.

From Calvinism, Puritanism, and Arminianism came the view that some had God's favor and that being successful would prove it. A better life was to be had by man operating in a free economy. Unitarian humanitarianism and the transcendentalism of Thoreau and Emerson provided counterpoint to economic man. After Darwin, it became common to hear of the survival of the economically fittest. Such considerations tend to support the claim that Protestantism is capitalism.

Consumerism replaces affect. Modern America is urban and very heterogeneous, and depends on specialists and impersonal central, rather than local, services. The unconscious ideology includes thinking about cost/benefits and *minimum* legal requirements. Mobility and urban social isolation reduce individual identity and interpersonal bonding. Schooling is not individualized. There is little place for warm emotional feeling. Since people need affect and since they no longer have a large family to supply it, they must find it elsewhere. They may seek it the false intimacy of large churches or television shows.

Consumerism serves as a substitute for other human satisfactions. Television insulates people from a feeling of identification and responsibility for what happens, rendering them spectators. Dissatisfaction seems to be increasingly manifested in religious rather than political forms. Some call for a return to the "good old days".

A strong and heterogeneous religious presence characterized rural America. Significant minorities came to America to form communities and practice their faiths. Although the spirit of the Enlightenment informed several of the country's founders, the enlightened attitude was not universal. For example, the Continental Congress of 1774 banned cock fighting, theater and horse-racing as well as banning British goods. (Withington, 1991).

Evangelical and revivalist efforts have been a characteristic of American life. On psychological grounds, some suspect that emphasis on group religious expression could increase to assuage guilt over collective wrongdoing in social injustices, wars and economic affairs. A more probable explanation would be the search of individuals for an identity among a changing and uprooted population. Group (as opposed to individual) migration should have a contrary effect, increasing the cohesiveness of the migrants.

The mass man of the demographers is the target of skillful and very well financed manipulation. The film industry and television increasingly produce in response to marketing needs rather than to other criteria. Similarly, politicians and politics are manipulated according to very skillful and expensive marketing. Great wealth is thus able to, and does, control the news, opinion and politics of the nation. The same professional marketing skill can change the calls for economic reform to become calls for "moral and religious" reform. (See also Reed, 1996 and Bill Moyer's *Call to Renewal's* Pentecost 2004 keynote address).

"We don't have any nuances in Texas", said a twice-elected President. Introspection is generally disdained in America, as is any form of intellectualism. Americans are relatively unaware of history, important in many other cultures. The individualist and alienated mindset becomes more isolated and manipulated as reality is increasingly defined through television. Simplistic credulity makes the people very susceptible to ideological manipulation, while selfishness hinders complete ideological conviction.

Three decades ago, a popular writer complained of: "our inane impulse to involve ourselves everywhere, to dispense arms and largesse and to try to be loved". There seems to be a genuine and totally naïve conviction that American values would be adopted everywhere, if only the ignorant foreigners could see what they are.

The American mass psyche has at least five characteristics. Eric Hoffer described certain defects in the American mass psyche: the worship of success; equating quantity with quality; valuing only the practical; being fascinated with the trivial; and being addicted to movement. We also have the "American Hustler", whom Hoffer sees as a plastic man adapting to change but lacking the ideology and the magic of communion.

Rokeach (1973) discussed contending values in North American society. The mechanisms of the consumer society involve distribution, not purpose. Missing are external goals, a sense of mission, of contribution- things that contribute to finding a "purpose and meaning" in life. Do such material values as comfort, pleasure, excitement, or titillation have anything to do with having a sense of purpose? To supply missing psychic elements, a revived interest in religion, or the search for an ideology, might be expected.

American narcissism and fundamentalism may be a response to changed conditions. Just as a tribal Rorschach may apply to only a third of the population, so are psychiatric generalizations tenuous when applied to groups. Perhaps fundamentalism and narcissism are each a response to a changing and threatening world.

Christopher Lasch saw the following factors as contributing to a change toward narcissism in America: (1) a dangerous environment (2) weakened familial and social ties (3) emphasis on consumption rather than production (4) media fostering of a cult of glamour and celebrity (5) disappearance of a sense of historical continuity and of posterity, concomitant with the disappearance of the extended family.

The psychiatrist Otto Kernberg said that narcissism was a

continuum and that clinical cases are only more emphatic forms. In these, superegos control from fear rather than from guilt, with punitive and sadistic forms said to dominate (consider the prevalent Hollywood formula of sex, violence and sadism). Primitive thinking produces reliance on magic symbolism, and leaves little room for ambiguity. Identifying with other people is said to be beyond the capacity of the narcissist.

Projection intensifies the impression of a threatening world. There is rigid separation of good and bad images. Stress might facilitate a rage that results in acting out rather than in repression or sublimation. With acting out, a megalomaniac self-image results, with rage and envy compensated by fantasies of wealth, beauty and omnipotence. There is a sense of emptiness and phoniness.

The inner-directed obsessive-compulsive is said to have yielded place to the chaotic and impulsive. If these psychiatric insights are valid, one has some explanation of the motivation for both fundamentalism and narcissism in recent decades.

Canada

Canadian attitudes demand restraint. North of the American border, a different society has accreted, essentially without a clear culture or identity. Canada was colonized for economic exploitation and never experienced Enlightenment. Quebec was kept under the thumb of a reactionary Church. English Canada was told that "peace, order and good government" were the reigning values, along with an implicit class structure. Canadian Attitudes.

There was never nobility in Canada and, with the exception of two cities, nothing approaching a European class structure developed. Without such leadership, the civil servants became the establishment. Essentially, the butlers rule the mansion. The basic values thus became conservative and stagnant, prizing order and riskless security.

European peasants were imported to farm along the rail lines leading west. Today, new immigrant entrepreneurs, including many Asians, provide commercial leadership. As immigrant stock gradually achieves political power, there will be increasing discussion while the society seeks to become a nation and articulate its own values.

Latin America

Latin America has a tradition of peonage and dependent mercantilism. The economy, the tradition and the culture establish an unarticulated ideology. There was a tradition and culture in Latin America long before the Ibero-Catholic invasion. The Amerindian population showed passive resistance to the invader's ideology. For five hundred years, dependency-religious, governmental and economic- has been fostered in Latin America. Class apartheid has been encouraged to facilitate control.

As an antidote to the dominant Catholic Corporatism, Comte's positivism was introduced by educated technical elites who sought to counteract the influence of the Church and to introduce a more modern economic view to replace the dependent mercantilism. Although positivism does not appear to have taken root, liberation theology emerged as an essentially indigenous ideology, using the symbols of Christianity and embracing the Amerindian socialist tradition, fostering the collective spirit of the small community. Vatican opposition to liberation theology had made place for a Lutheran "freedom theology" in Mexico. Recently Protestant evangelicals are achieving great success preaching an entrepreneurial approach.

4

IDEOLOGIES

Zionism is a contrived ideology . Whereas the Amerindian ideology comes from unarticulated cultural bases, Zionism has been contrived and manipulated according to changing political conditions. Weissbrod (1981) traces the changes in Zionism over seventy years. In 1917, it was a revolutionary ideology of labor calling for immigration to Palestine, thus resurrecting Israel and offering individual salvation through work in agricultural communes. The ideal pioneer would be a "new man" self-sacrificing and having little interest in material rewards. "

In 1942, the definition of "Zionism" had changed to mean immigration to Israel and setting up a Jewish state. This was especially motivated by Hitler's *Shoah* and the closed-door policy of many nations toward Jewish immigration. By 1946, talk emphasized the working class and social and national, rather than individual, redemption.

Irgun, Haganah and Stern terrorism against the British in such incidents as the King David Hotel bombing and such military terror attacks against the Palestinian Arabs as at Deir Yassin and Jaffa in April of 1948 were successful in removing the local populations to make way for Jewish immigrants.

"Zionism" seemed to yield to "Israelism" after some 750,000 Palestinians had been driven from their homes. By 1973, many young people were talking about "New Zionism", which gave a religious justification for the settlement of the occupied territories. Weissbrod notes that having *national* goals is convenient, for no changes in the social order are then required.

Demographics evoke tribal extremism. The ruling Likud party is far to the right of Ben Guerion's socialist Zionism, and the Jewish state is faced with a demographic problem. The territories occupied in 1967 contain far too many non-Jews. To make them part of a democratic Jewish state would recognize a non-Jewish majority. To withdraw to the 1967 borders would require the removal of almost a million Jewish "settlers" fostered by the Likud and subsidized by billions of American tax dollars. The policy of the Likud leader, Sharon, was to simultaneously foster settlement of Jews and the ethnic cleansing of Palestinian Arabs. The spirit of the times, or *zeitgeist* affects personal ideology. Israel's ethnic state concept is reminiscent of the spirit prevailing a century ago when former empires were breaking up. Will multiculturalism eventually supplant tribalism?

When we review the sources of personal ideology, it is apparent that the individual is strongly influenced by the tradition and the culture. Such influence could be said to produce a "collective unconscious" or "modal personality" dominating about one fifth of the individual personality. Propaganda could then create a multi-modal national personality with possible neurotic superego conflicts.

For society to survive and prosper, the culture must respond to the environment. To at least feed the people, economics must dominate ideology. Environmental and economic change will provoke change in the ideology, but the natural alternations of the expressed and the repressed will also bring change. The system must thus handle both diversity and change.

Socialization forms the child. The child gets basic beliefs about the world early. The culture also causes him to unconsciously form views. Parents articulate and transmit filtered bits of ideology. School and church consciously seek to indoctrinate the child with the established ideologies. The process is one of "socialization".

Peer groups, cults and social movements can also form special or counter-ideologies. Counter-ideologies tend to use the traditional words and symbols but put a special twist on them so that words become split-referents and have multiple meanings. The special ideology seeks a free ride on the established connotations of the tradition.

When people act on it, ideology ceases to be merely words. Personal ideology is highly subjective, but commonly shared beliefs find expression in physical action. Thus, collective ideology can become reality.

RELIGION

How is religion to be defined? William Alston says that to find religion one should see where the "divine" is sought or said to be and "what response is made to it". *Sacramental religion* locates the divine in things and in procedures. *Prophetic religion* (Judaism, Christianity, and Islam) focuses primarily on human society and its progression, emphasizing the divine word as revealed by the prophets. *Mystical religion* centers on transcendent unity with the universe.

Religion is a subset of philosophy. In practice, any organized religion may express sacramental, prophetic and mystical aspects. Since its focus is society, prophetic religion may emphasize ethics and morality. Confucianism, focusing on man, is a prophetic religion-philosophy. Communist China had a strong neo-Confucian influence. Said Mao Tsetung: "my god is the Chinese people".

We suggest that the religious urge is to seek understanding of and unity with the universe, while defining one's role therein. Nonetheless, the Abrahamic religions that are so influential in our world focus on socicty and the revealed word.

"God" is undefinable. If one asks a number of believers "what is your definition of God?", most will be unable to offer one. "God" is ineffable and a very general symbol that means different things to different people.

Religion has many dimensions: "Religion" serves many purposes and can mean many different :.ings. Glock (1962) postulated five dimensions to religion: (a) overt behavior in practice and ritual (b) emotional expression and satisfaction (c) seeking "knowledge" or "understanding" (d) the ideological satisfaction of belief e) propitiation and social integration. :

Religion serves individuals and society. Religion serves the needs of the individual and the needs of society. People want to have a sense of personal integration, of integration with society and with the universe. They want to understand their place in the order of things. They want to have hope and to feel that they have some satisfying purpose in life. They want to calm their fears. They want to transcend their bodies and their lives. Society, too, wants integration, order, and common purpose. For its part, religion seeks to satisfy conscious and unconscious anxieties, pretends to aid the understanding and control of the world, and supports social solidarity.

In his apologia, *Varieties of Religious Experience* (1902), William James makes the following claims for basic religious belief: (a) The visible world draws its significance from a greater, spiritual world, (b) Our true goal is to seek harmony with that greater world; (c) Communion with the spirit of that greater world is possible.

There is also the question of life's purpose. Religion reflects the questions of "how" and "why", the ethics and morals of existence. Fear, curiosity and desire for well-being are all motives.

Freud, in his *The Future of an Illusion*, suggests that gods have three principal functions: (a) to succor from the vicissitudes of nature. (b) To rescue from unkind fate and death. (c) To console. Freud further suggests that the religious illusions which men cherish are constructed out of their childhood memories and out of memories of the race. For him, religion was an attempt to dominate the real world by the wish world. He saw religion as a neurosis on the road to maturity.

There are many motives for religion. King and Hunt (1972), found these dimensions, among others, to personal motives for religion: (a) to communicate with spirits. (b) To hold a canned set of beliefs. (c) Reassurance for feelings of inadequacy. (d) Motives of selfish advancement.

There are several psychological foci of religion: On a psychological level, there are certain primary foci for religion: (a) an hallucinatory sense of unity with a maternal matrix (womb return). This is seen as repairing disjunctures in the personality. The union gives the sense of conditional approval. Feelings of shame are thus relieved; (b) A seeking to pacify the paternal (conscience); (c) The projection and reflection of self; (d) the dissolution of self. Since man is a social animal, his desire to dissolve himself in the stream of life may exist independently of desiring womb return. This "dissolving" may also be a seeking for "unity with the universe".

Motivations of first-year theological students: Webb (1966) found a group of first year theological students motivated by: (1) dissolving self into the greatness of god; (2) achieving peace of mind; (3) masochistic self-sacrifice; (4) finding meaning; (5) sociability; (6) partaking of mystical power; (7) womb return; (8) communion with spirits. A broad spectrum of needs, both personal and societal, exists even within a single religious group.

Religious needs are basic: Man wants both existence and to transcend that existence. There may be a basic need to feel that one exists, that one is a distinctive and valuable person. There certainly is an inborn drive to preserve that existence. The sense of reality is in part derived from others, and our personal feeling about existence depends largely on the reaction of others.

Transcendence implies the desire to identify with an existence that views life from a greater and higher perspective than that of self. Seeking escape, seeking psychic completion via union, etc., may represent the search for transcendence. Thus, man wants to exist and to preserve that existence, but his desires for transcendence may marvelously transform the drive to exist, such as by seeking martyrdom.

It is plausible, but not certain, that religious seekings group into three factors: (a) Seeking completion, fulfillment and integration. (b) Dissolving self in something greater, seeking immortality. (c) Desiring womb-return, wish-fulfillment. Can these factors each be served by a different expression of love? Are these also the seekings of ideology?

The socio-biologist Edward O. Wilson has proceeded from the study of ants to humans and thus takes a broad perspective of human effort. For Wilson, religion classifies a person, provides him with membership in a group claiming great powers, and gives him a purpose in life compatible with his self-interest.

Wilson claims that objectification, symbolic simplification and description of reality with images and definitions that are easily understood and unshakable are the first steps in organizing a religion. The savage models his Earth-Mother in clay, the peon adores gilded statues of the Virgin and ideologues use vast systems symbolized by a flag.

Emotional self-surrender: "Commitment is the second process of religion-making... commitment is pure tribalism enacted through emotional self-surrender", says Wilson in *On Human Nature*. We may see this as the conversion phenomenon, the embracing of the ideology.

Mythical explanation: Finally, says Wilson, there is myth: the narratives by which the special place of the tribe in the world is explained in terms that the believer can understand. Thus, religion and totalitarian political ideology may share some common motivations and satisfactions.

Religion and group survival: D. S. Wilson (2002) considers religion from the standpoint of group survival. In his thesis, small tribes cannot afford priests and governmental organization. Only when there are enough members in the group can specialists be afforded. The expansion and long-term survival of the group's religion, in competition with other religions, depends on the policies of the religion.

One unfortunate survival pattern is that of "kill or convert". This has been a good survival policy, as have been principles of maximum procreation, proselyting, forgiveness of members, etc. The extermination of one's enemies has been lauded at least since Deuteronomy 20 and the Talmud, lending religious justification to political objectives. When we are attacked on this basis by members of other religions, we may call them "terrorists", but they are convinced that they are doing the will of God.

Religion is also social conformity. Religion is seen as useful in maintaining the order of society. Gradually, its function changes from legitimation to consolation. The religion to which one belongs is largely a matter social learning and social pressure.

Superficial surveys are biased toward socially conforming responses. If ninety percent of people asked told a pollster that "yes, they did believe in God" were they sincere and, if so, would they have defined "God" as "nature", etc.? In Germany, those who declare a faith are taxed for the support of that faith and non-believers are not taxed. Social factors are strong: Of German Catholics so taxed, one-third said (*Spiegel*, 6, 2006) that they did not believe in God and half of the Protestants did not!

Conventionally religious people are more responsive to prestige, are suggestible and are seemingly always moving toward majority opinion. Forty-two percent of Starbuck's (1898) subjects said they were converted as a result of social pressure. (Today, this is called "moving toward majority opinion"). Atheists and prophets, however, respond to their own convictions. The prophet may actually claim to "know" and have talked with God, and thus is not troubled by the uncertainty of belief that may trouble others seeking to fit with the majority.

There are several possible motives for joining a religion: Possible motivating factors for accepting a religion include: (a) Social learning and conformity. (b) Transcendence, identity, integration. (c) Frustration and seeking solace. (d) Fear. (e) Hope, wish fulfillment, control.

Seeking "understanding" is a universal impetus to religion. Perhaps it aids the formation of a worldview and the finding of a place in the world. A canned belief system supplies this. In supplying the "why", illogic and inconsistencies may be acceptable as amorphous symbols are manipulated. Accepting the world as random (as many scientists do) seems incompatible with religious needs for answers and fixed points of reference.

Social learning and conformity are major factors in forming a belief system. Older studies have shown religious belief to be determined by: parents (67%); church (40%); social learning (42%); conformity (27%). Thus, two thirds of religious adherence was due to social learning and conformity, although other factors were also common. Socialization is also integral to forming the external conscience, the superego.

Other motives for seeking religion were: fear (51%); consolation (18%); mystical (17%); sex turmoil (16%). These were not exclusive i.e., many cited both a mystical and a sex turmoil motivation.

"Seeking unity with the universe" can take many forms, including "dissolving oneself in the leader". Ideas of warmth, peace, coming home, unity, joy, new reality, out of body experience, etc., all have been considered "transcendence".

The "mystical" seems to involve only a sixth of those who are very religious. Dreams, seeing light, hearing voices, have all been called visionary or "mystical". Gimello (1978) calls the mystical a "state of mind", which may bring a feeling of unity with the universe, a sense of the blending of opposites, a stepping out of the usual modes of thought, and a confidence in the reality of the experience, even though it is ineffable. Those who have experienced such right-brain phenomena are unshakably convinced that they are real.

The concepts of the sacred, spirituality and transcendence are interrelated. The "sacred" involves the individual's perception of the "ultimate reality or truth"; or of a divine object or being (Hill et al. 2000). Spirituality involves investing a part of daily life with the sacred. "Seeking" may be the attempt to identify and articulate the sacred. "Religion" usually implies a faith community and a validated way of seeking (organized religion). Scales have been developed to measure spirituality and religion. The Spiritual Transcendence Scale considers reported responsive contact with the sacred;

unity with the universe; and connectedness with past, present and future (Piedmont & Leach 2002). MacDonald (2000) found "spirituality" to factor: cognitive orientation; an experiential or phenomenological outlook; existential well-being; paranormal beliefs; and general religiousness. Hill and Hood (1999) list more than one hundred measures of religiousness, including "images of God" and the attitude toward death.

Externalizing in the leader. The threatening voice of father has been called the beginning of conscience, of the superego and of the call to action. That conscience will need to be removed from the self and externalized. Projected outside, it becomes the "voice" of God, the "orders" of a superior officer, etc. In the Catholic system, the superego is projected onto the priesthood. The believer achieves a symbolic integration of self in the leader (or the King).

Guilt is a manipulative handle. Fromm suggests that Western man has been encouraged to project all that is good in himself onto God and thus to feel vile and alienated. In religious terms, is God projected as the superego and the Devil as the id? Could a principal religious seeking be the relief of feelings of guilt? Guilt is a marvelous handle for manipulation. If natural feelings of guilt and social inadequacy are not sufficiently troubling, religion will actively seek to enhance the feeling of guilt. This is necessary to increase the demand for the solution offered- a reduction and accommodation of guilt feelings.

Someone is watching. The superego is the conscience that society imposes on us. We are quite aware of that conscience. Some psychiatrists postulate another, unconscious conscience. Some think it may be mother's lingering influence. This psychic presence may be projected as God. Could it also be the spirit of the Leader? Is "Big Brother" watching?

Womb return. Externalization may be accomplished by surrender to some external authority. If the god is projected as a sheltering and protecting mother, then the return to the womb, the union with a maternal matrix, is a surrender that brings relief from anxiety and guilt. This may help to explain the place of

Mary along with a Trinitarian god-head.

Union is feeling whole in a comfortable place. "Finding one's place in the world" involves explanation, conformity, and integration with that world on the part of the individual. To do this, the individual must also find a personal identity and seek personal psychological integration. The integration of the individual within himself and with the world is a complicated and interrelated process. Would return would achieve these goals.

Love is also humanistic benevolence: "Love" occupied a primary place in Christianity, in the expression of important Confucian thinkers, in Greek cosmology, and in Freudian analysis. Do these broad and diverse uses reflect only the elasticity of a widely used symbol, or is there a common nexus of meaning, a universal unifying principle? Recall that "love" may involve sex, adoration, projection, the herd instinct, humane benevolence, etc.-

Chinese *jen* and *li* could explain the universe: Wang Yang-Ming (c.1500) saw love (*jen*) in the drive to perpetuate the species, in the desire to preserve the self, and in the urge to dissolve the self in the universe. The ordering principle of the universe (li) could be discovered within one's self, expanded upon, and realized through praxis. Thus would one achieve unity with the universe. (*Li* is similar to the *logos* described by Heraclitus of Ephesus.)

Proper conduct towards others was also *jen*, which can also be translated as "the moral quality of humaneness". There is also a sense of *jen* that means "seed" or "growth". Chu Hsi (c. 1170) said that, with *jen,* man can find unity with heaven, earth, and all things- a sort of loving identification. It has been claimed that the entire Confucian Analects are an exposition of *jen.* http://www.wsu.edu/~dee/GLOSSARY/JEN.HTM

For Ch'eng Hao, principle, *li* merged with jen as the concept of reproduction, the spirit of life, the understanding of which yielded unity. By 1900, K'ang Yu-wei was calling jen "compassion" and the "universally diffused power of attraction".

Love was the dynamic tension that held the universe together according to Heraclitus. For Empedocles, love was the unifying force of the universe, as strife was the opposite. *Logos* was the ordering principle of the universe, to be apprehended by the psyche. Plato divided the psyche into intellect, passion and appetite, suggesting the ambivalence and plurality of man's psychic nature.

Is "love" really love of self? From these Chinese and Greek examples "love" is seen to include both the striving for universality and the striving for immortality. There is implicit in "love" the notion of attraction. The role of the self is unclear, but the dissolving of self in the universe is a goal.

If the self is understood as divided, ambivalent, pluralistic, and passionate, then the problem becomes more complicated. One may experience a captivating idealization, an adoration, but of what? Is it the self that is really adored, the part that represents the completion, the union, the universal, the immortal or the best? Does such a love allow man to affirm his own existence?

Is sex the primary motivation? The drive to reproduce is fundamental. Once accomplished, the organism may be expendable. In this sense of universal priority, the sex-instinct either subsumes or takes priority over the instinct of self-preservation. Is the urge to be with one's own kind, the *herd instinct*, attributable to the reproductive instinct? Is the attraction here the same as the attraction that forms a part of "love"?

Is ideological commitment both love and religion? From the foregoing, it would appear that love, adoration and dedication can satisfy the religious seekings relating to fulfillment and selfless immortality. We note that ideological commitment to a cause, leader and group would offer similar satisfactions.

The role of narcissism: Can love be paranoia and narcissistic megalomania? According to the Freudian organon, hysterics and obsessional neurotics can retain actual or imaginary love objects, but many paranoids turn the sex-energy inward, becoming narcissistic. The paranoid's end of the world vision is thus the very opposite of being in love.

Does belief in wish-fulfillment suggest narcissistic megalomania? As the infant fails to distinguish between his own body and the universe, so extraordinary belief in the power of wishes may indicate a primitive failure to distinguish between self and universe and, thus, a narcissistic megalomania.

Can one express narcissism by adoring a narcissistic leader? To be loved is the aim and the satisfaction in a narcissistic object-choice. Normal non-sexual love could be for the man who protects or the woman who nurtures, but narcissistic love could be for what one was, is, or would like to be. Narcissism may also be a way of coping with a threatening world, of answering a life that seems to hold no future and no strong ties with others."

Repressed sex can seek Armageddon. When sex-energy is focused normally, it can be applied in the religious direction of completion, fulfillment and integration. Ego is altruistically dissolved in the object choice and immortality is achieved through offspring.

If normal catharsis is blocked, passion mounts and expression may be sought via the dissolution of self in something greater, something also the locus of immortality and the beneficiary of altruism. Repression can beget regression and a return toward infantile narcissism, corresponding to the religious direction of womb return and magical wish-fulfillment. This can lead to neurotic megalomania, paranoia and end of the world fantasies.

Seeking unity with the universe. Joseph Campbell sees symbols and myths as objects constructed to shape the unconscious to respond to practical needs of society and existence. It is in trying to see beyond these contrived and fashioned objects that one seeks to find reality and union with the universe. "Mythology is psychology misread as biography, history and cosmology".

God

Defining "God" is difficult. "In the beginning was the *logos* and the *logos* was with God, and the *logos* was God" (John 1:1). The word *logos* is conventionally translated as "word", but the Greek usage at the time also conveyed the idea of "logic" or "reason" or "formula" or "ordering principle of the universe". This sounds very much like what is meant by the Chinese concept of *li*.

Ch'i or the power of God: Campbell derives as a universal principle that everything is the effect of a general power, back into which all must ultimately dissolve. He notes that science calls this "energy"; the Melanesians call it *manna*; the Sioux Indians *wahonda*; the Hindus *shakti*; and the Christians "*the power of God*". It also appears to be what Confucians call *ch'i*. Perhaps meditation might bring some to understand the universal force that lies beyond the symbols and the unconscious.

An amorphous deity offers advantages. "Libidinal" energy is so pervasive and diffuse as to be ineffable. Therefore, ritual, myths and gods serve as symbols to channel the mind to that ineffable something beyond. This perception of something beyond is obscured in Judaism, Christianity and Mohammedanism because they teach that the personality of the deity is fixed and humanoid, rather than amorphous.

Seeking the Kingdom of God. If *Luke* 17:21 is translated as "the Kingdom of God is *within* you", then we are talking about the individual. (An alternative translation is "the Kingdom of God is *among* you", suggesting realization of the Promised Land in the present world). Groups with an eschatological hope of the Kingdom of God on Earth may be in conflict with the conservatism of an established state religion. A similar perversion arises when such evangelical groups fall under the control of conservative monied interests. When a church no longer serves the social needs of a local congregation, it might provide an impetus to "isms", to reach that "Kingdom of God".

Ideology and religion offer the same major satisfactions. Love, projection upon and identification with a leader, and dissolution in an organization can gratify major religious seekings. These are also the principal aspects of commitment to an ideological movement. Religion, however, usually has a supernatural element, may have difficulty effecting political programs and may have no ostensible class or nationalist focus. This changes severely when religious fanaticism is coupled with nationalism and partisan politics. In today's world, political ideology may be yielding place to politico-religious ideology.

Both civil religion and traditional religion make appeal to some supervening principle, often called "God", which is deemed integral to the religion. "The Creator", "divine Providence", "Nature's God", "Supreme Judge", "Fate" and many other terms were used to this same purpose. At the time those terms were used in the American Declaration of Independence, both the spirit of the Enlightenment and natural law theory were prevalent. The framers sought to appeal to as wide an audience as possible. Such amorphous and general symbols are politically useful. Similarly, the "pursuit of happiness" was a code phrase for both local free trade and protectionism.

Wealth can be a God. Having seen mob violence in Amsterdam and having grown up with tales of the Thirty Years War, Spinoza thought that the mob needed to be diverted from its religious passions and to have its energies channeled by a civil religion. Instead of seeking sanctity, they should be induced to seek money. The civil religion should lead them toward rational, rather than emotional and imaginative behavior. Interestingly, Spinoza, in 1676, thought a liberal democracy with individual freedoms would provide the most favorable environment for such a civil religion to lead men to better things. For Spinoza, God was only nature and religious rapture could be found in seeking unity with the natural universe.

The definition of "God" is problematic. The variation among believers who attempt it is far wider than one would imagine. The definition is frequently (and with reason) avoided. Perhaps the quest to find "God" is the search to find oneself and to be integrated with the universe. Experiencing beauty can give a feeling of transcendence, as does the experience of awesome power. Energy is primal, but it can be personified through gods. The eternal is often thought to be divine.

The circle is a common religious symbol. Jung said that the image of a god is an obstacle to experiencing transcendence. The circle, however, Jung thought to be the most pervasive religious symbol, representing the self, the soul and the universe of enclosed space. The circle could symbolize integration and eternal continuity.

What of deities who are clowns? Consider the American Indian "trickster" or a comedian, such as Charlie Chaplin. Would such idols represent the self as projected in a problematic universe?

God is often a father-substitute. The common man projects his God as a father-substitute, thought Freud. Freud explained that the deity is endowed with the function of protection, of explaining the universe, and of defining the moral order, the rights and wrongs of conduct- the role of the father.

Is God close or distant? Broen (1956) found two entirely different attitudes among strongly religious people. Some thought of god as close and accessible. Others had a vision of an intolerant and distant god punishing an essentially sinful man. This might correlate with basic attitudes of trust or mistrust in mankind, and with the difference between natural and authoritarian religion.

Human nature as God: "Natural law has undergone a significant transformation. So, too, has "nature", which was often thought synonymous with "god". "In 'nature', we have a 'common good of man'... it is a combination of postulates and experiences... that people do not question, even if they belong to opposed systems", said Cardinal Roy in "*Reflections on Pacem in Terris.*"

God as "nature": "Nature" may be replaced with such near synonyms as "quality of life" or "values" when referring to human nature. The concept leads to a harmonization of wills and "ideals" with the image of society, which can be called the "spiritual order", according to Cardinal Roy. If we follow Cardinal Roy's reasoning, it would seem the "God becomes "nature" which becomes "common good" and then becomes "values". Harmonizing individual wills with ideals gives the "spiritual order" of society, which sounds very much like the politico-ideological order.

"God" is a projection of society, says Swanson (1964). Gods are projected models of the local human society. A diverse and specialized society will produce principal gods. A hierarchical diverse society will imagine a higher god, etc. Thus, society is the genesis of religion. Gods are, in part, the projection of the societal organization, and especially the personal familial situation (Hertel & Donahue, 1995). Myths are persistent and conserving, so the model of society projected may be an ancient one. God- society

God can be the self. Perhaps what is worshipped is really the self, dissolved in society and idealized. The Devil then becomes the repressed or rejected identity. It is useful to keep this insight in mind when one considers civil religions that create scapegoats. It is noteworthy that some non-dualistic Indian religions make this relation explicit- they recognize that the deity is really within the individual.

Bateson, in his *Steps towards an Ecology of Mind* suggests that the form of religion reflects the concept of "self". Thusly "totemism" is self completely absorbed by the environment, "animism" is self projected onto the environment and "gods" are the self projected away from the environment.

Progressive development of religious forms: Some claim that man first worshipped the spirits of objects, "animism". Then, an object became the symbol for something else, "totemism". Subsequently, religion was expressed in polytheism, henotheism (principal gods), pantheism and monotheism. (The "powers" attributed to Catholic saints, Mary, the Trinity, angelic hierarchies, etc. indicate the difficulty of classifying religions.)

"God" may describe the reality of the society. The first deity seems to have involved the female, reproductive, principle. This evolved into Great Goddess worship. As we begin to enter recorded history, Ishtar, Astarte, Isis, Cybele and Aphrodite continue the Great Goddess tradition. Soon, they begin to be joined by a young male god who represents vegetation. The young god dies and is resurrected annually. Religion might thus be the symbolic collective representation of reality, as perceived in the epoch.

For the Babylonians, men were to serve the gods and their needs. Man's destiny ended with death, with no after-life. The antithesis of that cosmic order was chaos.

God is a contractual partner for the Jews, As an ethnic religion, Judaism was essentially a contract for Yahweh to assure that his chosen people prospered, notes Northrup Frye. Words here assumed a legalistic rather than a mystical aspect. As the Jews became agricultural, rather than nomadic, Yahweh took on different attributes. The formation of a confederacy gave impetus to the monotheism of Yahweh. (One may recall that local gods do not travel well).

After Israel was conquered by the Persians (537 B.C.), Yahweh was given the function of assuring a day of vengeance in the future, a Day of the Lord, when the existing order would be overthrown, the nations would be judged and the Kingdom of God established on Earth. Yahweh is also the God of History, guiding the progressive evolution of the People of Israel.

Distress begets the myth of a redeemer. With distress, the religious idea of a "redeemer" evolves. The spirits of returning vegetation, such as the corn stalk, and of celestial bodies became the icons for myths of a resurrecting god in the Hellenistic Age.

Originally a Jewish heresy, Christianity became, with Paul, potentially universal rather than ethnic. The Roman emperor Constantine gave substance to the potential universality. The day of the sun god was adopted as the day of rest, and other amalgamations were effected. By 325, a council, seeking to unite three large factions, decided on a Trinitarian god.

The salvation sought by the intellectual is mental. That sought by the poor is often material. Generally, as the belief in magic fades, people become more interested in a total explanation of how things fit together in the world. The universal replaces the particular as religion develops. Religion is useful to the individual psychologically. As an instrument of coercion, pacification, and instruction, it is also useful to society and to rulers. This helps explain the transition to ideology and civil religions such as National Socialism and Marxist-Leninism.

Religion is a popular expression of philosophy in the sense that people seek to explain their lives and the world through religion. Many suggest that a definition of "philosophy" should include the specification that philosophy involves "reasoned speculation". *Speculation* is key, because dealing only with what is known would belong in the realms of science, history, etc. Thus, this view requires that philosophy deal only with the *unknown*.

God did it. Looking at the branches of philosophy known as "rationalism" and "empiricism", one encounters concern over the origin of universals, "innate ideas", "innate principles", etc. Such claims tend to reduce to "we have to assume some pre-existing logical rules before we can start thinking" and "since we don't know how these first principles got into our minds, we must assume that God put them there". Such considerations make it easy to claim that religion is, indeed, a subset of philosophy.

Logos, a potential intersection of the supernatural and the transcendental, was noted by Heraclitus of Ephesus (fl. 400 B.C.). He, and the subsequent Stoics, believed the World to be uncreated, but saw a *logos* or formula that balanced the natural strife of opposites in the continual flux of the natural world. The universe was thus seen as a system responding to natural laws that tended to harmony in an ever-cycling universe. Many names were ascribed to this "unity of the universe". It was often considered a sort of non-anthropomorphic deity.

Churches and Believers

Characteristics of believers: Brown & Lowe (1951) found significant distinctions between believing and non-believing university students. The believers had lower intelligence (50th percentile vs. 80th), but they worried less and were less introverted. Their interest patterns were narrower than the non-believers. Among the Bible-college students whom Brown and Low used as controls there was a significant tendency to lie to produce socially acceptable responses. There is often a difference between what people say they believe and what they practice. The Bible students were more stable, self-possessed, and had better inter-personal relations.-

The strong finding of authoritarianism among those who take their Bible literally may help explain the phenomenon of Christian fascism. Poythress (1975) performed a study and reviewed other investigations, concluding that anti-religious persons are more intelligent ($p < 0.01$) and less authoritarian ($p < 0.005$) than the religious. Both the Stewart & Webster (1970) team and G. M. Maranell found a clear distinction between conservative and liberal/social clergymen. Both groups exhibited anti-scientific attitudes or "superstition". Fundamentalism and theism (at a loading of 0.91) dominated the attitudes of the conservative ministers. The conservatives were not interested in supporting causes.

Although both liberal and conservative ministers of this fundamentalist church were superstitious, the outlook and ministry were different. The attitude loadings of the liberal clergymen were:

(a) Ritualism (.91)
(b) Superstition (.66)
(c) Mysticism (.64)
(d) Organizational Interests (.63)

(e) "Cause" Espousal (.57)
(f) Altruism (.54)
(g) Fundamentalism (.39)
(h) Theism (.39)

Guilt and its projection are learned. That children learn the religion of their parents and of their school is obvious. Belief is developed by overt conformity. Eventually, parental and group standards are internalized, providing the main components of superego formation.

Fear and the propitiation of an angry father-god help to account for religion, especially among authoritarians. Could this sort of analysis be applied to Iran, with its tradition of the absolute father and of projected violence?

Handling of aggression differs. The superego may be harsh, (possibly, it has been suggested, in proportion to the cultural pressure forbidding aggression towards parents or other authority figures). This guilt is then directed inward until released by being projected out onto the Devil or out-groups. One study found that Catholic and Baptist children tended to internalize aggression, whereas Jewish children tended to externalize it. Such externalization skips the guilt and its consequent projection.

Responsibility can be projected from the self. When the authoritarian says: "I only follow orders", we see the mechanism of projection at work. The Catholic system, for example, facilitates projection of the superego onto the priesthood or authorities.

Prophetic religion becomes revelation. In prophetic religions, God is the powerful and distant father who commands the obedience of men. God's will is revealed by the prophet who proclaims the new worldview. The written word later dominates in the prophetic religions, and revelation becomes law.

Religious propagators were characterized: Weber classified the propagators of the major religions: (a) Confucianism- the organizing bureaucrat; (b) Hinduism- the world-ordering magician; (c) Buddhism- the traveling mendicant monk; (d) Islam- the world-conquering warrior; (e) Judaism- the wandering trader; (f) Christianity- the itinerant journeyman.

A church differs from a cult or a movement. Cults, movements, sects and churches are among the forms of religious organization. A church says Weber, may be characterized by: (a) A professional priesthood (b) Dogmas and rites are systematically defined. (c) It asserts the equality of all members in the faith. (d) It asserts universal and unique dominion. (e) There is a compulsory aspect to the organization. (f) The church claims institutional, rather than individual, charisma.

The assumption of a body of scripture and of an institution existing apart from the society underlies much of the thought published by Westerners. However, the religion may be the society itself and need not depend on scripture (China may be an example of this).

Denominationalism, institutionalization, and authoritarianism meet religious needs. The individual has certain "religious" needs that are better satisfied in a group or institutional way. The institution can offer and inculcate a canned set of beliefs with group reinforcement and social solidarity. People with strong religious beliefs grouped on the factors: institutionalization, denominationalism and authoritarianism (Brown, 1962).

Fundamentalists are often fearful and social authoritarians. Members of a conservative fundamentalist church formed three clusters: authoritarians, the fearful, and the socially ambitious (Monaghan, 1967).

There is little relation between church activity and ethical behavior: Cline & Richards (1965) found almost no relationship between church activity and conduct according to religious principles. People overtly active in institutional church affairs seemed to be exploiting their relationship to the church. Within any organization, the goals of the founding movement are altered by those wishing to foster their own interests. Such extrinsics predominate.

Conservative fundamentalists and social liberals form two groups. One study found American churchgoers in two distinct clusters: the "conservative fundamentalists" and the "liberal socials". A similar division was found among conservative and liberal ministers of a fundamentalist denomination. Conservatives showed fundamentalism, theism, and superstition. Conservative fundamentalist ministers had dogmatic, ethnocentric, rigid, views and values. They had a negative view of man, exhibited insensitivity and called for law and order.

The liberal ministers of the same denomination, by contrast, had an inner sufficiency, a positive view of man, and a sensitive, existential outlook. Liberals saw religion as mystical, altruistic, idealistic and oriented to the church as an organization. They were ritualistic and mystic, rather than theistic. Liberal ministers would support causes, but conservatives would not.

Are one's standards internal or external? In attempting to predict the behavior of believers, it should prove useful to ask whether the outlook is conservative or liberal and to then determine whether the person is driven by internal or external standards. This would yield four categories. One suspects that extrinsic conservatives would predominate in proportion to the prevalence of authoritarians. Factors such as frequency of church attendance, religious group activities and performance of ritual religious duties have been used as measures of religiosity or extrinsic orientation.

An "intrinsic" religious orientation has also been identified by the sixteen item Quest Scale (Altemeyer & Hunsberger 1992) and appears to well distinguish the "questers" from the religious fundamentalists and their prejudices. Concern with a purpose in life, with a sense of mission, with finding meaning in situations and seeing the unfolding of life as part of a larger plan have been used a criteria of an intrinsic or spiritual orientation.

Urban religion. A rural society and an urban society require different religious expression, and the rural immigrant moving to the city will seek others of like background. They will tend to form a religious grouping that differs both from the rural milieu and from the established city churches (See Gardner, 1982). Urban religion must provide a philosophy of life for daily interaction with strangers in the midst of pluralism of values, and still maintain an ostensible continuity with the rural past.

The Sephardic Jews immigrating to Israel faced a situation analogous to that of rural people migrating to a new urban environment. They were marginalized by the dominant Ashkenazim Jews. Rabbi Ovadia Yosef organized the Sephardim into an effective "civil society" with services, a political party (SHAS) and an ideology of returning to the religious law and practices. Essentially, this was an extension of their older custom of having community life center on the synagogue, with an added element of organized political participation.

A cult or sect cannot claim universality. Similarly, it must allow enough freedom of conscience to permit others to join. As a community of the elect, only members may be in a position to know and judge each other. Those who would join must usually demonstrate their suitability and willingness to abide by group standards. They must be prepared to be independent of the rest of society while highly dependent on each other.

The sect may also appeal to those with unusual desires. Fabian (in Halperin, 1983) found Jamaa followers enjoying the impoverishment, suffering and boredom that resulted from membership in the sect. (How prevalent is masochism and how much do the satisfactions thereof explain participation in other such movements?)

A movement may arise when the established institutions no longer serve the needs of many people. If their psychic and physical circumstances become disquieting, people will seek to orient themselves and find comfort in new forms of religious expression and organization. They will thus seek a new philosophy (or a return to an imagined "Lost Paradise"). Is the religious pilgrimage a means of breaking away from old structures, of swarming (like bees) in search of new inspiration and orientation with others who are dissatisfied?-

Seeking security is an important motive. Religion can offer standards and a secure place. When one loses the security and protection of a stable place in a stable society with known standards, he feels threatened. He may also perceive economic and physical threats. He may wish to relieve this anxiety, powerlessness, aloneness, and doubt. The individual may seek to associate himself with a group in which he can find a place and feel secure and to which he can refer for standards. Perhaps fascism offered similar advantages.

Continuity is usually claimed in religions. In offering succor, religion will typically serve to unite the older tradition with a response to the newer needs. A semblance of continuity, control and dignity will be preserved while substantive changes in philosophy are made to accommodate new conditions. One may find "scripture" continually reinterpreted to accommodate such changes. A religious or political movement will usually claim the legitimacy of tradition while developing a compensating ideology for the changed conditions that threaten the psyches of adherents. Even a revolutionary movement will claim to adhere to certain traditional principal values of the civil religion.

Finding salvation through the movement. A group gives protection, a movement promises salvation. A religious movement is still a mass in motion. There is a common seeking, rather than a stable structure. The usual motives for religious seeking may be present, but something creative and renewing is also sought.

A movement wants charismatic leadership and salvation. General slogans, such as "peace", "life", and "justice", may be voiced. In joining a group, one seeks a protected place. In joining a movement, one is often seeking salvation from dissatisfaction. Universal generalities characterize salvation religions. A person disoriented and seeking security will want such simple and seemingly complete explanations of things.

Can a movement's evangel be universal? Economics, political conditions, social structure and family ties as well as individual personality affect one's acceptance of a movement. The movement is essentially a swarming of the discontented seeking a new ideological and organizational structure. The mass in motion is detached from the traditional structure. Better material conditions, a new unity, an integrating worldview and set of values are sought. The goals of the movement must be most generally expressed if it is to find wide acceptance.

A universal evangel is desired, but the evangel must change as it interacts with different cultures. Is the desire for unity compatible with pluralism? How would a rural society, based on kinship, homogeneous culture and shared fate, integrate with the urban pluralist society of interdependence among strangers? (Could global communication overcome tribalism by forming a universal culture?)

Religion serves society and the individual. Religion must make the central value system meaningful, relieve alienation and allow personal integration. Society and the personal psychology of a particular individual must be integrated through the value system. Society socializes the individual, molding his consciousness, establishing the central values and furnishing the basis for the abstraction and projection of deities. Both the unique and the shared experience of the individual determine his personal psychology. The efforts of religion must serve the moral order of society as well as seeking to integrate the individual with society and with himself.

Religion stabilizes the state. The established religion is linked to the stability of the state, as is evident in the Orthodox faith and as indicated in *Regina v. Woolston* (1729). "The attack on religious dogmas resembles the attack on the legal foundations of the state" (Similar views were expressed by the English courts in *Traske's Case*). "All current symptoms of decay are but the result of the absence of a definite, uniformly acknowledged philosophy. This results in uncertainty toward the great problems of the times", said Adolf Hitler.

Many motivations are common to religion and ideology: Basic religious seekings include: (1) seeking completion, fulfillment and integration (2) dissolving the self in something greater, seeking immortality (3) desiring womb-return, wish fulfillment. These seekings could be satisfied by adoration and dedication, such as conversion coupled with enlistment in a group with a charismatic leader. In this, the psychological motivations of religion and of political ideology appear to be the same. Political Religion.

The achievement of the Kingdom of God on Earth-the soteriological promise- is common to both religion and to organized ideology. Unless one feels distress, he feels no need of salvation. By contrast, the primary concern of the ruling classes is not for salvation, but for legitimation. All "isms" assume that the logic of their ideology promises salvation. What is offered is a consistent world of promise and a refuge from the insecurity of the real world. The human desire for a feeling of worth may have to rest on the promise of what one may one day become.

Religion and ideology as neurosis management: Theology, like obsessional neurosis, deals with problems that are basically insoluble. Similarly, totalitarian ideology can never achieve its goal. According to Freud, civilization is only possible through the sublimation of the individual's aggression and his current neurosis. Religion and ideology could thus be viewed as neurosis management.

Common factors of religion and political ideology include: to explain the world and give one a place and purpose in it; to provide a feeling of security; to provide transcendence; to define good, evil and boundaries; to offer the "conversion" and "salvation" experiences; and to provide parental substitutes.

Religion and Ideology address the same issues. When J. M. Yinger in 1977 asked some Asian university students what the great issues were, they replied: the problem of meaninglessness (60%); of suffering (54%) and injustice (38%).

Seemingly, these future Asian leaders might as easily be satisfied by a political as by a religious ideology.

A political ideology can be a religion. Ideology seeks both to explain the world and to change it. If there is no program of political and social action, does an ideology exist? Manipulated or absorbed, ideology is either an instrument or a vehicle of domination. Is the appeal made to the social man, to the "new man", or to the "inner man"? Since neither religion nor ideology is rigorously defined, these questions help to highlight the possibly differing emphasis and the common nature of ideology and religion.

Religion, apart from any supernatural or pastoral aspects, delivers the same satisfactions, often serves the same ends, and uses the same means, as political ideology. Religion can be a political ideology and a political ideology can be a religion. Non-religious ideology, however, offers little union with a maternal matrix or sensitive pastoral care.

With both religion and ideology, a set of symbolic relations takes the place of real relations and individuals become subjects, seeing themselves important in the whole. In this sense, we have a "return of the repressed".

The rationalizations of civil religions were called the "sociology of knowledge". When we talk about "natural law", "social contract" and the "rights of man", non-religious ideological systems began to enter politics. For Marx, such concerns represent a "false consciousness" whereby the "reality" of economic exploitation is masked from those exploited. Karl Mannheim and Max Weber published in a similar vein, claiming that life circumstances or unconscious rationalizations of class interests are the real basis for ideologies. This study is sometimes called the "sociology of knowledge.''

In civil religions like Marxism and National Socialism (Francois Bourricaud, 1985) the ideology is concerned with the totality of life, providing a worldview, promising salvation, considering itself sacred, mingling knowledge, power and faith and seeking uniformity. Religion must make its message clear by using easily understood symbols. In Hitler's Germany, rituals and liturgical forms expressed the Leader's worldview.

Churches can get involved in politics. When priests speak of morality and law, when they acquired property and power, they then began to rival the power the state would exercise. Government and priests both sought to control the same turf. The also work together, especially when political leaders seek legitimation.

The claim of divinely ordained laws is a recurring ploy of both priest and king. The Egyptians claimed that Thoth gave the laws to Menes; similarly, it was the god Shamash who gave Hammurabi his code; it was Yahweh from whom Moses received his commandments and precepts; and it was Egeria who revealed the Roman law to Numa Pompilius. A Chinese emperor was "the son of Heaven".

The Canadian prime minister, Pierre Trudeau, evidenced the overlapping of his religion and his politics, saying: "the basis of a socialist ideology is to work out a set of human values for the fostering of which society is held collectively responsible", and "I am attempting to implement in the political sphere many of the programs which the Pope advocates in the spiritual sphere".

Modern Buddhist churches are often involved in politics and there seems to be no view that scripture and church are separate for the society served. Huntington suggests that only India and some in the West believe in the separation of church and state: in Islam, God is Caesar; in China and Japan, Caesar is God, while in Eastern Orthodoxy, God is Caesar's junior partner.

"The only religion which understands the true way for the individual and society to achieve happiness should try to send persons into the political world." Soka Gakkai, 1965 (Japanese Buddhist Party). In the foregoing we see a claim of the possession of unique truth and the call for political action.

In addition to power, thought control is sought by the religious authorities. "It is not for the state, or even for political parties... to try to impose an ideology that would lead to a dictatorship over minds, the worst kind of dictatorship. It is for cultural and religious groupings... to develop in the social body...those ultimate convictions on the nature, origin and end of man and society," said Paul VI, in *Octogesima Adveniens*, 1971. Thus, dictatorship over minds is seen as the worst kind-to be reserved to tradition and to the Church.

Our feelings are externalized, projected and symbolized by the religious and political systems constructed for us. The needs that these ideological frameworks satisfy are known. Man seeks to feel good and whole, to understand the order of the universe and to integrate with that order. His role in the universe must appear significant, his fears must be abated and he must be given hope, either for this world or for the next. Man also wants to transcend his body and his earthly role; for this, he needs to believe that he serves a higher purpose. Those are also the needs that an ideology should fulfill.

The state cab be God. Man can dissolve himself in the state. As a projection of the social organization, the created "gods" allow society to worship itself. Patriotism is a similar act. Religion always has at least one purpose- to make the individual feel better mentally. It usually has the additional purpose of making him serve better. In this latter aspect, religion does not differ from organized ideology.

Different religions serve different worldviews. Does one see "time's round", or "time's arrow"? For example, the Eastern ideologies generally assume the effacement of the individual and the endless cycling of history. Buddhism and Confucianism have non-linear views of history, but in Japan the teleological (God's purpose) outlook of Shinto was said to prevail. The Western view of the world has a Judaic-based selfcenteredness and idea of progress (teleology) toward a Kingdom of God, as is found in its successors, Christianity and Islam. Different religions serve different worldviews and different cultures. Shintoism, for example, finds gods in everything and extols the beauty of nature. Such a feeling would combine the motives of achieving integration and self-affirmation.

The leader may be viewed as God. Bellah (1957) suggests the complete integration of religion and politics in Meiji Japan.

There, the leader was the symbol of the collectivity and the nexus with the divine order. Loyalty was the highest virtue. The demand for unconditional loyalty has a religious character.

When Leighton and Opler (1946) analyzed the belief of the Japanese in their Emperor, they found a uniformity of belief concentrated upon a single symbol. "It was as if our flag, constitution, religion and family feeling were all focused on one object." The Emperor was all ideal things to all men and was each man's salvation.

Beliefs purport to explain the world, but they are more emotional than logical, biased by the culture and altered by the situation and psychology of the individual.

Totalitarianism forces conformity and focuses on itself. Dominant values channel action within a context that includes a dogma of a worldview and ultimate goals. Totalitarian religions and modern civil religions serve these action-oriented functions. The main distinguishing factors of totalitarianism appear to be the use of force to achieve conformity and the subordination of all other aspects of life to the dogma.

Dogma unites the unattached. Hsu observed (1961) that the individual who lacked attachments to other people would be more likely to attach himself to dogma, to objects and to associations. North American society seems like this. The individual in a transitory society, denied affective ties and unable to attach himself to permanent objects, would then seek to unite with associations and with dogma. The fluidity of that society would inhibit the affective bonding possible through associations (formerly characteristic of North America). Dogma would then emerge as the affective and cognitive cement of the society. (Might this apply to modern reactionary fundamentalists?) .

Basic insecurity is a common motivating factor for totalitarianism. A basic attitude of trust or mistrust will be formed in the very first years of life. The majority will be dominated by mistrust and will seek the reassurance of totalitarian or authoritarian systems.

Inconsistencies cannot be recognized. Man has curiosity, coupled with a limited tolerance for ambiguity. Recognized inconsistencies or contradictions cannot be accommodated by the average mind. Perhaps this is more pronounced in Western societies. Mental integration is avoided by attributing inconsistencies to the desire of the leader or by claiming that systems received whole from authority are perfect. Ritual contributes by fostering an uncritical dissociative state. Calling attention to inconsistencies will provoke agitation and hostility in the believer.

Symbol, rite and ritual are necessary for unity. "In no religion can men be held together, unless they are united in some sort of fellowship through visible symbols or rites", said St. Augustine. Symbols can take on the importance and meaning that we vest in them. A flag, for example, can represent a nation. People can die for it or be shot for not respecting it. Yet, in reality it is only a piece of cloth. The flag is often used in rites and rituals designed to mold thoughts and actions.

A symbol is a thing that stands for something else. When used together with other symbols, complicated concepts can be created and conveyed. The Christian communion ceremony uses only indifferent biscuits and poor wine, yet it suggests transubstantiation and membership in the community of believers. God and the Devil are symbols for a duality of opposites. Young children and primitives may confuse the symbol with the thing it represents. Adults may not agree on exactly what a symbol is supposed to represent and thus vagueness in a symbol is useful in obtaining wider support for it.

Symbols channel the thought of the faithful. The symbol system itself will reference both the concrete and the abstract, will condense, will be somewhat ambiguous and will establish arbitrary boundaries, postulating further opposites or dualities. The more elemental and simple the symbol, the greater is its flexibility. Symbols channel the thought of the faithful.

As magical religious behavior begins among primitives, the incantations are oriented to the needs of *this* world. With the introduction of symbols for unseen forces, magic becomes a symbolic activity. Symbols can be negative. For example, *tabu* may forbid something individually desired.

If man's desires are dual, consisting of the expressed and the repressed, then his projective symbols will reflect this. Dualities include god and devil, moieties in the community, and important aspects of the economic and social order. Myth will usually provide an additional symbol, an imaginary one that purports to reconcile polarized dualities or moieties, e.g. the Kingdom of God.

Symbolism can express a mystic union of two ideas. A symbol then acts to concentrate and order the emotions. Symbolism pervades ritual and rite. A rite is a single act seeking to mold individual consciousness. A ritual is a totality of rites. Monotonous repetition of the same acts dulls the individual personality and sense of judgment while unifying the community. Such *li* are much prized in Confucian societies.

For the individual, ritual can serve as neurotic obsessive-compulsive activity. In groups, rites serve to enhance group expression, solidarity and control. Jung claimed that the symbolic elements of all literature are "primordial images" or "archetypes" arising from the "collective unconscious of mankind". Skar (2004) has suggested that the Jungian "archetype" is expressed in the developmental proclivities of the human brain.

Ritual is a major influence in forming human consciousness. Symbols are important tools of ritual "The whole sacramental economy is based upon natural signs or symbols imprinted on the human psychology" said Pope Paul VI. Dorahy & Lewis (2001) found dissociation (the ability to separate belief from sensory input) highest among practicing Catholic youth, but not among Catholic students.

Myth functions as the background support for ritual. Ritual persuades men to share a common view and to form a common mind. Jane Harrison found that Greek myth and drama grew out of ritual. Ritual is the dramatic element in religious life, myth is the epic.

If ritual takes precedence over myth, then the role of the ruler as leader of ceremonies becomes very important. In the older Chinese culture, leadership in such ceremonies signaled the rank of the individual. In totalitarian states, the leader performs the duties of the shaman.

Nazi ritual paralleled Roman Catholic ritual. The Fuhrer's speech replaced the hymn at the beginning of the service. The loyalty oath to the Fuhrer replaced the Credo. The memorial to the martyrs of the movement replaced the Mass. For baptism, the Nazis had a ceremony called "consecrating the name". Düsseldorf even began a cult of relics about a Nazi martyr.

Primitive minds use personified animism. The need of children and primitives to personify things could explain their view that all nature is animated. In the Fifteenth Century, according to Huizinga, things had to be explained in terms of human-like spirits.

Symbols, mysticism are superbly combined by television. Like Augustine, the medieval Christians saw everything in the world as a symbol for some other thing or other symbol. Mystical thought often works with signs that are between images and concepts. In its reduced use of magic rites, Protestantism deprives its followers of much mysticism. Does television reintroduce the mystical into our lives?

Words impose idols. "Men imagine that their reason governs words, whilst, in fact, words react upon the understanding and this has rendered philosophy sophistical", said Francis Bacon. On his deathbed, Confucius said: "the secret is to control the language".

Idea association holds that concepts are formed by mentally joining and repeating events in space and time. We know that this is done by connections within the brain. According to Pope Paul VI, "the whole sacramental economy is based upon natural signs or symbols imprinted on the human psychology".

The mixing of symbols permits the analogical inference of induction. Then, the inference of deduction and dogma can take over. The repeated chanting of slogans is a modern example of language symbolism used ritually to form individual and group attitudes. Commercial radio did this for a long time. Television is now doing this.

Ideology is created in our mind. The world we know exists within our minds. Humans habitually try to impose structure and continuity. The only world we know is the one that exists in our minds. This is the world that we have built or accepted from the descriptions of others. It reflects our individual experience with the world others have presented us.

A myth represents collective experience. Collective repetition, becomes a part of the collective mind. "There is no small difference between the idols of the human mind and the ideas of the divine mind... between certain idle dogmas and the real stamp and impression of created objects as they are found in nature", said Francis Bacon.

Ideologies may deal with hidden explanations and with what is becoming, rather than with what is. Ideology nonetheless seeks to provide a worldview that is accepted as total and certain.

Destutt de Tracy and those first called "ideologues" sought a free, but totally rational and scientific society. Their approach offered an explanation of what was wrong, presented a corrective program of action and conflict, envisioned an organization of society and sought dedicated intellectuals as cadres.

J. C. Davis called ideology "a set of ideas aimed at action with a simplistic explanation for what is wrong, who and what are to blame and what must be done". Symbols replace people. The world is explained, alternatives are limited, decisions are justified and solidarity is enforced. The foregoing describes "ideology" in one common and pejorative sense, that of "organized" ideology. There are, however, more general ways of understanding "ideology". Any use of abstraction or symbol, for example, may mark the beginning of ideology.

In a created ideology, L. S. Feuer sees: a myth that does not change; philosophical doctrines that alternate in a regular pattern; and the promotion of the interests of a special class.

The Chosen have their myth. The worldview of the age and the outlook of a particular class form the starting points for an ideology. Starting from a worldview, organized ideology develops a social myth. This myth is then said to reflect history. Typically, ideology asserts the existence of a select people and then seeks to dramatize and anthropomorphize the historical process. This is a very integral part of Hinduism.

Organized ideology has for its domain the socio-political sphere. It always deals with the social and political relations of man. In the social-political domain, how much can be proved? Are there any limits?

Reality is represented in the mind with words, symbols and pictures. Our perception of reality is not reality, and our perception is influenced by collective views of others as well as by personal factors. Those interested in controlling thought try to be first to establish symbolic connections in the semantic memories of the young. Memory and thought are arrangements of these representations of the real world.

As the symbols and connections are joined, science becomes semiotics, while philosophy and religion make belief become explanation. Such moving from paradigms to examples without benefit of theory can turn us into mystical robots (this is often intended).

Ideology must promise a better life through action in order to gain adherents. Getting a better material life requires politics. Being political involves appealing to experiences and desires, including the desire for power. Thus, we come to a definition of an ideology as an "action oriented system of ideas focused on the social-political milieu".

Organized ideologies offer facile explanation. Formalized ideology appeals to the emotions, and is not pragmatic. Adopting a canned set of beliefs is easier and is more congenial to the submissive authoritarian mind. For these and other reasons, ideology is easily accepted.

Forming an individual's ideology. The following contribute to forming the ideology of the individual: (1) Worldview of the tradition and the culture. (2) Attitudes unconsciously absorbed from others. (3) Filtered worldview received from parents. (4) Reality as established by personal experience. (5) Symbolic structures of religion and philosophy. (6) Indoctrinated views. (7) Special ideologies of peer groups. (8) the "Lived" ideology of economic organization. (9) Influence of the *zeitgeist* and media. (10) Consciously adopted ideologies. (11) Adapted or constructed ideologies.

Ideologies easily replace each other. Perhaps fashions in ideologies alternate between the mystical and the deterministic. Kant, for example, was succeeded by pragmatism. The ideology of the older generation can become repressive dogma to the younger generation. Youth wants an ideology that will topple the establishment and make room for a new elite. Similarly, intellectuals want a mission and influence. Ideology can be an outlet for repressed ego.

The replacement of one ideology by another is relatively easy because the emotional motivation among true believers is similar, because ideology is a vehicle for obtaining release from psychic tension, because the symbols are flexible and because the susceptible want to get their view as an already integrated system.

Alternative ideologies are excluded: A single frame of reference excludes alternatives. Typically, an ideologue knows only one frame of reference and therefore does not recognize alternatives. Without alternatives, rational choice is not possible. Ambiguity would cause mental unease.

The ideologue must repress, change, or reinterpret the evidence. Dialectical logic is a way to accommodate such facts. History can be explained as the continuing resolution of opposites, of the thesis and the antithesis. Essentially, the unwelcome is labeled as the "antithesis of the thesis". Naturally, the ultimate expected synthesis must be as the ideology predicts. XE "Hegelian dialectic as explanation"

Ideology often speaks of "process" and of the future. It is also easier to justify an extreme position if one claims that his idea is in the process of becoming reality. As the ideology becomes a closed system, outside news is blocked. Events and actions are explained as the result of processes described in the myth and the worldview. The ideology seemingly becomes a self-fulfilling prophecy. Not surprisingly, some actions are taken simply to make the predictions of the ideology appear valid.

Economics create an unconscious ideology. For Althusser, the lives men lead also constitute an ideology, an unconscious, one that is ultimately determined by the way the society earns its bread.

The Devil is needed. Being one of the select and initiated, and possessing the exclusive truth, one may think he has a duty to be authoritarian and intolerant of those not sharing the revelation. In a conflict with unbelievers, it is useful to have a closed, intolerant community. In seeking to create such a community, it is useful to point to an enemy. In people seeking to form a new identity or ethnicity, one may define oneself by the "other" that one is not. Thus, collectivist Asians with new pride may point with distain to the selfish individualism of Westerners, etc.

The enemy is the repudiated, the "not" which defines the boundaries of our identity. Totalitarian ideology focuses both devotion and repudiation. Hate is useful in developing a spirit of community. Evangelism can improve unanimity and, within the community, make ideology seem more like reality. It can also generate hate against outgroups. Altemeyer and others have shown that such prejudice characterizes fundamentalists and authoritarians.

The Infallibility of the leader must be claimed: Certainty and unity requires that the leader must be thought to be always right. Even if a decision appears bad in the short term, we must assume it to be good in the long term. When the modern world began to threaten the Vatican, the Pope was declared infallible. If the old leader were infallible, what is left for the new leader? To change policy under these circumstances, it becomes necessary to denounce the "cult'' that made the old leader less than infallible.

The new rulers will purge those revolutionary ideas that might be used against the new establishment. It was, for example, a serious revisionist heresy in the Soviet system to use Marxist principles to criticize government policies.

The influence of art on the right brain is strong: The right hemisphere of the brain is involved in ideology and the right brain is important in art. Ideology celebrates a cultural ideal. In public art and in great buildings, the lower classes can identify with the elite and their values. But, the artist is often a non-conformist. If his works are hostile to the establishment, then the majority (always weak conformists) will feel their value system threatened.

The independence of the artist and his potential effect upon the public cause both Church and state to seek to control his work. Art can celebrate life independently of any ideology. The art of film and fiction lets one describe and hope for other worlds. Art is a competing, polytheistic religion. To have no public art offers no source of pride. To have independent ideals is threatening, so organized ideology restricts art.

The brain's hemispheres: Art employs the right brain, while ideology both seeks to dominate the semantic connections of the left brain and sources from the symbols and gestalt of the right brain. Art is highly symbolic. Some suggest that the technical rationality of the left brain uses the economic man. The left brain can posit logical extremes that may be life-destroying.

How does ideology express totalitarianism? Do the ideas deal mostly with socio-political topics? Is the set of ideas incapable of objective proof? Does it make assertions about value? Does it use terms like "mission" and "vocation"? Does it claim that its doctrines are certainties? Is the belief system resistant to new information? Does it deal more with things to come? Does it advance the interests of a special class? Are loyalty oaths required? Does it seek to control the facts reaching the public? Does it distort and oversimplify? Does the end justify the means? Is it intolerant? Is there moral absolutism? Does it forbid ambiguity or doubt in belief? Is the thinking Manichean, binary, black or white? Is an overall worldview provided? Does it claim that its worldview is total? Is the overall worldview applied to daily life? Is principle more important than the concrete? Does the logic lead to extreme positions? Is the set of ideas deductively organized? Is it paranoid? Does it try to set up a closed community? Does it seek to arouse hatred against out-groups? Does it seek to be authoritarian? Does it offer a myth of the historical process? Does it reject all that would permit its overthrow? Is the leader infallibly right? Does it prevent choice among attractive alternatives?

Philosophy and Ideology: "The philosophers have only interpreted the world-the point is to change it" said Marx's *Feuerbach*. All definitions of philosophy are subject to dispute, so we must content ourselves with looking at a few characteristics in order to distinguish philosophy from religion and ideology.

Philosophy deals primarily with speculation. Philosophy should be rational and systematic, without passion. Although it may develop principles for how life should be lived, philosophy is oriented toward contemplation, rather than action. These characteristics distinguish philosophy from articulated ideology.

Civil Religions are a national formulation. Religions seek to satisfy the psychological and social needs of men. They invent stories and explanations to answer questions of origin, cause and ultimate purpose. They seek to guide socio-political behavior and expressions. In the sociopolitical domain, when traditional religion is strong, civil religion is weak, and vice versa.-

The formation and guiding of attitudes and behavior is effected by establishing, manipulating and modifying a system of symbols. The symbols convey a vision of how life should be organized. Rituals dress the imaginary vision with an aura of reality and seek to motivate individuals according to the vision.

Traditional religions incorporate the idea of deity. To have the widest possible acceptance, this symbolic concept of deity must be amorphous. Religions in the Biblical tradition seek to promote the idea of a male, anthropomorphic deity. Other traditions had god-kings, the Sun, Earth Mothers, etc. Some anthropomorphic character is attributed to such symbols in an attempt to explain intent, motivation and causality in the universe. The civil religion will reference the "founders", heroes and the leadership.

"Civil religion" is the understanding citizens share about the origin, purpose and destiny of the state. Included are assumptions about a national character and permanent national identity. Civil religions may assume that there are some principles that transcend the state. Such principles can come from traditional religion, from international treaties or from supra-national bodies, etc.

The symbols of civil religion must be sufficiently flexible to encompass changed conditions and bigger territories. A national flag, for example would be a more ecumenical symbol for a nation than would a confessional god. A building or monument could be made a transcendent national symbol. Historical figures can be inflated to become secular saints or demigods. In both fascist Europe and in modern America, the expression "family values" became an ecumenical symbol for moral conservatism.

The national civil religion contains an "origin" myth concerning the creation and purpose of the state and will set out the putative concerns of the people concerning national values, heroes and ideals. This framework will seek to suggest cohesion and common purpose to a diverse community.

The leader's projects will be explained in terms of the civil religion, rather than reflecting real motivations. Such "scripture" can always be so selected as to forward the goals and style of the national leader. Policy will be dressed as morality.

The nation may be presented as the exemplary "City on a Hill"; as a "Chosen nation", as the vehicle of God's will in the world, etc. Psychologically, a mass democracy can envision the people themselves as the national hero and the polity thus permits a form of self-worship. If the "rescue" of a foreign nation is sought, this may be a form of self-rescue.

Self-interest has been dressed as "Manifest Destiny", the "White Man's Burden", "Making the World Safe for Democracy", etc. Withal, there is an element of millennialism. Although it is not at all exclusive to them, the Abrahamic religions have shown an intolerant desire for world domination. The American Puritans were Calvinist dissenters seeking to establish in the New World a theocratic state with the millenarian promise of a "City on the Hill". Implicit was the conviction of a superior way and a duty to bring that way to the World at large.

The United States has assumed that it is the champion of "democracy" and "freedom". These terms are defined only as America defines them. In 2003, the Secretary of State, Rice, announced that the United Nations should be replaced as the World authority by a coalition of "democracies". Naturally, the United States would lead and would decide who was a "democracy". Engaging in military aggression and numerous illegal acts, the American president announced that he was "bringing democracy" and "fighting the axis of evil" in a "global war on terror".

The American government has assumed an evangelical role in striving for empire. Imperialism feeds on itself and exhibits pleonexia, knowing no limits. A superior culture is claimed, as is the imperative to bring that culture to the uninitiated. Such was the claim even in ancient Athens and in China.

In the Mexican War and in the Spanish-American War, "Manifest Destiny" and the alleged abuse of Cubans by the Spanish government were drummed as justifications for American aggression. In World War I, the American president claimed that he been chosen by God to "show the way to the nations of the World how they shall walk in the paths of liberty" (cited by William Pfaff).

The civil religion includes the national myths with their "chosen glories" and "chosen traumas" of the state. The symbol sets are today referred to the "national discourse", but most will recognize it as ideology. Identity, individual and national, is intimately linked to the civil religion.

Globalization and media saturation can severely impact personal identity. For space and time are compressed and the world intrudes on the local (Kinnvall, 2004). Development and privatization often destroy old structures and cause unemployment for the middle and lower classes. Such threats to identity are met with attempts to strengthen or recreate personal identity. Resort may had to simplistic fundamentalist-like formulae to restore a feeling of knowing who and where one is.

One's identity as a member of the nation state may give a group-like feeling. If one depends upon his group identity, does his personal identity change to that of the group? Does the group identity change with events? Under threat, the identities of self and "other" receive emphasis. The "other" must then be projected and dehumanized to justify his destruction. This helps to explain group violence against minorities.

Is the "American Way of Life" a civil religion? Nationalism can be seen as an answer to heterogeneity and religious pluralism. Herberg, for example, saw the "American Way of Life" as the basic religion of the American people. (There is a unifying set of values, sacred writings, saints, ceremonies, fervor, etc.). It sees the country as the "Promised Land" and holds "democracy" to be sacred, without being at all sure how democracy should be defined. Enlightenment ideals, as embodied in the Declaration of Independence, form part of the creed. However, the specific application of that creed is a source of continuing controversy. In less urban areas, specters of Puritan theocracy seek to reassert their influence. Whether there is, or should be, a "Social Gospel" or a democratic "Social Contract" is discussed from time to time. Withal, there is an ethos of pragmatism, materialism and of progress through technology. American Way of life.

The American civil religion is much influenced by the current way the ideology is expressed in the "political discourse" (Hapson & Smith, 1999). The resurgence of the Christian Right was created by political activists who sought out a religious framework to aid their goals (R. Reed, 1996; W. Martin, 1996; M. C. Moen, 1992).

Of long-standing influence are the myths of the frontier ingrained in the American subconscious, with ideas of the extermination of evil races and the identification of laissez-faire capitalism with virtue (see Richard Slotkin's works).

The permissiveness and lawlessness of the 1960's favored a psychological reaction among many. Simplistic minds yearned for authoritarian guidance. The long, binary, indoctrination of fundamentalists makes the reception of such "guidance" from religious authorities especially easy.

The reactionary religious ideologist Tim LaHaye outlined his tactics in *The Battle for the Mind* (1980). In the reactionary religious ideology, Biblical injunctions are mixed with political goals and much use is made of vague catch-phrases that create an aura of dissatisfaction and anxiety, while promising amorphous solutions. "Liberal humanists", "religion of secularism", "welfare cheats", "crime in the streets" etc. are contrasted with "family values", "morality", "tradition" and "individual responsibility", etc. As long as the goals are left vague, general, and unspecified, wide acceptance and endorsement is found.

Political dissent is heresy. If there is a civil religion of nationalism dissension would then approach treasonable heresy, and serious dissent could take primarily religious, rather than political, form. This seems to have been an important factor in the collapse of East Germany where the Protestant churches led protests.

Individualism is repudiated. Dissent is no more popular with a civil religion (nationalism) than it is with the Vatican.

Serious political religions tend to be anti-liberal and anti-individualist. (In the American version, an exception is made for economic individualism) Since many of those joining a movement are seeking relief from feelings of isolation, they, also, do not want individualism.

One in the hands of a greater power no longer feels either isolated or responsible. When that "greater power" is able to organize mass rituals, institutionalization occurs. One thinks of very large evangelical churches and religious rallies. The Nazi mass rituals illustrate this in a civil religion.

The ideology of the leading people serves more general goals than the superstition of the peasants, for it seeks to respond to the needs of the era, the spirit of the times and a broader perspective. Such ideology is less likely to be in response to a feeling of isolation. Organized ideologies tend to promote both a particular myth and the interests of a given class

China seeks collective harmony and experiences recurring issues. Ideas of collectivity and of harmony supervene in the expressions of Chinese philosophy. In the long history of China, basic questions have included: a personal leader vs. a ruling principle; transcendence vs. immanence; the mystical vs. the physical; stasis vs. change; the teleological vs. the circular; selfishness vs. altruism; unity vs. plurality; and thought vs. force. These are essentially the same issues dealt with in Greek and Western philosophy. The key difference is that the dominance of a collectivity, and therefore the importance of harmony, is not a major theme in the individualistic West.

The psyche and zeitgeist invite alternating philosophies. As religion for the common folk serves to express changing outlooks and conditions, so does philosophy perform a similar function for the intellectual. There is also some ground for suspecting that the doctrines of successive ideologies alternate between the mystical and the deterministic. Feuer, in his *Ideology and Ideologists*, suggests that every claim of a philosophy can be mapped to some particular aspect of the psyche. A given philosophy satisfies one aspect of the psyche and suppresses another. For example, determinism downplays spontaneity, voluntarism frustrates the desire for order, and empiricism rejects fantasy.

Ideology and Ideologists

One sees a rotating return of the repressed. Accepting a philosophy represses some psychological desire, and the succeeding wave of philosophy will furnish an outlet for the previously repressed psychological desire (Feuer). Thus, successive philosophies are seen to alternate and to vent psychological opposites. The psycho-historian E. H. Erickson sees alternations between carnival and atonement. There may also be an alternation between the security of proclaimed certainty and the insecure doubt of relativist attitudes. Freedom brings an uncertain and threatening world. Pluralism weakens the strength of conviction. Choice begets uncertainty and calls for the restoration of certainty.

Doctrines develop according to changing times. The *zeitgeist*, or spirit of the age, is important. The Renaissance flourished as the secular nation-state developed. As the Renaissance dawned, men began to perform for each other rather than for the Church. As nation-states became more powerful, a doctrine to protect individuals became needed. Between the Reformation and the French Revolution, the air was filled with talk about "natural rights" and the "social contract".

To the True Believer, the world must appear as the doctrine says it should. Descartes saw men as sharing the structure of their minds, rather than the objective world. All was process. If all is process, then all is change, all is becoming. What, then, are facts? Did Newton really supplant Descartes? Can True Believers really think scientifically?

5

CULTURE AND SOCIETY

Culture is the idea of how life should be lived. The myths of a culture must point to a vision of life accepted as a shared ideal. The common set of symbols and history, passed on from generation to generation, forms much of society's traditional culture. Having a vision of how life should be lived ought to be different from the limited aim of the business corporation. Can capitalism recognize this?

The image of man depends on time and place. Makers of myth put their stories in the ethos of the time and place. For the Middle Ages, society was made up of the faithful; for Locke, of property owners; for Hobbes, of acquisitors; for modern Americans, of job holders; for socialists, of workers.

Berelson and Steiner (1964) categorize the images of man: from Greek philosophy, as one of virtue and reason; from Christian dogma, of sin and of love; from the Renaissance of power, will and nationalism; from the economic view, of class, property and money; from the psychoanalytic, of sex, ego and self; from the behaviorists, of programming, environment and group-perceived reality. Confucians place great importance in the character of the leader and the leading individuals.

The town culture and individualism shape Western development. The townsman choosing a monarch in preference to a feudal lord could find himself more oppressed. To defend against too powerful a monarchy, Locke claimed that personal rights to life, liberty and property were inalienable. The myth of a "social contract" developed. This was a useful fiction, for the alternative is to face up to unpleasant domination. In America, the *Federalist Papers* sought to describe a balanced and pluralistic system that would secure the rights of the individual.

The culture often determines the priority of the individual's psychic elements. Even within the individual, a question of authority arises- how is he to order the priority of his psychic elements? The individualism of the West seems selfish to many cultures, but even Communist China has recognized the power of selfish economic motivation. How to best harness such motivation for the general welfare is still unresolved.

The political organism exalts the collectivity. To the Greek sophists, "man" meant the individual man. To Socrates, self-questioning, or *logos,* was the way the individual could determine for himself what was good and what was evil. Plato, on the other hand, said that man could only realize himself through collective expression.

Conflict arises between the claims of the individual and the needs of society. If the individual knew his own best interest, he would, thought Rousseau (1760), realize himself through society. Rousseau saw the relation of man to the collectivity as a matter of the "general will", not of agreements.

The Hegelian collective mind: Hegel (1800) defined "mind as a system of individuals realizing their potential by being incorporated into increasingly complex forms. As modern times approached, many communities had dissolved into atomistic individuals. National Socialism solved this by explaining that the individual derived his worth from his membership in the tribe.

A society closed to outside influence is likely to be authoritarian or totalitarian and conservative, with values that are static and rigid. The prime requirement in the closed society is ostensible conformity. Human nature seeks to reduce psychic tension. The closed society responds to this desire. The idea of fixed occupational categories can easily be implicit in a closed society (Echoes of this are to be seen in the papal encyclicals and the "Christian Corporate State" of Austria under Dollfuss.) Even in an open society, if economic mobility ceases, social class becomes important. Thus, the psychological comfort of order has powerful implications.

The Closed Society

China was a closed society. In China, religious ethics required that the individual comport with the values of order, conformity, propriety and moderation that prevailed. In an agricultural country, this fostered a closed society.

Toward the end of the 8th Century, Islam became a closed society. Effectively, the religious and temporal powers were both held by the ruler. Free interpretation of the Koran was ruled out. In Europe, at the end of the 12th Century, the dark night of the Inquisition began to descend. Europe, too, became oppressed.

An open society allows the introduction of new ideas and change. In the open society, development can take place. America was not a totally open society. Connecticut authorities banned Locke's *Letter on Toleration* (1689). The rulers of that state did not favor freedom of religion. Those Puritans who fled England for America did so to establish *their* denomination as dominant. In the American colonies, compulsory tithing and suffrage requirements penalized any but the dominant sect.

A new world of clashing closed societies? As the dialectics of Hegel replaced the openness of the Enlightenment, a new philosophy of intolerance and confrontation presented again in the Western world.

Release from mental tension is offered by a simple and closed intellectual system that explains the world and offers the promise of coping with fate. In the closed society, the repetition of images and clichés is mutually reinforcing. What chance for development or progress is there in a world composed of mutually hostile closed societies?

Concrete freedom comes only through the state. Hegel thought that the rational individual ought to draw on the organized resources of the state, and realize himself only through the state. The individual had to be "formed" to do this. By conforming, the individual would serve his own rational ends and thus be "free". When ordered life is maintained by the state, the individual, said Hegel, enjoys "concrete freedom". It is noteworthy that Canadians speak of "peace, order, and good government while Americans praise "life, liberty and the pursuit of happiness."

Freedom was defined as submission. Hegel's "spirit" is considered as satanic as is Freud's *id* by some Islamists. Calvin's view was that true freedom consisted in voluntary submission to the will of God. For Rousseau, it was total submission to the "general will". Submission to authority is the primary characteristic of authoritarians.

Society may imply conformity and witch hunting. In Salem, as with inquisitions, coercion of socio-political conformity was sought through accusations of witchcraft. If the individual seems to have power apart from the group, then the idea of "*mana*" may arise. Unstable times and weak government cause people to seek objects to blame for misfortunes. Such times may also involve a crisis of values- the search for more adaptive attitudes versus a return to imagined old verities. The witch-hunt tries to suppress change.

Social specialists (teachers, priests, prophets, editors), as articulators of values become targets in unstable times. The threat of an accusation of witchcraft may serve to enhance ostensible conformity. Another political characteristic of witchcraft, Michael Kunze suggests, is that it always represents apostasy and can thus only a member of the community can be called a witch.

A state may not be a nation. There is a difference between a nation and a state. As the sole possessor of legitimate force, the state is the mechanism of government. The state may be subordinate to Party, Church, Leader, possibly even to the "Folk". The "nation" implies an entity apart from mechanisms and legalities, a community of common spirit.

Has the nation local or transportable gods? Historically, the more important gods had been concerned with the great forces of nature. As the Greek city-state arose, the gods were local. Like the patron saint of the village, the local gods were not easily transportable. A god takes on new qualities in response to the needs of his worshipers. The god of a tribe or of a clan is more easily transportable, less place-dependent, than the god of a city. A tribal god is more suitable for political expansion.

Can pluralist and totalitarian evangels coexist? A logical culmination of political authority is the concentration of all authority, religious, family, tribal, etc., into a sole source, creating a pleonexic unity. Once this is achieved, further power would call for an imperialistic evangelism, but, if this is not possible, then isolation would be the preferred policy. How could a pluralist representative democracy achieve such a unity? What dialogue is possible between the pluralist and totalitarian evangels?

Hegel called the state "the march of God within the world". In this, he seems to have been a precursor of Fascism Hegel viewed states as autonomous individuals. He argued that the state was necessary to insure fair dealing and to curb the selfishness of corporations. The ethical responsibilities of the state were great.

The modern state has now become powerful enough to restructure the social order and to thoroughly "form" individuals. Such forming occurs both intentionally and unintentionally (as with the cultural effects of television. Should we foster the independent individual or should the individual realize himself through the collectivity? The argument has been going on since the time of Socrates and Plato.

The choice between the pluralist and the closed society is not obvious. Although we may pay lip service to the idea of liberty, few of us, probably less than fifteen percent, are really comfortable with freedom. The Roman Church and the great movements of recent times, National Socialism, Fascism, Marxist-Leninism and Resurgent Islam- all express the collectivist, integralist, option and castigate pluralist individualism.

The influence of economics is primary. Prosaic economics eventually wins over transcendence. Economics and cultural differences are principal determinants of the worldview in different nations and culture is strongly influenced by economics. Thus, there will be differing national ideologies depending on local economics and not all ideologies will travel equally well. Just as the gods were a projection of local society, so do local economics affect the worldview.

Values and Attitudes

Instrumental cultures integrate societal means and ends. Consumer cultures do not. The idea behind these terms is that an instrumental culture that separates institutional means from societal ends can adapt innovation more easily than can a culture such as the Chinese or Islamic, which ostensibly seek to integrate means and societal goals. Values are the moral order.

The relative priority of values and their relation to each other represent the moral order of a culture. In the long run, the moral order must facilitate adaptation and survival. Thus, the physical, economic and political environment shapes the values. Kant may be interpreted as saying that man must serve values, rather than that values serve man.

Value orientations are fundamental. Kluckhohn and Strodtbeck suggest these basic value orientations: (1) is man basically good or as evil? (2) is his relation to others lineal, collateral or individualistic? (3) is more emphasis placed on the past, the present or the future? (4) is it more important to do, or to be? (5) is one subject to nature, at one with nature, or master of nature? Should we call these values or attitudes? Are they factors of the individual personality or of the social man? Are they sufficient to determine the moral order?

Attitudes and worldviews characterized. The following terms have been used in anthropological literature to categorize the attitudes and worldviews of groups of individuals: (a) Seeing the world as friendly or as hostile (b) Seeing man as good or as evil (c) Feeling autonomous or feeling independent (d) Feeling subject to nature, as one with or as dominating nature (e) Being active or being passive (f) Being purposive or being existential (g) Emphasizing the past, the present or the future (f) Being inner-directed or other-directed (g) Being conservative or liberal

(h) Being conformist or being independent (i) Being a member of the group or being an individualist (j) Being religious or being a freethinker (k) Particularism vs. universalism (l) Having specialized or having diffused relations (m) Benevolence vs. selfishness (n) Being a leader or a follower (o) Tending to save or tending to consume (p) Tight control of impulses vs. loose control (q) Emphasizing the political or the economic (r) Emphasizing controlling or doing (s) Preferring the theoretical or the practical (t) Emphasizing the aesthetic or the carnal (u) Seeing others as lineal or as collateral. (v) Recognizing titles or recognizing achievement (w) Challenging, depending on, or avoiding authority (x) Favoring fatalism or favoring scientism (y) Being open or closed minded.

If the values and attitudes change, then the society will change. Consider the social order, the way society is organized. If that changes, then values and attitudes must correspondingly change or there will be social conflict. Just as older people are less inclined to change their attitudes and values, so are traditionalism and conservatism strongest among populations least accustomed to new stimuli, such as rural dwellers.

One can seek change in a direction opposite to that that one really desires, by reaction formation. Although change produces anxiety, people yearn for some variety. The suppressed aspects of the personality need to find expression. The illusion of alternatives and progress also requires some change. Static poverty does not produce as much desire for change as does a reduction in the standard of living. High anxiety invites totalitarian ideology rather than liberal reform. Threat may cause the culture to emphasize attitudes thought to be needed. Such emphasis facilitates change but may lead to reaction formation, where the overt conduct is the opposite of what one really feels.

A nation's values change. The family and the culture do much to form the individual. How much is the culture the summation of the psyches of the individuals who form it? How do we explain change? Recall that the dominant philosophies seem to alternate, so that what was repressed in one era finds expression in a succeeding era. Do the dualities of individual character find similar expression in the national character? Much domestic controversy arises over the delay in recognizing and acknowledging change in a nation's values.

International society needs a common set of rules, institutions, values, and shared interests. It should also have a common culture. Much of the Western world expresses what Huntington has called the "Davos Culture"- the commonalities shared by the powerful figures who annually assemble to review the economy and state of the world at Davos, Switzerland. From Davos, there appears to be a Western vision of a universal civilization, but those values are not universally shared.

Are there six religio-cultural zones? Ronald Inglehart has coordinated much research seeking to quantify worldviews. Religions and historical differences shape values. On this basis one may postulate six religio-cultural zones: Confucian, Orthodox, Latin-American, English-speaking, Roman Catholic, and Protestant. Should India and Islam be called additional zones?

Do "tradition" and "survival", with their antipoles, map cultural zones? Through his factor analyses, Inglehart (2003) postulates two axes of polarization: *traditional vs. secular-rational* and *survival vs. self-expression*. He suggests that the transition from industrial to postindustrial society brings conflict between materialist and post-materialist (survival vs. self-expressive) values. Survival values are emphasized under a life of poverty. However, the collapse of a social system will give even more emphasis to survival values. In the Islamic world, the people of Saudi Arabia, Turkey and Iran place more emphasis on secular-rational and self-expressive values. This is said to be a reflection of their relatively greater wealth. Such a classification would suggest that these societies might progress more rapidly, but what of Malaysia?

Saudi Arabia was found to value self-expression highly, whereas Orthodox countries did not. Autonomy was lowest in Africa (78), Latin America (75), and most Islamic nations (74), compared with Protestant Europe (37). It is still early days in the attempt to quantify values and democratic institutions, but the effort is worth following.

Man is easily malleable by the group. In considering human nature, we observe that speech and symbolic reasoning capabilities, coupled with an imperative for social living, make men especially flexible. There are many forms of responses to basic urges, many forms of drive reduction. Man's sense of reality is partly derived from others and he is susceptible to ideology.

Man can and does adapt to a wide range of real and imaginary social organization. Parsons saw the functions of the social system as: (1) adaptation to milieu (2) achieving objectives (3) organizing links among people (4) providing values and a common ideology. Man is a social animal. In a group, a man may take on much of the character that the group wishes him to assume. He is economically and socially dependent on others.

How are those relations to be structured? Structuring relations with others is the essence of man as political organism. In both Confucianism and in Chinese Marxism, groups mold and correct the individual. American society seems to be more dependent on peer opinion than are societies with strong hierarchies.

Role identification alters the man. How others regard us and how we regard ourselves seem crucial to feeling whole. The regard of others emphasizes one's role in society. Role identification may be another way in which the external culture is incorporated into the individual personality.

Key cultural institutions serve to mask, control and channel conflicts. If the nature of man is deemed selfish, aggressive, competitive and playful, then it may be argued that the key institutions of the culture will provide rules which mask and dampen these tendencies while allowing room to maneuver and to negotiate changes in these rules. Engagement requires one to pretend that it is not just a game. Key cultural institutions are thought to include churches, films and television.

Loyalties may be ethnic, clannish, or based on the extended family more than nationalist. Primitive man and his family have been categorized (Diamond, 1974) as individualistic, not viewing society as organized and existentially reacting to the merits of each situation. A family is a fundamental political organism that gives stability to society. (Keep in mind the interpretive paradigm that sees the state and the leader as replacing the father's role in the family.)

If the world seems a hostile place, authoritarianism is invited. The child brought up to see the world as a place of threat may tend to become conservative and authoritarian. Anxiety, neuroticism and strength of opinion group together. When combined with institutionalization, denominationalism and authoritarianism, one has a profile of a religious ideologue (Brown, 1982). Such people would see God as a distant and intolerant father-figure (Broen, 1956).

Is it a friendly world? A warm and supportive childhood would tend to foster the feeling that the world is a friendly place. One with such an attitude may be open, accepting of others, tolerant, altruistic and directed by inner standards. Such were the characteristics of fundamentalist liberal clergymen (Stewart and Webster, 1970; Maranell, 1968). Theists among liberals would tend to see God as close and accessible.

Harmony does not require uniformity. Confucius (550 B.C.) said "The man of superior quality aims at harmony, not uniformity, the small-minded at uniformity, not harmony" (*Analects* XIII, 23). In the turbulent times that he lived in, he advocated that the thinking man should seek to perfect himself, and his family. If the ruler did this, his character and attitude would permeate the society.

Is man basically good or evil? Individualist ideals were in contrast with those of the Legalists (e.g. 255-207 B.C.) who saw man as fundamentally evil and requiring comprehensive laws and police to permit society to function. Mencius (300 B.C.) saw man as basically good and Hsün-tzu (270 B.C.) thought of man as basically flawed and requiring much formation.

Will paternalism, maternalism, or a fatherless culture obtain? According to Faber, the particular culture establishes whether the influence of the mother (supposedly basic trust and love) or of the father (authoritarianism) will prevail. The paternal culture of the West is now giving way to a fatherless culture. Perhaps such a society will go through an adolescent, existential phase. The eventual replacement may be a media-created father-figure who defines the values and path. This phase could emphasize submission and authoritarian faith. Is such a speculation that a fatherless culture would yield to a Fuhrer consistent with experience in Germany or elsewhere?

Conservative fundamentalists see human nature as evil. Monaghan (1967) found that conservative fundamentalist church members grouped psychologically into the authoritarians, the fearful, and the socially ambitious. Conservative ministers viewed human nature as evil and were dogmatic, ethnocentric, rigid, and depended on group approval (Stewart and Webster, 1970). Adorno's authoritarian profile resembles the "archetypal conservative" of Glen D. Wilson. Indeed, authoritarians and conservatives share many traits (McCloskey, 1953). God, for such people, is often projected as ominous and powerful.

Altemeyer and others have factored the authoritarian personality to dimensions of aggression, conventionalism and submission to authority. Altemeyer (1988) postulates fear and a "feeling of righteousness" as an underlying reason for aggression. Ethnocentrism, religious or otherwise, implies an "us vs. them" attitude and prejudice. This combination easily leads to hate and persecution.

The group may be more important than previously thought in evoking the less desirable aspects of the authoritarian personality. J. Duckitt has found that those with an intense yet insecure identification with important groups are activated by a perceived threat to the group.

Submission can show authoritarian aggression. Authoritarians may show authoritarian aggression, by submission to authority and by conventionalism. The relative importance of these characteristics may vary among individuals (Funke, 1999). Oesterreich suggests that a child under threat will normally flee to the protection of a parent. If the child fails to develop personal autonomy, then this aspect of the authoritarian personality will be set.

Threat changes the group. Stellmacher and Petzel (2005) point out the importance of group identification to the authoritarian individual and say that it is the threat to the group that is determining. A personal "Social Identity" may serve as a vector opposing the complete identification of an individual with a group. Levine (2005) indicates that perceived threat can change an authoritarian individual from a relatively open quest for information to a closed-minded search for confirmation.

Stress splits the paranoids, narcissists and the libidinous. Freud and subsequent writers have suggested that, under stress, groups of a certain natural size (100-150 persons) will tend to break into psychological factions. Such factions are thought to be: the narcissists, the aggressive paranoids and the libidinous. These factions will seek a leader who resonates to their own particular pathology. One can easily think of the vainglorious or the paranoid leader, but what of the libidinous? Among the apes, the Bonobos quell stressful situations by sexual interchange. Perhaps entertainers, rock stars, etc. serve as such objects of superego projection (are the Bonobos) in our society.

Man's symbolic projective system changes with the organization of society. Since the gods reflect the organization of society, the gods will change when society's organization changes. Polytheism is appropriate to nature worship. When the king becomes important to society, it may also be believed that *mana*, psychic potency, is hereditary. Ceremonies and cult objects give the priest-king increasing importance. The god of a tribe is less site-specific than the god of a city and thus could have a wider appeal.

Community begins when there is a sense of common identity and shared fate. An individual has the multiple identities of family, party, class, ethnicity, occupation, culture, nationality, religion and ideology. Interactions among members of the community establish the social structure. The collectivity can be qualitatively different from the individual. To the ancient and to the native mind, it was alien to think of an individual life spent apart from the community. Hegel thought the great periods of Greece and Rome to have occurred when the individual saw his own interest as inseparable from that of the community. In Greece, after the classical period, the sense of community spirit and responsible participation diminished.

***Gesellschaft, Gemeinschaft, and Kultur* convey ideas of worldview**. Hegel said that civil society arose from the marketplace. German thought can reflect *Gesellschaft* and *Gemeinschaft*. *Gesellschaft* is the rational society of the corporation. Most Western thought takes this view of society. The German word *Kultur* conveys more the sense of *Gemeinschaft*, the sense of community.

The individual's desire to conform may take precedence over principle and even perception. Solomon Asch, in 1956, found that 76% of people would change their report to conform to what others said. Zimbardo and Anderson (1993) suggested that such reporting was external and that changing inner beliefs would require informational persuasion.

Is there a collective psyche? Does society have a psyche different from the individuals who comprise it? Does society mold the individual or do individuals in the aggregate mold society? Overt behavior depends on the culture and rules of the society. In primitive societies, the sanctions are limited, usually being only death or exile. A "shame culture" is used to secure compliance with tribal customs. This contrasts with the legalistic, father-imaged "guilt culture" of our modern world.

John Dewey defined society as a set of group habits or institutions that fit together. For him, the function of education was to assure that children were molded to accept these group habits. The psychiatrist Wilhelm Reich claims that the authoritarian structure of society, especially family, school and religion- determines individual character. We may note findings that personality is influenced over 40% by genes, 25% by a shared environment and 35% by individual environment (Borkenau 2000, Rushton 2004).

Values differ in different societies. The long Chinese experience developed Confucianism, which has three principles to assure order and the harmony of the individual and society: (1) be conscientious and altruistic; (2) do the job for which you are fitted and do it well; and (3) continually compromise with others. A society's existence depends on shared common values and on the maintenance of order among the individuals comprising that society.

Is society with church and state a single unit? Maintenance of order requires that the state be as extensive as the society. Ideology tries to mold a uniform society and treats "society" as a single unit. Christianity's insistence on the difference between god and Caesar introduced a discrepancy between the social and the political that is still causing difficulty in the West.

Land and City

Feudalism had little political organization. As serfdom disappeared, revenue became the essential relation of landowner and peasant. The personal ties of duty and responsibility dissolved. Priest and Church provided some focus for feelings of community. The story of government and culture during the Middle Ages is really the story of the Roman Church and its hegemony over the Western world.

City life brought changes. With the rise of the town, wealth was no longer being based solely on land and it became movable. Personal acquisition arose as another value to replace feudal ethics. Hegel saw marketplace competition as the genesis of modern society. The town offered more independence. Kings became more autonomous, for they could get funding from bankers rather than from feudal lords.

In the West, cities were trading centers. In China, they were administrative posts. This may have helped diversity of thought to develop more in the West more than in ancient and medieval China. Contacts with traders also brought many new ideas to the cities.

The city furnishes the basic model for Western political organization. The modern state operates as one city. If the social community is the only natural unit, then nation-states and empires are unstable patchworks without the natural cohesion of a social community.

Without common values what will hold a nation together? Today, corporations and the mass media are determining vectors, creating an isolated individual who can respond only as a consumer to a remote and imaginary unity created by advertising.

Media now create instant mass psychology, consequently facilitating mob reaction. Mob action is "characterized by a sense of freedom, power, and lust for destructive aggression" (Kernberg, 2000). The susceptibility is further increased by television, whereby individual integration of information is reduced and violent moves providing quick resolution are illustrated.

Should the state serve man, or should man serve the state? If state and society are identical, the control of the individual (and thus society) benefits the state. Does the state become the purpose, rather than the servant, of life? The structure of society is the political organism. The organism uses the state as the administrative apparatus. The organism speaks for society as a whole, but its voice is controlled by the ruling class. The values and myths of the society are provided partly by tradition, but are, for the most part, articulated by the ruling class (with some competition from artists).

UTOPIA

A utopia represents an unobtainable ideal. "Utopia" is taken from Greek words meaning "no place". Describing a utopia is also a way of criticizing the present. Thus, utopias are normative and depend on time and place. A utopia can be a mythical description of a world to come. Writing about a utopia usually attacks the existing order and provides psychic release. As an ideal, it may be the *unreality* of the visions recounted that give them a magical presence.

Utopias have aspects of myth, religion and ideology. A utopia shows the hopes many of the people at the time of the writing. Considered with science fiction, such writings can explore how we came to be the way we are, what our nature really is, what is happening to us and where we are really going- as Atwood noted.

Utopia offers a myth of past or future perfection. In utopia, there is a teleological faith in the ability to achieve a better social life, usually by expressing a different human nature. Implicit is belief in the possibility of achieving the millennium, the equivalent of the Kingdom of God on Earth. One may also mention the Lost Paradise, the golden age of nature in the past, with which the present is contrasted. Returning to a golden age was a recurrent theme as, in the early 1990's, Islamic fundamentalism became rampant and an era of consonance of faith with life was imagined.

Thomas Moore's *Utopia* (1516) was influenced by reports of the discoveries in the New World. Moore had seen the enclosure movement and questioned the justification for private property. He disdained commerce.

Campanella's *City of the Sun* (1627) projected the worldview of the Italian Renaissance. He introduced thoughts about radical social policies and deism. James Harrington argued, in *Oceania* (1656), that agrarian societies could survive only if limits were placed upon the acquisition of land. *Oceania* took a mechanistic view and was most concerned with the constitutional structure and the economic foundations necessary to stability. Morelly's *Code de la Nature* (1755) talked of a society regimented to achieve communism.

Utopias presume teleology and progress. Belief in the possibility of achieving the ideal society through rational organization increased during the Enlightenment. The 18th and 19th Centuries appeared to think that progress was inevitable and that man could be perfectible.

In China, K'ang Yu-wei (d. 1927), in his *Book of the Great Concord*, thought the chaos of capitalist individualism would yield to the unity of a single world civilization pervaded by *jen.* This vision of future benevolence and harmony is not typically Eastern, for the East generally puts the Golden Age at the beginning. Earlier Chinese writings of this sort describe a sort of heaven on Earth, located beyond explored lands, e.g. the *Paradise of the West* (Chi Tun, 314-366). In 1947, B. F. Skinner's *Walden II* saw utopia being achieved through behaviorist social engineering. His *Beyond Freedom and Dignity* (1961) furthered these ideas, emphasizing the environment. Peter Singer's *The Ethics of Globalization* (2005) continued the genre.

Utopias are dateless but ideology is for now. Karl Mannheim sought to distinguish utopias from ideologies by claiming that the adoption of a utopia would shatter existing systems, whereas an ideology usually preserves the appearance of fitting in with history and with prevailing worldviews. In both cases, one deals with an imaginary society, but with ideology one may act as though the imaginary were real and thus make portions of the dream (or nightmare) come true.

There is also what is called the "anti-utopia" or dystopia, wherein the evil doings of the present are extrapolated to their inevitable logical future. Orwell's *1984*, Huxley's *Brave New World* and H. G. Wells' *War of the Worlds* are of this genre.

Alienation

"The Youth Movement is not intended to be made up of the contented and of the satisfied, but is to embrace the tormented, the discontented and the unhappy," said Hitler. Scales seeking to measure alienation have assessed feelings of "powerlessness", "meaninglessness", "normlessness" and social isolation. Alienation.

"Alienation" may be an estrangement from self, from other people, or from society. Stokes (1962) sought to measure alienation in terms of political trust; Rosenberg (1956), trust in people; Campbell (1960), of confidence in the efficacy of the political system; Srole (1966) in terms of anomie [disorientation, normlessness]. Alienation implies a lack of identification, of trust, and of satisfaction. It is said to be common among working-class whites in the U.S.A. It is often accompanied by a feeling of powerlessness. However, in a given society, the feeling of being normless and without meaning may increase with prosperity at the same time the sense of being powerless and socially isolated decreases (Neal & Groat, 1974).

Society's losers may try to establish a new society Moral discontent may give rise to reform movements. Psychic discontent may provoke the search for new values or a new social milieu. Several different senses of alienation may be present simultaneously. Indicators of alienation include: normlessness, futility, powerlessness, lack of will, estrangement, lack of purpose and a feeling of worthlessness.

Distrust of man is a form of alienation: Feeling isolated from society or from the world is fairly common. Is a basic mistrust of man alienation? Is "original sin" a statement of mistrust in man? It can be claimed that Stoicism, Epicureanism, Hedonism and Cynicism all evidenced such a basic mistrust of man. Puritanism was another philosophy that distrusted the nature of man. One scholar has noted that Protestant fanatics felt so alienated that they could never cease trying to purify themselves and the external world.

The market system is alienation from humanity. Religion evidenced the alienation of man from himself, thought Marx. He saw alienation in many of man's other activities. There was alienation in factory labor, in class divisions, in the exploitation of classes, in ideological domination, and in both competition and in monopoly capital. He saw the market system itself as an instrument of alienation, and private property as a basic concept alienating man from society and from his true nature. Salvation would be found in a return to man's proper, social, existence.

How to perfect oneself and the World? Both Christian and Marxist dogma saw man as alienated and offered him a hope of redemption. "Original sin", or guilt, is a form of alienation. In seeking to relieve a sense of alienation, the individual may elect to try and change himself, to try and change the world, or both. The Confucian view is that by seeking to perfect oneself, one may approach perfecting the world.

Sex, urban economic life, and media offer alienation. Economic life in a modern city environment forces alienation. One sees people but has little contact with them. Economic change or expansion destroys stability. Similarly, people sitting at home and receiving preformed images from television are alienated from their fellows and from reality. Eric Fromm thinks that modern emphasis on sex represents a pathological alienation from the real world.

Elitism is also a form of alienation. Hitler claimed that separation from the customary standards of society made men willing to do any assignment. Loyola required that his Jesuits "make ourselves indifferent to all created things". News media create a scenario of constant threat. How can the lonely individual compare notes with his fellows to determine what valuable and what is real?

Alienation exists in Iran: The daughter of the Shah of Iran described events in Iran as being a sort of alienation. In terms of change, the people had experienced in ten years changes most peoples would have experienced over a period of a hundred years. This created mental stress. Children were not surrounded anymore by an affectionate family. In previous times, all one had to do was to listen to what the father or the chief of the tribe said and that settled all. Suddenly, people were alone. When the Ayatollah Khomeini returned to Iran, he was welcomed by the poor and the alienated. This was essentially the same sort of constituency which welcomed Christianity in the First Century.

Filling the void of alienation with hope. At the end of the Roman Empire, said Hegel "the unhappy consciousness" prevailed. He saw the individual as feeling isolated. As a contra-hope, Augustine offered the illusion of a "brotherhood" of Christians. Does the alienation of modern man invite cults and movements to fill the void?

Seeking identity may cure alienation. The search for "meaning" in life may refer to goals, purpose, interest, and satisfaction, or to finding a significant and important place in the universe. The lack of these may be called anomie, angst, or alienation. Is the alienation of youth a serious phenomenon, or does time adequately repair it? The adolescent lacks the integrated identity, the inner resources, of the mature, and is quickly alienated by routine.

Circumstances alter the man. "I am myself and my circumstances", said Ortega. Life in society requires that a man must change in order to conform. This state of "*alteracion* differs from alienation in that it is normal and is connected with the belief system absorbed from society. Man modifies his conduct to conform to the society. The "rejecting of the world" seen in adopting religious fanaticisms a step beyond *alteracion* and represents alienation from society and can be lead to political fanaticism.''

The alienated neurotic becomes fanatic. Is it neuroticism that prompts the ideologue to seek canned answers and have a closed view of the world? Facts incompatible with that worldview must be rejected. Brown (1962) found that anxiety, neuroticism, and strength of opinion grouped together, and that a fixed belief set, institutionalism and authoritarianism were also closely correlated.

The anxious neurotic will be intolerant in his views and seek the structure and the support of a group. "Go search for people who are hurt by nature, those with inferiority complexes, who crave power and influence... the sense of belonging to a powerful organization will give them a feeling of superiority for the first time in their lives" said General Sudoplatov on recruiting KGB hit men.

The psychologist Rokeach sees alienation as giving rise to feelings of anxiety. He speculates that the hopelessness and anxiety generate a sense of worthlessness that engenders a compensating drive for power and status.

In strong ideologies, the neurotic component seems pronounced. The Protestant fanatics were tormented by guilt and self-hatred because they could not live up to the demands of their religion. Philip Greven, in *The Protestant Temperament*, noted that the Puritan fanatics were preoccupied with removing any sense of personal worth in themselves. (Michael Walzer's *Revolution of the Saints* discusses Puritanism as the origin of radical politics).

The inevitable internal psychological conflict often resulted in a broken will. This was thought to be a sign that they had become "true children of God". Exaggerated passivity may be a defense against great rage (reaction formation) and might reflect a fear of dependency (Goldberg, in Halperin, 1983).

Since the Protestant fanatics, said Greven, suppressed their own wills, they could not allow freedom to anyone else. A totalitarian system convinces even the leaders that they are superfluous. Only through the ideology do they have any hope of transcendence. Fanatical acts can occur when the self, (the being of independent will), is rejected as evil or worthless. The leader or the cause then becomes the surviving being and will.

Times of Change

In the Greco-Roman world of the First Century, there was great insecurity. Belief and value systems had weakened. These conditions aided the development of the Christian movement.

The latter Middle Ages, up to the 13th Century, were a time of optimism. Population increase and the rise of the textile industry toward the end of the century created alienation. Increased mobility, weakening of traditional authority, and displaced masses of unemployed caused anxiety. When Charles VIII invaded Italy (1494), the world was fractured into secular states and the Middle Ages were over.

The Renaissance opened a greater world. Men were no longer considered serfs. In psychological terms, the Renaissance has been seen as a revolt from a negative external conscience. The individual started to feel and enjoy his own value. The absence of conscience could also lead to great excesses.

Circumnavigation of the Earth, the Reformation and the invention of the telescope are said to have marked the Modern Age. Toynbee saw the Reformation as breaking the unity of the clergy; the rise of the vernacular languages as rupturing the unity of literate men; and the French Revolution as breaking the unity of the aristocracy and the start of wars of peoples rather than of kings. This was a period of great change.

Change created threats. The loss of religious unity made for insecurity. Rapid economic changes caused social dislocations. National wars made for rapid political change. Rousseau and Marx introduced new political theory. Kierkegaard changed religious thought. Nietzsche talked a violent philosophy and Freud debased man.

"Progress" implies change. The 19th Century had to meet the threat of revolution. In the first half of the 19th Century, idea of "progress" was common. But, "progress" implies change. Ideas of liberalism and democracy, of socialism and Marxism, also implied change. Population pressure and the search for markets fostered imperialism. Imperialism needed a justifying rationale, and social Darwinism (''survival of the fittest") served.

The colonized try to adopt the invader's ideology. The old way of life was destroyed by imperialist invaders. Thus, belief in the old ways and in the old ideologies no longer served the colonized. There seemed to be no choice but to adopt the values of the conquerors. The conquered became second class citizens in their own land who could never fully assimilate the imperial culture.

The colonized needed new ideologies. For example, American Indians evolved the Ghost Dance religion. This has been seen as an attempt to establish whites and Indians in an ideological universe and to offer the Indians the millenarian promise of a restored world. The Boxer Rebellion in China included similar ideologies.

In more recent times, the effect of Western cultural imperialism is often an improvement in the economy, followed by a feeling of threatened or lost identity. The locals then seek to restore their religious and cultural identity, perhaps by a seeking fundamentalist return to an imagined better age.

The "modernist crisis" is the name given to the efforts of the Catholic Church to adjust its ideology to the 20th Century. Liberalism, for the Church, meant the industrial revolution, economic determinism and materialism. Deification of the state, the identification of God with history, the ideology of laissez faire and the materialism of science were challenges that had to be met.

A new elite favoring violence arose. By 1900, Georges Sorel (said to have inspired both Hitler and Mussolini) was talking of a new social elite that would use violent direct action to lead the masses forward. Changes in society and a spreading Russian revolution threatened Europe. In popular philosophy, reason gave way to individual existentialism. Pessimism coexisted with utopian visions.

"Without war, the world would degenerate into materialism", said the Chief of the German General Staff, von Moltke, in 1880. The First World War demonstrated the collective lunacy that could be achieved with ideological unity. "War's "purifying bath of steel" was lauded by postwar German sources (Bracher, 1982). War was seen as achieving progress, uniting moral, scientific and material transformations. Stress, tension, nihilism and such authors as Sorel seemed to combine to seek a relief in "decisionism" and Armageddon.

The sacrifice of nihilism: the use of scarce resources to slaughter Hungarian Jews in 1944 has been cited as an example of "nihilism", of a sacrificial policy from moral rather than practical concerns. Hitler also made a nihilistic remark to the effect that, if Germans did not win the war, then they deserved to be destroyed.

The sense of rebirth may come with greatly changing times. Abraham Hoffer says that the "born again" include the True Believer and the American Hustler. He feels that a sense of rebirth has occurred in the World during the past hundred years. There were mass migrations. There was nationalism and other variants of the Chosen People theme. There were revolutionary movements that offered the vision of a Promised Land. All contributed to a sense of rebirth. This period of change has also exposed a plastic human type, as evidenced by the True Believer and the American Hustler. Hoffer's works lucidly discuss this phenomenon.

Media generated crisis, change, and weak ideology call for a strong ideology. What can capitalism offer beyond a good standard of living? With inconsistent values there is social alienation and unease. The media create a climate of constant crisis. Media make cultural change more evident. This potentiates change. Change affects different parts of the system at different times, increasing stresses. Religion and philosophy seek to accommodate the changes, but also induce change. The weak then yearn for strong, fundamentalist ideologies.

A change to severe economic or physical insecurity can make people want a new deal or order of society. Some will want to return the world to the way it was said to be. A new myth may arise that seeks to satisfy by saying what is in the process of becoming. A philosophy of resignation may also appear. Such are the typical responses to times of change.

6

THE MASS

The mass is society without a soul. "The face of the age is that of the unsheltered man. The masses claim that there is no god, hence man is worthless and slaughtered in great numbers, because he is nothing," said Karl Jaspers in 1931.-

Ortega y Gasset saw society as without a soul. Society can be defined as a group of individuals who interact according to rules and assigned roles. The relations of one person to another had meaning, but the usages of the collectivity were subhuman. How could one then speak of a *volkgeist* a "spirit of the people"? Confucians would argue that, once formed, the good character of the individual would permeate society.

Is existentialism a response of the individual to the consumer society? Do we have a society where people have no purpose other than to consume and to produce? Are we bobbing along on a stream of history over which we have no control? Is this the ethos of our era? Objectively, the world of the individual may be meaningless. Subjectively, to the individual, his immediate world may be the most important thing on Earth. To some, existentialism was a philosophical bridge between the objective insignificance and the subjective importance of the individual. It allows the individual to posit his own values when the articulated values are found to be wanting.

The masses revolt against responsibility: When people no longer belong to stable special interest groups, the character of politics changes. Tocqueville saw equality as isolating men and causing them to think only of themselves. Mass psychology replaces enlightened self-interest. Mass society has a leveling effect where the individual is reduced to a demographic insignificance. The individual is no more, counting only as part of a statistic.

By contrast, intelligent voting requires that one act responsibly and make difficult choices. Alienated mass man lacks the psychic strength to function responsibly in a democracy and the mass wants to follow a leader. For Ortega, this refusal of responsibility was the "revolt of the masses".

The psychic inflation of the group: Has the rational man been abandoned in favor of the existential group-man? Members of a group often feel a sense of omnipotence and freedom from the normal restraints of society. Freud sees this as a mania evoked by the fusion of the personal ego and the group derived superego. Jung calls the phenomenon "psychic inflation". This is the gang mentality.

Man must be moved by some ideal or illusion to consciously act in a manner that is superior to, or goes against, his personal interests. What of collective illusion? What happens when an entire community shares a biased myth, when there is a nation of ideologues? The mass can then act self-destructively under psychic inflation.

The practical man resists sweeping ideology. The empirical attitude differs from both ideology and religion. The practical man who asks: "does it work, and how useful would it be here?" has a mentality alien to that of the ideologue. Such an empirical attitude seems to develop slowly among individuals, in contrast to ideologies that sweep across groups.

The leader replaces the worthless self: "Anyone who wants to win the masses must know that the way to their hearts is not objectivity, which is weakness. The key to them is will and power." "The great masses of people are not philosophers, often they can operate only on faith." "The masses love a commander more than a supplicant and feel more satisfied by a doctrine which is intolerant than they do with freedom. They don't know how to use freedom and it makes them feel abandoned." The foregoing quotations are from Adolf Hitler, who has demonstrated his effective understanding of the subject.

Nationalism was a sort of mass movement, **embracing all classes.** Society had come to be identified with the nation-state. The industrial revolution and imperialism set people loose from their roots. Loss of the old psychic support structures alienated many people. The First World War ruined European social structure. Without a structure, how can one find protection or take effective action? As news spread of the Russian Revolution, even people who were apolitical wanted to join movements.

Is nationalism a form of religion- the industrial age equivalent of the "world religions of agrarian societies" as Gellner suggests? What modern vectors separate ethnic identity from national identity? Most studies assume the Western linear and teleological view of development. What of the East and its acceptance of "time's round" or of the Confucian view that all is process and change with time never repeating? (Hall, 1998).

Action potential rises with class interests and nationalism. Totalitarian movements do not involve classes, but are made up of masses. Thus, a significant characteristic of mass society is the absence of shared class interests. The mass must be given a shared objective. When the individual becomes lost in the mass, does he lose a feeling of self, of identity? A movement offers a place to someone who feels superfluous.

Television establishes reality. Interaction with the world is the usual way of establishing reality. If most communication comes from a TV screen, what reality is established? This is another peril of the alienated mass man.

The mass enfolds the narcissistic individual within it. To have no place in the world is to lose identity and self-respect. The personal and isolated was thought by the Greeks to characterize the animal nature of man. Mass man, before he joins a movement, would thus be seen as selfish and asocial. Some think that narcissism is the dominant psychic pathology of our era. The narcissist is styled as selfish, vain, shallow, empty, dependent, demanding and angry (Lothane, 1983). By joining a movement, one might hope to cure or to redirect such alienation.

Epictetus defined the "lonely" man as surrounded by others with whom he cannot establish contact. Feeling outside of any community, feeling rootless and superfluous, being unable to compare views of the world, all these have been styled as "loneliness". In the atomized and competitive society, is meaningful communication possible? Will Internet fora meet the need? Without the hope of immortality either from glory or from religion, how does modern man find transcendence? Must he then become part of a swarming mass?

Mass man requires psychological compensations. Rokeach and Hoffer each touch on the following points.

(1) Psychologically, a missing psychic component may require compensation.
(2) Can unreasoning faith then compensate for insecurity?
(3) Does hustling substitute for ideological purpose?
(4) Does pride replace self-respect?
(5) Can collecting things replace the illusion of progress?
(6) Can generalized desire replace transcendent goals?
(7) Can joining organizations replace a feeling of community?
(8) Does independence and disorganization now cause us to seek invented satisfactions?

The mass is susceptible to psychic epidemics: Do the psychological characteristics of the mass man differ from those of the individual? Jung saw masses in motion as expressing the collective unconscious, a "psychic epidemic". In a crowd, it appears to be the mass, rather than the individual, that thinks. Every mob, however, has its leaders.

The Inquisition in its witch hunting stage could be viewed as a form of mass psychosis spread by the religious orders. One factor was the idea of purging self and community of everything that was alien and unclean. -

The mass in politics responds directly to the leader. Why have the mediation of a representative legislature? Does a civil religion provide psychologically sufficient communication between the masses and the leader? In mass society, conformity means following the leader.

As the processes of society become increasingly impersonal, the individual will increasingly become the mass man. Political economy deals with numbers rather than with people. Today, demographics describe people and the bureaucracy is anonymous, says Trow.

Television as Religion

Ideas are dangerous, especially when media men act as priests. Belief influences both our perception and our actions. Since ideas can affect belief (an important instrument of social control), ideas are dangerous. The decline in the influence of the Church and of authoritarian governments has left the media to form public opinion and provide leadership. Media hosts and anchormen have become the new priesthood. Earlier, the shaman or priest, along with the chief, articulated the higher goals of the community.

The media man is a sort of priest. Today, it is the media personality who increasingly discharges a goal-articulating and judgmental function. The worldview of the media person is constrained by the set of characters who make up his special environment. The media person is not trained to function as priest or prophet but, as a function of his popularity, this becomes his role. The media, however, must entertain and excite, producing for short attention spans. "News" may be created to meet advertising audience needs, notes Trow.

Television functions as religion. Fore's *Television and Religion* sees television as the primary expression of moral attitudes and values in today's society. Television offers a religion of instant, infantile, personal gratification in an imaginary world. Such a religion is completely at variance with ideals of altruism, transcendence, and community.

In a perceptive article in the *New Yorker*, "Within the Context of No Context" (Nov. 17, 1980), G. W. S. Trow offered several insights about the action of the media in modern American society. Some of these ideas are paraphrased here. Counting takes the place of judgment. Only things that could be counted were important. Those things with high counts were boosted even more. People sought a false intimacy for reassurance. The culture acted in a childish way. News is mostly reported without history or context for judgment.

The mass is molded by television. If we recall how children form their worldviews, the values and reality that television conveys and establishes are threatening. Most of us, including media personnel, belong to the "now generation" and have our consciousness formed by television. The culture is now being transmitted via consumerism. Fashion changes rapidly and with little cultural resistance. There is a risk that a psychic void of materialist consumerism may be quickly replaced by values of a very different sort.

Initiators of Change

The prophet-messiah initiates change. All things are lawful unto me, but not all things are expedient" (St. Paul, 1 *Corinthians* 6:12). Radical change is called for only in times of crisis. The prophet-messiah is usually marginal to the established society. He seeks to make society, religion and man better, purer, or "cleaner". The prophet, "self-righteous and independent", is more preacher than priest. The prophet need not belong to organized religion. He can be the lay leader of a secular movement .

Millenarian prophets offer hope to the poor. When, for political reasons, the Pope wanted European knights away and involved them in the first two Crusades. The dregs of society also swarmed. There was a chance for loot, and having a mission gave them a role. The confused and poor, the power base of the prophets, receive a promise of hope.

A salvationist religion should appear to meet the needs of the masses. There is a desire for a personal savior. We may recall that the Greek *soterios* implied "lord" or "protector", although today it is translated "savior".

Prophets are often paranoid. Norman Cohn reports (1957) that the Carmelites attempted a retrospective psychological analysis of Jean-Antoine Boullan (1824-1893), the mystical leader of a large sect in eastern Europe. The Carmelites saw Boullan as a typical paranoid, obsessed by delusions of grandeur and of persecution; intelligent, audacious and driven by insatiable cravings. He would both dissimulate and force his way. It may be that prophets of secular religions, such as Mao, Stalin, Pol Pot , Hitler, etc. were also paranoid.

Some mystics are thought to begin with an exaggerated introversion. Later, they relive childhood fantasies. In a study of six English Messiahs (Matthews, 1936), half were thought to be paranoid schizophrenics, one merely paranoid, one manic, and one hysteric. (Dare one mention that Joan of Arc was a hebephrenic schizophrenic?).

Millenarian messiahs have magnetism. Norman Cohn, in his *Pursuit of the Millennium*, has developed the histories of some millenarian leaders. He says that all these messiahs were eloquent, had commanding bearing and possessed strong personal magnetism. The millenarian leader pattern varies. The founder of the Mormon church, Joseph Smith, has been presented (Halperin, 1983) as typical of the fraudulent and successful millenarian leader. Another modern leader was Placide Temples. His personalized Bantu Philosophy seems to show him alternating in the roles of Catholic priest, anthropologist and sect leader.

Two main factors have been noted in exalting the prophet-messiah. First, there is the god/father-figure operating as a priest-king. Secondly, there is the member's projection and identification with the personal greatness of the leader.

The prophet-messiah must also offer the follower membership in a group and the chance to find identity in such membership. Hitler offered the common man a partnership in the greatness of a future Reich. Was this a version of the "Kingdom of God" on Earth?

"The majority of men have no opinions. These have to be pumped into them from the outside. Without someone to command, chaos would reign over mankind", thought Ortega y Gasset in the 1930s. Hitler would oblige. Kant (1790) spoke of an "enlarged mentality", able to think for everyone else. Carlyle claimed that men required heroes to worship. For Germany, Hitler's latest statements formed the only principles. Such an unrestrained system must exhibit pleonexia- an unrestrained appetite for power.

Jung said that the political leader who claimed to reflect the general will would be compensating for a feeling of impotence.

The leader then feels anxiety about the potential loss of power and a vicious psychological circle seeking pleonexia grows.

Extrinsic religion implies extremism. Liebman (1978) shows that, when religion is external rather than within the individual, a tendency to extreme positions exists. Confidence is increased as power increases, but the insecurity remains. In bad times, the mass will support a millenarianist who will lead them into increasingly extreme positions. Successors reestablish faith by disassociating from the previous "cult of personality".

Hitler

Adolf Hitler was a Messianic leader. Before knowing of Hitler, Goebbels wrote that Germany was seeking a great prophetic leader. John Luckacs categorized Goebbels as a "prototypical example of an unhappy German neo-idealist". From a lower-middle-class Catholic family, he did not like his father and hated anything middle-class. Hitler became his father-image.

"All current symptoms of decay are only the consequences of the absence of a definite, uniformly acknowledged philosophy, and the resultant uncertainty toward the great problems of the time." "The function of organization is the transmission of a definite idea, which always arises first in the brain of an individual... this idea cannot be transmitted until the authority of the spiritual founder... is regarded as unconditional." The foregoing quotes are from Adolf Hitler.

August Kubizek's *Young Hitler* reports that Hitler had a very strong conscience. Once he had an idea, no alternative existed. He felt responsible for everything. In Erickson's analysis, Hitler had a fear that he might be nothing. To evade this possibility, he became deliberately anonymous when young. From this point, he could only rise. A woman writer who met Hitler said: "He is inconsequent and voluble, ill poised and insecure. He is the very prototype of the little man".

As a youth, Hitler had admired Karl Luger, mayor of Vienna in 1900. Luger's party was a Catholic movement and Luger saw himself as the general of a popular army. Hitler was, himself, a

Catholic, although in later years he was not a practicing one.

The hysterical leader attracts other hysterics. The hysteric believes in his own lies. Jung thought that Hitler exhibited traits typical of the hysteric: lack of introspection, self-admiration and extenuation, denigration and terrorizing of one's fellow man, projection, lying, impressing. It was, he thought, a form of hysteria characterized by believing one's own lies.

Dissolving oneself in the leader is common. W.C. Langer studied Hitler for the OSS and noted that most Germans surrendered their personal judgment to Hitler. Thus, his person became incorporated into the psychological integrity of his followers- they dissolved themselves into the leader.

It was clear that Hitler offered a new identity to Germany's adolescents, thought E.H. Erickson. Hitler's personal psychology resonated with the frustrations of millions of adult Germans. Does one adapt his personal neuroses to those of the leader, or does the leader express the collective neurosis?

Hitler's childhood was thought "dangerous, uncertain and unjust. His impulse would have been to hide from it", said Langer's team. In Hitler, there seemed to be a libidinal attachment between mother and son resulting in a basic feminine identification. There was also masochism.

The army provided an identity for him, but Germany's defeat in World War I left Hitler in a near-hysteric state. His reaction was said to "identify with the (imagined) aggressor" and seek to manifest traits that were the opposite of his feminine weaknesses. A similar repressed feeling of weakness may have characterized Hitler's German audiences.

Hitler treated his mass audiences as feminine. In speaking, he began hesitantly and approached hysteria as rapport was established. There appeared to be a regenerative circuit between the neurosis of the Fuhrer and the neuroses of the people, each fostering excesses in the other. Fear produced grandiose pleonexia in the search for security, as giant buildings had earlier sought to symbolically compensate for lack of confidence.

Hitler had a strong personal magnetism. Many attributed this magnetism to his apparent fanatical belief in himself. This sort of commitment to a cause is far more dangerous than an interest in women or riches, for such a leader will sacrifice himself and everyone else for his cause.

The weak hate weakness. Eric Hoffer, in *The Ordeal of Change*, says that a sense of inadequacy and impotence motivates the weak. Thus, they hate weakness and they hate themselves. The weak will gladly surrender themselves to one who appears strong. Social crisis, the need to feel secure, and even the desire for identity and importance, can make the weak masses want to follow a strong leader. Coupled with this is the fact that submission characterizes all but about seven percent of authoritarians (Altemeyer 2004).

Does the idea of being "born again", as Hoffer suggests, mean becoming like a child, a dutiful, protected, member of a family, following the dictates of a father-figure? Those low in self-esteem are sensitive to the opinions of others and are thus easily influenced (Hovland et al., 1959). Being in a structured situation allows the individual to feel powerful and protected at the same time. It has been noted that members, as distinguished from fanatics, do not seek martyrdom. Members will wither away if the movement weakens.

Mass commitment can overcome alienation. "The true believer finds in mass meetings the visible confirmation by thousands of the rightness of the new doctrine," said Adolf Hitler. When an individual becomes lost, a movement or an organization can offer a place.

Unamuno claims that only through fervid commitment can man escape from the despair of meaninglessness. Further, says Unamuno, belief and action constitute reality for man. Hegel thought that man could, through speculative philosophy, detach himself from the world and achieve a spiritual rebirth. Both Unamuno and Hegel claimed mind over matter, but Unamuno seemed to better understand the True Believer.

Passion is the inverse of confidence. Can passion serve as a substitute for confidence? Religious beliefs are defended more passionately than are issues of fact. Those lacking confidence may display more passionate conviction than the normal person. Conformity of belief is most sought when belief seems threatened. For example, when the world does not end as predicted, doomsday cults redouble their recruiting efforts.

As the member becomes a true believing group member, responsibility is shifted from the individual and projected onto outsiders. (In Milgram's experiments, obedient personalities, when told to torture a victim, tended to blame the victim for the torture). Aggression, submissive obedience to authority and obsession are said to characterize authoritarians (Butler 2000).

The fanatic becomes inhuman. "At times I was overcome by gloom and malignant fear. Then I saw before me a doctrine, comprised of egotism and that, as mathematic-like laws, will lead to victory. But in doing so, it must put an end to humanity," said Hitler.

Jung saw fanaticism as arising from doubts about personal conformity. These doubts are repressed. To prove that he conforms, the insecure person behaves in a fanatical way. Repressed feelings often find outlets in destruction (Middendorf, 1976, Arno Plack, 1974).

Orders are the categorical imperative. Many of those who were called criminals at Nuremburg believed that they had done no wrong. This appears to have been a reasonable judgment on their part. Eichmann, a psychiatrically "normal personality", had a perfectly clear conscience. Only if had he failed to follow orders would Eichmann's conscience have bothered him, said Hanna Arendt. Eichmann's categorical imperative was that he should try to exceed his orders and do his best to execute the will of the Fuhrer.

Fanaticism and Terrorism

Fanatics as idealists: Totalitarian supporters often display altruistic selflessness. Fanaticism, religious and political, can be a form of idealism. (Eichmann referred to himself as an "idealist".) The mechanism may be similar in the case of those possessed by spirits. This permits escape from a conflict situation and allows responsibility and guilt to be projected. Such "possession" is most likely to occur among the oppressed.

The projected Devil is necessary. Hostile parents can induce evil tendencies in the child. It then becomes useful to project both the parental attitudes and one's malevolent tendencies onto devils. The devil is the repressed. To struggle against something makes it real. One then really depends on it. The Devil is psychologically necessary.

The paranoid reaction uses denial and projection. Serious frustrations may precipitate the paranoid state. People who are tense, insecure, and mistrustful of self are more likely to be paranoid. The paranoid causes what threatens him from within to seem to threaten him from the outside. Evil is projected onto that outside world. One then seeks to isolate oneself from that world.

Fantasy and projection involve psychic inflation against a target. When reality yields to fantasy, can conscience and the old rules still function? If the leader encourages the mob, then the leader and the mob potentiate each other and psychic inflation exists. A single, simple target of projection is sought. Then the mob and leader sanction each other's behavior.

Purification is part of the terrorist subculture: The more perfect the ideal, the more guilt man feels. The torment of such guilt may be projected as prejudice or vented as destructive violence. "You must think of humanity, past, present and future, as one great body that requires surgery... all acts that further history and socialism are moral acts", said an instruction manual for Soviet agents.

Performing violent acts removes the terrorist from society and commits him to the subculture. Professor Fenarotti talking about his former students who became active in Italy's Red Brigade said that a lack liberal confrontation, open-mindedness or dialogue contributed to their mind-set, as did Catholicism. Politics was viewed as something filthy in need of purification that could only be cleaned up through blood sacrifice.

Asceticism and martyrdom are religicus attitudes. Juan Sebreli (1985) expands upon the connection between certain Catholic schools and the violent fanaticism of the Montoneros in Argentina, naming particular schools and Catholic youth organizations, priests and former seminarians. Sebreli focuses on psychological characteristics of irrationalism, sectarianism, asceticism, the idea of sacrificing self for humanity (martyrdom), the seeking of absolutes and the "adoration of death". Similar considerations apply to certain radical Islamic mullahs and their activities.

Henri Atlan (1985), Sabino Aquaviva and Jose Aranguren have sought to identify the links between religion and terrorist violence in Italy. Since Argentina has a great cultural connection with Italy, it is not immediately clear whether only Italian-style Catholicism is implicated.

The end justifies the means. If the True Believer sees the world as a conflict between good and evil, one implementing the revelation sees himself as a savior. The God-appointed savior can do anything, since the divinely ordained end justifies the means. Insecurity leads to violent movements.

A cold hater may commit terrorist acts. Timothy McVeigh, who bombed a federal building in the USA, and Mohammed Atta, who led the group attacki[illegible] New York's Word Trade Center were "austere, self-righteous and highly controlled". Atta's resentment and anger were given sanction by being on the side of the "righteous".

Factors common to such violent ideologues: (1) distrustful of and alienated from women (2) introverted and of superior intelligence (3) blocked in chosen occupational path (4) emotionally withdrawn and socially adrift (5) having undergone a conversion experience (6) having grandiose fantasies about the consequences of his actions (Meloy, 2004).

Psychological motivations of terrorist violence vary among social-revolutionary, religious-fundamentalist and nationalist-separatist movements. This is further complicated when a movement partakes of religious and nationalist aspects, etc. It has been claimed that social-revolutionaries include many schoolboys rebelling against parental authority- but this is not the case with Palestinians seeking revenge for the Israeli murder of parents (Post, 2005). It is thus difficult to generalize about "the terrorist" when situational and group organizational factors loom so large.

Palestinian suicide bombers have been motivated by patriotism, vengeance, recovery of dignity, individual or group identity and communal self-defense They are said to come from highly religious families and to unquestioningly accept what they are told by religious authorities. Their operations are styled "martyrdom", rather than "suicide". A fusion of individual and group identity takes place. (Post, Springzak & Denny, 2003).

A study of thirteen such bombers (Nolan, 1966) found them unmarried, aged 19-25, of devout family, educated in fundamentalist centers, having had a close relative killed by the Israelis, having lived in concentration camps, unable to find work, being too poor to pay for studies and having a strong Palestinian identity (Lester et al., 2004).

Soibelmann (2004) interviewed five Palestinians who had failed in such bombing attempts. They wanted to recover their personal dignity and to carry a message to their Israeli oppressors. They saw no alternative way. For all, abuse at the hands of the Israeli military created a strong desire to restore personal dignity.

Ideals of "justice", "truth", "purity", personal dignity, honor and land were important to these bombers. Islam and their Palestinian culture reinforced these ideals. Several had originally had a neighborly attitude toward the Israelis, but, as the Israeli oppression increased, they became more intense in their religion and moved to an extremist group.

Political violence in Pakistan seems common to the culture and is practiced by both the government and opposition parties (Khan, 2003). Disillusionment with the system may cause the individual to feel that violence offers the only chance for improvement. There, an "instrumental" rather than a psychological, mainspring exists. Khan emphasizes the distinction between individualist (idiocentric) and collectivist (allocentric) cultures and says that Pakistan is about 60% collectivist. Thus, the cultural context may define the motivations for terrorism.

In the Schwartz Value Survey (1992), motivations of power, achievements, hedonism, stimulation, self-direction, universalism, benevolence, tradition, conformity and security were applied to members of Pakistan's secular, violent, MQM party and to the large Islamist and nonviolent JI party.

Psychological attitudes can differ among parties. Despite its revolutionary goals, 93% of the JI party members were against violence and embraced the values of benevolence, security and conformity, de-emphasizing hedonism, power and stimulation. Violence correlated most negatively with benevolence and universalism and most positively with hedonism, stimulation, power and idiocentrism. The 89% violent MQM party members most valued hedonism, stimulation and achievement.

7

SPIRITS AND ISMS

"Lastly, there are the idols which have crept into men's minds from the various dogmas of peculiar systems of philosophy, and also from the perverted rules of demonstration, and these we denominate idols of the theater; for we regard all the systems of philosophy... as so many plays brought out and performed, creating fictitious and theatrical worlds." Francis Bacon, *Novum Organon.*

We will survey the development of various philosophies and ideologies to see how these develop through time and inform the present.

Surplus brings hierarchy. Even very primitive societies organize themselves in two groups, or *moities*, and then develop procedures for regulating the interaction between them. As surplus becomes available, hierarchies develop and are fed from that surplus.

Legitimizing myths arise to rationalize the hierarchy and wealth and power become positive social values (Silvanius and Pratto, 1999). After myth, we encounter a socially constructed reality (Shcrif, 1937, Asch, 1956), where exclusive control of information by the mass media (Chomsky, 1989) is able to influence inner beliefs (Zimbardo and Anderson, 1993).

Organized ideologies tend to promote both a particular myth and the interests of a given class. As religion for the common folk serves to express changing outlook and conditions, so does philosophy function for the intellectuals. The ideology of the upper classes serves higher goals than the beliefs of the peasants. The ideology of the rulers must keep with the spirit of the times as well as the personal concerns of the common folk. There is also some ground for suspecting that the doctrines of successive ideologies alternate between the mystical and the deterministic.

The psyche cycles between poles. Feuer, in his *Ideology and Ideologists*, suggests that every claim of a philosophy can be mapped to some particular aspect of the psyche. A given philosophy satisfies one aspect of the psyche and suppresses another. For example, determinism downgrades spontaneity, voluntarism frustrates the desire for order, and empiricism rejects fantasy.

Since accepting a particular philosophy represses some psychological desire, Feuer claims that the succeeding wave of philosophy will furnish an outlet for the previously repressed psychological component. Thus, successive philosophies are seen to alternate and to vent psychological opposites. The psycho-historian E. H. Erickson sees a basic alteration between carnival and atonement.

Doctrines accord with changing times. The *zeitgeist*, or spirit of the age, is important. The Renaissance grew with the secular nation-state. Men began to act for the mirror of each other rather than for the Church. As nation-states became more powerful, the times needed a doctrine to protect individuals. Between the Reformation and the French Revolution, there was a lot of talk about "natural rights" and the "social contract".

Philosophy becomes doctrine becomes "ism". Once philosophy hardens into doctrine, it becomes an "ism". Historicism, for example, asserts that vast sociological laws can be known that will forecast the course of societies. A person claiming special knowledge of such laws may see himself as a prophet. Nineteenth Century American imperialism was carried on in furtherance of the alleged "manifest destiny." of the nation. Some imperialists cited "the white man's burden" as their excuse for imperialism.

As with a kaleidoscope, one can observe elements of philosophic thought combining, opposing and splitting. To speak of "spirits and isms" is to suggest the links that preceded the modern civil religions. To provide a longer context, one can consider the Greek experience and some aspects of Chinese and Indian philosophy. The latter are in sharp contrast to the "spirits and Isms" that stem from the intolerant fundamentalism of the Zoroastrian-derived (Jewish, Christian and Muslim) religions and their secular sequels.

Chinese history illustrates basic issues generally encountered in political philosophy: (1) a personal leader vs. a ruling principle; (2) transcendence vs. immanence; (3) the mystical vs. the physical; (4) stasis vs. change; (5) the teleological vs. the circular; (6) selfishness vs. altruism; (7) unity vs. plurality; and (8) principle vs. force. Those are essentially the same issues dealt with in Greek and Western philosophy. Ideas of ethics, collectivity and harmony pervade Chinese philosophy. The key difference is the dominance in China of a collectivity and its harmony. The West has been more individualistic. The implicit teleology of development leading to the Promised Land on Earth is pervasive in the West and contrasts strongly with the Eastern view.

Transcendence contrasts with immanent practicality. By 1650, the Chinese world seemed wholly material and called for pragmatic and rational explanation. With Tai Chen (1750), China had its own version of positivism. In the late nineteenth century, the need to improve things evoked a return to idealistic praxis.

Life is competition, thought Hobbes. (1588-1679). Thomas Hobbes saw man as common and the state as a business, in keeping with the *zeitgeist*. Why should the individual desire what is good? The nation-state and mobility for the individual were both new. Hobbes saw life as a competition, a meaningless race with no goal other than winning. To keep order, a strong monarchy was required. For Hobbes, social conflict resulted from the nature of man. (For Locke, only a few people caused the trouble in society.)-

A merchant could choose the integrated corporate state of Fascism. Does the merchant see society, economic relations and government as a single thing? For Hobbes the virtue of society rested in the merchants, for they could replace Church domination. In the "Kingdom of Darkness" portion of the *Leviathan*, Hobbes showed the Papacy as exercising such domination.

The Enlightenment gave emphasis to reason, citizenship and the nation-state. Descartes thought that truth could be found by introspection. God began to reside within man. Reasoned subjectivism received emphasis. In the 1700's, men began to think independently of religion and to identify with their nation-state. The ruler became the symbol of the state, rather than the owner. The ruler's "subject" became a "citizen". The middle class values became the values of society. Reason, science and progress received more attention than religious claims. Deism became popular as the Enlightenment spread. The deist god was a "clockmaker god" who set the machine in motion and stood back.

The Enlightenment and Reason

"State of Nature" and "Social Contract" were fictions serving ideological argument. Human reason was applied to the natural world. The rational method was thought "scientific". Progress came through the application of science. Progress in material things would lead also to the perfection of man. Talking about the perfect "state of nature was a way of seeking a new order of society, as was "social contract" theorizing. Locke's *Essay on Human Understanding* (1690) portrayed the human mind as being fully determined by experience. Education, according to Locke, could thus be arranged to achieve a more perfect human. Some took a different view. Burke, for example, saw society as a growing organism, a non-rational process, (much as, today, the idea of random chance is replacing Darwinian evolutionary survival). There were also the unenlightened: The evangelical movements of Methodism in America and Pietism in Germany were popular in conservative areas.

Rousseau, then Romanticism

Rousseau's "new man" and the General Will: "It is impossible to separate morality and politics. Those who want to treat them separately will never understand either", said Rousseau. Men, as they are, are not fit for liberty, says Rousseau. Therefore, a state must be created which will mold them. In this process, voluntary associations and dissent are not to be allowed. There will be a civil religion. Disobedience will mean exile or death.

Seemingly influenced by monastic life, Rousseau saw a special education and an egalitarian society as producing a new type of man, who would have no desire to counter the general will. "Education" was to produce voluntary submission to the General Will.

There was to be a one-time surrender to the state. By submitting to a regime that he selects, the individual achieves "true freedom". Such submission is to be irrevocable. Where law was sovereign, how could sovereignty be limited? In this, Rousseau agreed with Hobbes.

Those who possess power are the ones who articulate the general will. Rousseau's version of the "social contract" gave the government absolute power over all citizens. The citizen makes a one-time surrender of his body and his property to the state. This is a voluntary and complete surrender to dissolve oneself in the realization of the general will. Thereafter, it is the general will which determines man's relation to the collectivity.

Government knows the general will best. "Our will is always for our own good. People do not always see what is good for them and are often deceived", said Rousseau. The general will is what each person would wish if he knew what was good for him. After the revolution of 1956, Janos Kadar told the Hungarians that there was a distinction between "the wishes and the will of the working masses", and the true interests of the workers. The Communist Party knew the "true interests" of the workers and this was justification for calling in the Soviet army.

Government will prevent inequality. Justice, for Rousseau, meant preventing inequality among men. Capitalist society required competition. Winners and losers result, and the winners institutionalize the inequality. Rousseau foresaw a society were all men enjoyed equality. He spoke from a milieu of class privilege.

Materialism evokes Romanticism. Enlightenment rationalism and the materialism of the times evoked a reaction. From a study of late 18th Century English novels, one author derived the following as general views of the times: it was a sad era; civilized life was too complex; man was overwhelmed by the material. The French Encyclopedists called for reform. By 1800, the rationalism of the Enlightenment was being faulted for "lack of heart". Reason was the *verstand* of the bookkeeper. What was needed was intuition, *vernunft*, and romantic feeling. The romantic spirit tends toward idealism at the expense of practicality.

Romantics such as Rousseau, Herder, Schiller and Goethe were to express the feeling of the times, to articulate the *zeitgeist.* Jung claimed that the Enlightenment's stress on individualism tended toward egoism, uncontrolled selfishness. This could produce a compensatory reversion to the collective man. Hegel's counter ideology of historical and economic determinism and dialectic proved useful for Marxist-Leninism and Fascism.

Some claim that the scientific attitude, is, itself, mythic. Rubem Alves points out that our scientific culture has some dubious assumptions: (a) to "know" means to be able to duplicate. (b) Social phenomena determine consciousness. (c) Imagination and mysticism are sick. (d) Normality consists in adaptation.

For Kant (1724-1804), people were by nature selfish and sought to advance themselves at the expense of others. Civilization was the process of controlling and channeling this competition. The same sort of control was needed among nations.

Kant saw history as continuous progress towards the ultimate realization of a worldwide ethical commonwealth. He thought intuition could distinguish between the noumenal (ideas) and phenomenal (senseperceived) and then achieve a synthesis. In this, he presaged Hegel and Romanticism.

Joseph de Maistre (1753-1851) called for the Church to control things. Thoughts about the ideal state of nature and the perfectibility of man put in doubt the Christian dogma of original sin. This was not de Maistre's view. He thought that baser drives controlled men. To make them behave, coercion was required. Reason was to be avoided, said De Maistre, for what one man could demonstrate, another could refute. Thinking for the group was to be done by the Roman Catholic Church. For de Maistre, the Church was the basis of the collectivity. De Maistre also had some thoughts about the importance of language: "language is the thought of the race expressing itself." The words "race" and "tribe" were becoming common in German writing.

The counter-Enlightenment posited human will and was a reaction to the waning rationalism of the Enlightenment. Fichte, Hegel, Goethe and Schopenhauer expressed poetic ideas of passion . "Rules are like vestal virgins, unless they are violated, there will be no issue". Thus did J. G. Hamann, the Pietist, express his voluntarism. "Voluntarism" is a philosophy wherein will or passion is valued more than economics or logic. Reason gave way to passion.

"God is a poet, not a mathematician", said Hamann. The movement came to be known as *Sturm und Drang*. The Pietists wanted a sort of new Medievalism with guilds, rather than free trade. They wanted a system of land tenure that would keep men on the land and they wanted a revived and universal Church. There soon appeared developments that have been classified as pre-Romanticism, Pietism, romantic Hellenism, German nationalism and *Sturm und Drang*. The writing of J. G. von Herder marked the culmination of these stages.

Pietism sought the devotion of the whole man. Religion was to include all of life. In Germany, love of fatherland became part of Pietism. The Pietists claimed that direct communication with God was possible. They were both emotional and greatly concerned with self-discipline. Perfection in this world was sought. Hamann was to argue for emotion over rationality, and thought that "absolute dependence" was what characterized religion. In this, he seems to represent the German Pietist tradition. In *Pietism as a Factor in the Rise of German Nationalism* (N.Y. 1934), Koppel S. Pinson follows these developments more fully.

When the United States was created, the Enlightenment was the spirit of the age. To achieve the good life, attention would be paid to the checks and balance of governmental power. There was no talk of creating a new kind of man. Individualism and free enterprise were praised. In France, however, the Revolution hoped to change men's behavior in a uniform way. In America, pluralism and the separation of powers were seen as ways to protect the individual. This pluralism is a fundamental distinction, for it is integral to totalitarian thinking that truth is one.

Tocqueville saw democracy as incompatible with liberty. The tyranny of public opinion could be worse than the tyranny of a monarch. There would be a preference for easy success and quick enjoyment over future benefit. Men would strive for riches rather than for glory.

The passions of the mob would militate against statesman-like careers. There would be few illiterates and also few who were very learned. The interest in equality would make superiority unappreciated. Equality isolates men because it makes them concentrate on material possessions and consider only themselves. (Tocqueville was writing c. 1832. Does it sound like today?)

The despotism of the democratic state would want to keep people as children. "What remains but to spare them the need to think and to spare them the problems of daily life?" Was America a "despotism" or a "tyranny of the majority"? Tocqueville thought a compromise likely to result between an administrative despotism and the sovereignty of the people. He saw the worst possible outcome as the concentration of public power in an individual or in a committee responsible to no one.

"Engineering the World" was the approach of French intellectuals. France had experienced a rapidly increasing population and inadequate food production. The growing bourgeoisie had been kept from power. Marx saw the French Revolution as essentially an operation of the middle class. This idea also influenced Fichte and Novalis. With the elimination of a nobility and the establishment of equality, material possessions became the primary distinction among men.

The Declaration of the Rights of Man and of the Citizen (1789), established equality of rights in liberty, security and property. Having equality of rights is not the same as having rights. Rousseau thought that normal society militates against equality, and thus legislation should promote equality.

Does alienation also result from equality? With equality, do men lose their feelings of responsibility and become selfish and isolated? When superiority is resented, is mediocrity fostered? Is equality really desirable?

The French Revolution let society worship itself. Mass participation characterized the new approach to politics. Mosse thought that the French Revolution initiated the practice of letting people worship themselves in a political framework. Mass revolution requires that the power of society exceed the power of the state. The French Revolution established the middle class in power. It then increased the power of the state until it equaled the power of society. Could revolution continue?

Romanticism (1780-1830) supplanted rationalism. Rationalism attempted to explain politics in terms of abstract principles rather than as the balancing of interests, and was thus idealist and ideological. De Rougemont described Romanticism as a passionate attack on the material, the logical, and other male-type obstacles to realizing the feminine principle. Romanticism, as a reaction against the rationalism of the Enlightenment seems to exemplify the psychological alternation of dominant philosophies.

Distinctions between the individual and the outside world, between feeling and thinking, between belief and knowledge, weakened. The German Romantics would call the "reason" of the Enlightenment the "*Verstand*" of the bookkeeper. "V*ernunft*", transcendent intuition, was the logic of the Romantic. In Germany, Romanticism was anti-French and counter-revolutionary.

"Novalis" (1772-1801) [F.L.F. von Hardenberg]. He was an influential poet who glorified medieval unity. The Enlightenment and the Reformation both served to break that unity. German Romanticism raised royalist nationalism against revolution. Novalis, in his *Annals of the Prussian Monarchy* (1798), said that the state would create feelings of love, faith and devotion. He saw these feelings being realized in a mystical communion with the ruler of the state. The self would be dissolved in the leader.

Friedrich von Schlegel (1772-1829) was the leader of the German Romantic movement. After converting to Roman Catholicism, he immediately moved to Vienna to accept a court appointment from the Catholic Emperor. From Vienna, Schlegel proclaimed that the best preserver of civilization was the Roman Catholic Church. He cited the Middle Ages as the great era when political and religious powers were nearly one. Since language shapes thought, claimed Schlegel, nations speaking the same language were the fundamental elements of history. For him, the state existed only to foster the nation.

F. D. E. Schleiermacher (1768-1834) provided a religious version of Romanticism. He took the Christian relation to Christ as a model for his definition of religion. He saw religion as the feeling of being absolutely dependent. The thing adored need not acknowledge the adorer. Such dedication was seen as distinguishing the adorer.

For Schleiermacher, all thinking occurred as dialogue. A common language was therefore necessary to a common philosophy. The need for dialogue made membership in social and religious communities necessary. He saw Pietism as furnishing a basis for a romanticist philosophy of religion. Later, Schelling would use symbols to objectify myth.

F. W. J. Schelling (1775-1854), like Kant, saw history as a teleological progression toward the perfect state. While Fichte saw the world as a construction of the personal ego, Schelling thought external forces shaped the individual consciousness. He defined "God" as the revelation of the divine in man. It was through the willful acts of the individual that God was revealed.

Johann Gottlieb Fichte (1762-1814) said nationalism created and expressed the general will. His early writing was much concerned with religion. Later, he became more concerned with the German state as a form of religious expression. The vocation of man, claimed Fichte, was to create a moral order. This moral order was the essence immanent in all men.

Fichte thought a universal reason common to all men. That universal reason would achieve perfect love freedom and unity. (There was still the striving for union with the "One" of early theology, but now the "One" was human society.) If we speak of *li* instead of *logos* or universal reason and *jen* instead of "love", we seem to have a reprise of the Confucian views of Chu Hsi (d.1200).

Fichte called for the annihilation of the individual who would thereby lose himself in the state. The ego would be realized through the state. The economically self-sufficient state would practice a culturally isolationist nationalism aiming for absolute "unity".

Fichte urged that education be used to create a united Germany that, through purity of race and character, would lead the world. Children were to be separated from their parents and prepared for a life of dedication and duty. Rigid state control, together with the educational indoctrination, would assure that each citizen would do what he ought.

The future would belong to those who knew how to impose their will. Such egos would not be subject to conventional morality. Heine foresaw, in 1834, the day when "armed Fichteans will stride onto the scene with fanaticism that can be restrained neither by fear nor by considerations of utility".

Hegel (1730-1861) thought that the most important function of the ruler was to achieve the moral unity of the state. "Unity", "wholeness", "oneness" and "integration" are keywords in Hegel's philosophy. The complete subordination of the individual to the state in achieving unity was also basic to Hegel's thought. The individual achieved his "highest power" and "immanent purpose" by losing himself in the service of the state. "One must worship the state as a terrestrial divinity", said Hegel, for the freedom of the human spirit could only be realized when the individual dissolved himself in the state.

Custom, derived from the experience of the folk, was most important. In achieving unity, the laws of the state would be consistent with custom. The course of history showed the unfolding of the absolute mind. As individuals grouped themselves in more complex societies, "mind" became "spirit". The *volkgeist* was the historically determined folk-spirit or national genius of the people. It could be called the "God of the folk". Human thought thus became the externalization of the mind of god. For Hegel, the state, representing the folk-spirit, demonstrated the highest expression of the divine mind. Politics was now a religion.

History reflected a progression wherein opposites were synthesized. The Hegelian dialectic became a universal philosophical tool (1600 years after the Indian philosopher Aryadeva had elaborated it). The dialect resembles the Confucian ideas of *Yin* and *Yang*, applied to concepts.

History, explained dialectically, was the successive realization of a world spirit, embodied in the state. To be rational, the individual must conform to that higher rationality, the state. He must get in step with history. Reason and religion became identical in Hegel's view. What was religion but philosophy in symbolic form? Positive freedom came through the philosophy that man could transcend his material constraints and be reborn. This expressed a religion of the state. The state was the highest expression of morality. What of freedom? The freedom to act within limits was only "negative freedom". Positive freedom, as Hegel saw it, could only be achieved when men dissolved themselves in the state.

God's mind is revealed through the Folk. For the German Romantics the *volkgeist*, or spirit of the people, became the mainspring of the culture. The state was the collective mind. Around 1814, a rationale for German unification was sought. It was then that the exaltation of "race" began in earnest.

Beginning with Kant, there was a growth of ideas that led to an action-oriented ideology. Did the ideology form the national consciousness or did it simply reflect and potentiate it? (As far back as 1510, the "Revolutionary of the Upper Rhine" had published a racial myth of socialist unity and violence). From Kant to Political Action

The state becomes God. The psychic factors that caused men to invent gods persist. If gods are projections of the social order, then the state itself may easily be the object of worship. Many seek to deify the state. For many, the state replaces the parents. The state has not, as yet, developed religious-like techniques for calming anxiety or giving warm affect.

Nationalism can be seen as self-worship through symbols. In 1500, Fortescue wrote a book wherein the "realm" was more than the sovereign, being described as a religious, mystical thing. The monarch came to serve as a symbol of both the nation and the state. As a unifying symbol, the monarch could later be replaced by the idea of citizenship.

Renan suggested that a common history, especially a myth of common struggle, combined with a will to live together were necessary to make a nation. Nationalism and Romanticism seem to have begun together. Mosse argues that symbols then became the essence of nationalism. A liturgy of national myths and symbols enabled people to worship themselves in a political religion.

Nationalism, conformity and xenophobia occur together. Hatred of things foreign was psychologically linked (Bracher, 1982) to attitudes of nationalism, paternal authority and violent insistence on conformity. Windish said that the nation-worshiper loses himself in the collectivity and then adores it.

For xenophobes, the foreigner represents the unbeliever who threatens a loss of the identity one has received from the collectivity. The foreigner is also a useful target for the projection of aggression. Baiting the foreigner reinforces one's own identity and helps relieve anxiety.

The industrial revolution caused great social changes. In the view of Will Durant, the Industrial Revolution was accompanied by democracy, feminism, birth control, socialism, the decline of religion, and the economic interpretation of history. The steam engine marked the industrial revolution. As peasants became industrial workers, there arose a new sense of futility and alienation. Mass migrations produced the feeling of rebirth. Nationalism conveyed the idea of a Chosen People, and revolutionary movements moved toward a vision of a better world.

The polarization into rich and poor became more evident. Education and commerce were means of social advancement. The new bourgeoisie set the values for society, offering hope to the ostensibly God-fearing, diligent and clever.

Alienation resulted in social revolution. Toward the end of the 19th Century, travel and communication was increased for the wealthier. Laborers lived like machines. Feelings of community had been lost and individuals were isolated.

Uprooted former agricultural workers felt themselves unneeded. People became quantities in the economic calculus. With the Industrial Revolution, as with the Nazi and Soviet revolutions, man served the revolution, rather than the revolution serving man.

Positivism advocated social engineering. The word "positivism" was coined by Auguste Comte about 1825. The essential idea is that only propositions concerning facts can be objective. Belief in progress and optimism were part of the positivist culture. Comte foresaw social engineering by a political elite of managers. The rational and scientific formulation of the laws of human sociology, were not to be questioned by a "vain and at times seriously disturbing curiosity". Consensus and authority above politics would control events. Liberty would be restricted to keep things within the plan.

Positivists thought sociologists could function as priests. Comte thought that Roman Catholicism, divested of its supernatural aspects, would provide an ideal model for the new positivist society. His *System of Positive Polity* described a religious utopia. There was a positivist catechism, a calendar of the saints, a hierarchy of sacraments and a priesthood. (This continued Napoleonic precedent). The priesthood, made up of sociologists, would control education and public morality and would be available to arbitrate disputes. They would lack temporal power. The temporal administration, as distinguished from the planning, would be given to captains of industry.

Positivism was embraced by Latin-American technocrats who sought an alternative to the Spanish Catholic colonial corporatist tradition. In Brazil and in Mexico, positivism became the ideology of national liberation movements. Brazil, particularly, was influenced by the positivism of Comte

When Barreda brought positivism to Mexico in 1867, he changed the positivist motto "love, order and progress" to "liberty, order and progress". Vasconcelos later sought to give this an emotive, racist twist, speaking of the "Ibero-American race". The Mexican revolution had no doctrine. Some suggest that Diaz adopted positivism as an official philosophy to counteract liberalism and yet remain away from Catholicism. A mystical reaction developed in Mexico shortly after 1900, with Madero, Vasconcelos and others.

Does logic describe reality better than intuition? Are particulars the reality and universals only wishful thinking? Samuel Ramos talked of a humanistic middle course between the positivists and the romantics. By 1930, the cultural humanism of Ortega y Gasset began to be dominant in Mexican philosophy.

Determinism sees events as predetermined by prior events. One may claim that history follows a general trajectory based on economic and environmental factors. If the world is deterministic, then values are of little use. Dialectical materialism seems to be much more popular than determinism.

Materialism posits the brain and broad trends. As a philosophy materialism has two basic aspects: that thinking is determined by the physical construction of the brain; and that the course of history is determined by the interaction of broad trends. With its emphasis on the physical, science is materialist.

Illusion and hope are most important. People soon realize that the material goods of the consumer society do not bring happiness. The illusion offered by hope is always greater than reality. The lessons here are that illusion is much more important than material satisfaction and that materialism is therefore not a popular basis of ideology. Nationalism and religion are strong social vectors that are not adequately determined by economics alone. Materialism as an explanation has its limits Thus, popular ideologies are likely to oppose consumerism.

Empiricism holds that experience, rather than reason, is the basis of knowledge. Locke denied that any ideas could be innate. John Stewart Mill would urge that all was psychological and inductive. Bertrand Russell pointed out that the principles of inductive logic cannot themselves be inductively derived. The empiricist sociology of Malinowski and Boas, for example, tries to take a minute and factual look at a particular society and explain the society inductively in terms of the observed facts. Induction cannot be as popular as facile Gallic deduction from sweeping premises.

Nietzsche expressed repugnant pessimism and nationalism. For Nietzsche, all human behavior could be seen as the will to power. Christianity, said Nietzsche, is born of weakness, failure and resentment. He thought it the enemy of the body, of sex, of power, of joy, and of freedom, reason and honesty. As Nietzsche progressed towards madness, the repugnant was emphasized. Spengler and others made these concepts a part of nationalism.

Nihilism appealed to scientific pessimists. As it originated in Eighteenth Century Russia, nihilism believed only in scientific truth and claimed that all evil stemmed from ignorance. As seen in France and in Germany in the Twenties, nihilism conveyed the idea that destruction was true expression. A bloody pessimism, rather than progress, characterized the teleology.

***Volksgemeinschaft* implied the separateness and community of the German people.** Anyone would have an equal chance of success. Pan-Germanism appeared during the opposition to Napoleon. Around 1854, Gobineau popularized the idea of Nordic superiority. The Pan-Germanic League was organized in 1864.

Toward the end of the Century, Wagner and his son-in-law advanced the idea of German superiority. By 1908, the Pan-Germanic League's explicit objectives included the "continuation of the German colonial movement". The League was soon fostering ideas of racial superiority over Slavs and Jews and was making anti- capitalist statements.

Naumann's Mitteleuropa (1915) proposed a German dominated confederation from Arabia to Holland. A myth soon developed, supported by such ideas as "*Geopolitik*", which saw geography explaining history in Germany's favor.

Panslavism sought to replace the Hapsburgs with Russia. Kireyevsky (1806-1856) explained that Western ideas were undermining the Russian social system and religion. The Russian spirit, he thought, lacked the violence and competition of

European life. True order and social justice were believed to prevail in Russia. The *Philosophical Letters* of Chalayev (c.1830) spoke of the Slavs as the Chosen People. The Slavs, of course, were to be the defenders of Holy Mother Russia. By 1849, there were attempts at political organization of Pan-Slavism in the Habsburg Empire. This received support from the Russian Orthodox Church's notion of a "Third Rome".

Imperialism

Imperialism is ancient. As early as 1750 B.C., the Chinese emperors sought to give barbarians the benefit of Chinese culture. The Persians (c. 500 B.C.) claimed that their empire-building was a divine mission. In Ancient Athens, Pericles explained that "to be under our rule is not to be dominated but to be privileged". Aggressive war, said Aristotle, was justified only against those peoples obviously destined by nature to be slaves.

From 1450 to 1750, England, Spain, Portugal, France and the Netherlands installed empires in America, India and the East Indies. The English got economic benefits and exported a surplus of labor by assuming what they called the "white man's burden".

A frenzy of imperialism occurred in the period 1870-1914. Nations, such as Germany and the United States, who had missed out on early efforts to gather colonies tried to quickly take what was left. Certain American leaders plotted to realize their "manifest destiny" and seized possessions of a weak Spain.

War and Iraq reflect recent American imperialism. The Spanish-American War (1899) was conjured up by an officer on the Naval Staff in Washington (W. T. Mahan), the influential Senator W. H. Taft and the newspaper publisher William Randolph Hearst. The war was executed as part of a plan to obtain coaling stations to support a fleet needed to advance American commercial interests in China. The pretext for the war was a fabricated story concerning Spanish abuse of Cubans. An explosion that sank a U.S. vessel in Havana harbor provided the final excuse.

A century later, another commercially-dominated regime waged a war of aggression against Iraq. A former U.S. intelligence official explained the motives as (1) control of petroleum resources (2) removing a threat to Israel (3) advancement of a Neo-Conservative plan of American advanced bases and commercial empire. Various excuses were advanced, including the cruelty of the Iraqi regime and fictions concerning terrorism and weapons of mass destruction.

In the intervening period, the U.S. repeatedly invaded Latin American countries to establish governments favorable to American business interests. Said Smedley Butler, former commandant of the U. S. Marine Corps: "I spent most of my time (34 years) being a high-class muscle man for Big Business, for Wall Street and the bankers. In short, I was a racketeer, a gangster for capitalism."

With the capture of Hawaii in 1893, the period of overt aggression for America began in earnest. An era of more covert action began in 1953, with American changes of regime in Iran, Guatemala, Chile and Vietnam. Defeat in the latter adventure brought on more overt invasions of Grenada, Panama, Afghanistan and Iraq.

Can a nation-state expand? Nationalism fosters the nation. Can a nation-state expand without losing its national character? When people identify with movements and races, national boundaries are crossed. As when the god of the tribe replaced the god of the city, the "culture" or the "civilization" or the "universal religion" must replace nationalism. Ideological imperialism develops, but can empire be consistent with nationalism?

An imperialist nation cannot integrate its conquests. Roman imperialism had sought to make conquered peoples an integral part of the imperial system. However, with an expanding nation-state, the conquered do not fit in and cannot be integrated.

Did imperialism arise to foster commerce, to develop markets, to export manpower and capital? Does the survival of capitalism require constant growth? Can this expansion only be halted by the clash of rival imperialisms? If imperialism were the expression of the bourgeoisie, would bourgeois values be imposed? In imperialism, the misfits and the bourgeoisie found a community of interest, and the misfits were exported.

Power gives influence. Economic power brings military power and political influence. East Asia is rapidly growing in economic power and the West is declining. Population, geography, economic output and military force are all factors determining power.

A universal civilization, such as envisioned by Islam or by the Neo-Conservatives in America, requires universal power. Attaining universal power seems most improbable and thus continuing conflict may be expected. If a supra-national institution, such as the United Nations, could be invested with sufficient power, then conflict could be avoided. How likely is a voluntary ceding of such power by different civilizations?

International Law is not now really "law". It is the agreement among sovereign states concerning the rules under which they will act. Sovereign states can do as they please concerning such rules.

With the Atlantic Charter in 1941, Roosevelt and Churchill proclaimed that (1) resort to force would only be had in self-defense or when authorized by an appropriate international body (2) human rights would be protected (3) free trade would be fostered. Subsequently, the United Nations, the World Bank, the General Agreement on Tariffs and Trade, the Geneva Conventions, the International Criminal Court and other such bodies were created.

As the Twenty-First Century began, the United States found itself as the world's only superpower. A coterie in Washington formulated the "Project for the New American Century" (1997), a plan for the military advancement of American commercial interests throughout the world. The planners specifically sought to undermine the United Nations and international law. Apparently conscious of the culpable nature of their deeds, the planners obtained legislation authorizing the dispatch of US forces to rescue any American officials who might be brought before the International Court.

Existentialism placed the individual against the world. It is essentially a resistance to supervening ideologies. Existentialism seeks to justify the importance and freedom of the individual personality. It arose in France and Germany immediately after World War I. Existentialism is ill-defined, but certain characteristic themes include: a rejection of determinism the absence of externally imposed values, a sense of the absurdity of life, and a sense of freedom and personal responsibility for choice.

The ideas of Schopenhauer underlay much of existentialism. He suggested that, if the whole process of the universe is without purpose or meaning, then illusions and philosophies are invented to lend a purpose to an otherwise meaningless existence. Kierkegaard offered a religious expression to existentialism.

For Sartre, emotion is a total way of relating oneself to the world. Passivity, on the other hand, is a "degradation of consciousness", permitting the "bad faith" of the state. The real essence of human consciousness is, for Sartre, its separateness from the rest of the world. Reality is process, history. Thus, total perception of the world would require history as well as a dialectic between being and consciousness.

What effect can the moral choice of an individual have, in the face of the sweeping forces of history? Sartre thought that the individual might hope for understanding, but not for influence. Sartre suggested "being" as the individual's response to a sense of "nothingness".

Changing philosophies can reshape reality. Fashions in philosophies partially reflect the worldview and spirit of the times. These are often mixed with the manufactured myths of those attempting to articulate ideals for the society. If such a philosophy or myth is learned early enough, it becomes part of the unconscious belief system and thus, for the individual, is reality. Another aspect is that one's attitude toward a situation is often of greater importance than the fact.

Scientific, deterministic and materialistic views were attributed in the original Darwinian evolutionary outlook. If evolution is the result of chance, many assumptions of Western thought are shaken. Our world-view may then more resemble that of the Hellenistic Age.

Philosophers contribute to the set of ideas prevalent in the general discourse. Perhaps only students and intellectual activists adopt the articulations of philosophers directly. This process can be traced by examining the diaries of certain Japanese university students (Ohnuki-Tierney, 2006). There was, at the time of WW II, a general attitude of dissatisfaction with the social inadequacies and selfishness of capitalism. In general, the German Romantics of the Counter-Enlightenment resonated with the students. Fichte, Schelling, Hegel, Schiller, Goethe, Novalis, Hoelderlin and Schlegel appealed, as did the philosophical activism of Nietzsche and the idealistic formulations of Marxists.

The spiritual emptiness of Western society created a demand for an idealistic, religious-style fervor. The dissolution of the individual to become identified with the nation and its people was an important change. Devotion and self-sacrifice were facilitated by this ego transference. A mental unification of the land, nature and homeland took place. The reaction to colonialism and imperialism was nationalism and the demand for self-determination. The attitudes for conflict were in place. Today, similar attitudes exist, coupled with the rapid economic development of the most populous countries. It portends an unstable situation.

Zen Buddhism plays little part in the development of Western ideology. A bit like existentialism, Zen allows the individual to estrange himself from the "reality" that oppresses him. Estrangement or alienation is a pervasive phenomenon in modern society, but we have little in the way of philosophical or religious mechanisms to cope with it. We seem, instead, to be condemned to suffer the televised father-images of God-messiahs evoking movements.

The vacuum of consumerism needs filling. The emptiness of selfish consumerism may create a desire for a stronger faith. Ideology replaces personal, subjective reality with a seemingly stronger symbolic reality.

As the wheel of time changes, so do the isms alternate. Spirits, isms, and philosophical fashions usefully indicate trends in the spirit of the times. When particular isms predominate among specific peoples, then we have ideological myth. What the dominant ideology suppresses continues as a destabilizing element that may, in its turn, to become dominant, a "return of the repressed".

Fundamentals keep resurging to affirm identity. Revolutionary movements often appeal to simple fundamentals. Religious fundamentalism generally holds that there is one set of teachings that contains sufficient and invariant truth about men and their relation to deity. Today, there is a resurgence of fundamentalism cast as religious ideology. The religious framework promises more security through certainty of faith, community and identity.

The church group offers communion and a refuge from political oppression. As it did in the former East Germany and as it seems to be attempting in China. When common folk move from their rural environments to the cities, they leave the social network and former rules behind. The state schools foster nationalist symbols and secular approaches to life's problems. TV offers examples of extraordinary lifestyles. The police and military may effect political repression. Fundamentalist church groups are a response to these pressures.

Government and religion can be coexist in different ways. A fundamentalist movement can follow different strategies. Revolution will seek total power to remake society with force. By withdrawal, the sect can operate undercover and apart from society. A reactionary strategy will align itself with state power and seek to control state schools and media. A policy of accommodation may see electoral politics with alternative media and schools.

Fundamentalisms are found on all continents. As the 21st Century began, Hindu, Israeli, American, Hindu and Islamic fundamentalisms became disturbingly evident. In each, the mass of adherents sought refuge from the insecurities of the rapidly changing social and economic conditions that surrounded them.

Whereas "revivalists" want to restore the faith among the believers, the "fundamentalists" want everybody to conform to their beliefs, both in religious and in political matters. Often, the times are thought to require direct and possibly violent action. Fundamentalists need a basic scripture or set of rules, be it the Torah, Bible, Koran, Communist Manifesto, Little Red Book, or Fuhrer's orders.

Leading individuals and inner-groups controlling fundamentalist worship add additional motives-nationalist, political, racist, organizational and personal. An authoritarian, intolerant, and dogmatic attitude is usual among adherents. The action programs, however, differed, depending on the motives of the leadership.

Continuity in the goals of action programs is always claimed. But with skillful manipulation by the leadership group, the goals may even reverse without the followers being aware of it. Constants include: subordination of women and elimination of reproductive choice; hostility to homosexuals and to freedom of expression.

American fundamentalists, historically, hated bankers and were leftists. Today, they have been conditioned to articulate a mixed set of goals: to associate patriotism with religion; to oppose disarmament and to favor militarism, international aggression and hegemony; to oppose world government and international organizations; to favor "free enterprise" and to oppose "socialism"; to favor the dissolution of public schools, etc. Clever (and profit-oriented) leadership has reversed the political understanding and goals of the evangelical/fundamentalist community. The techniques of manipulation are becoming so sophisticated that ordinary folk believe that such programs are sanctioned by the Bible and are really what the individual himself desires.

Fundamentalisms have certain common features. There are assumed to be certain traditional verities. An ordered society will conform to these verities. The family is supposed to be a micro model of society (and possibly of an idealized moral order as well). The proper raising of children is deemed to be of prime importance and may be thought to be a means of creating a better and more moral society.

Times of transition induce anxiety. In times of change, fundamentalism may become emphasized as a means of preserving identity. Uncertainty about one's circumstances may be answered with loud assertion of "fundamental verities" that "do not change". Similarly, forming exclusive circles of like-believers isolates one from the threat and contamination of new ideas and worldviews.

Syncretism, the idea of blending in other views, is seen as an especial threat. Fundamentalist leaders may seek to limit education, control education, or even create special institutions of higher learning that will indoctrinate the standard view and discourage independent thought.

Society, state and religion are classified as different entities, but, in reality, they blend. "Fundamentalism" is thought to reflect a rural worldview, but it may be an urban creation. New religions originate in cities. The life of the city involves includes brief interactions with strangers and differs from the reciprocity of the little community. Population pressure and globalization force country folk into cities. The newcomer has lost his old community and is confronted with many different lifestyles and values. A similar situation exists for the foreign student. Under these circumstances, a special, political version of "fundamentalism" may be accepted.

Characteristics common to Jewish, Christian and Islamic fundamentalists include:

(1) **Intolerance**. There is only one true faith. Therefore, pluralist views are not protected and should be suppressed. Views are either for or against the faith. Those not in support are treasonable and satanic. Such an attitude may be called dualist, binary, black and white, or Manichaean.

(2) **Absolutism**. The faith is absolutely perfect, complete, without error and not subject to change

(3) **Revelation and prophesy**. History is unfolding according to a progressive plan revealed in the scripture and interpreted by the prophet. We live in a special time when the advent of the New Order is near. The final combat with the forces of Evil is neigh and extraordinary actions will be required.

(4) **Scripture**. There is a definitive statement of the faith, usually written, which is claimed to be infallible and true. In fact, such a canon is interpreted differently depending upon the needs of the interpreter.

Five features of fundamentalism were suggested by Ammerman: (1) inerrancy of scripture, (2) evangelism, (3) pre-millennialism, (4) biblical literalism, (5) separation from non-believers or from schismatics. Whether a "fundamentalist" must embrace *all* of these attitudes is uncertain.

There is an eschatology of progress towards the Kingdom of God. From the Iranians to the Jews and thence to the Christians and the Muslims came the novel idea that history proceeded to a perfect society in an ascending line instead of endlessly repeating in great circles. This teleology of "time's arrow" rather than "time's round" underlies millenarian efforts to mold a better world.

The apocalyptics of fundamentalist Christianity disturb the teleological vision. The role of the dual gods of good and evil is disputed. Are we in an intermediate stage (*John* 17:11-16), or in the proximate End Times of Armageddon, Tribulation, and Rapture? Since the world is seen as a combat between the two forces, a promised resolution should serve to improve belief. Must such apocalyptic destruction disturb progress toward a better World? Influential fundamentalist leaders claim that identification with Israel is essential for personal salvation, and welcome a clash of civilizations in Palestine as bringing on the Kingdom of God. If a national leader were convinced of this, his policies could prove disastrous.

Lutheran Protestantism rejected ideas of Armageddon with article XVII of the Augsburg Confession, but the ideas persist among Adventists, Baptists and other sects. Such believers are said to make up as much as a third of the American electorate and to accept the Biblical Book of Revelation as an inerrant predictor of events.

Serious thinkers have claimed an interdependence of Protestantism and capitalism. Max Weber started this thesis. Such ideas are mixed with Old Testament views and guilt-ridden paranoia to produce the current American fundamentalist mindset. Paradoxically, the less advantaged groups in America who had formerly embraced populism have been told that their faith requires political and economic conservatism. In Brazil, fundamentalism is being embraced as a way to personal economic betterment (in contrast to the quietism associated with the Catholic Church). Protestantism- capitalism

The upsurge of megachurches with thousands in the congregation and the success of television evangelists with audiences in the millions reflect media-style marketing of the services provided. Entertainment, "feel good" messages and advice for success generally follow any induced guilt and financial extractions during the service.

A mass, once put in motion by media techniques, becomes increasingly volatile. It is entirely feasible for one popular preacher to suggest an implementation of a social gospel and immediately influence thousands of affiliated church groups toward charity and group responsibility rather than individual success.

Some minds understand "the Kingdom of God is within you" (Luke 17:21) as suggesting the idea of "my mind is the universe" and see individual and collective progress toward a better World. Others start with the same premises and claim that; with faith, eternity is *now*. Fundamentalists, indoctrinated with ideas of Armageddon and "The Rapture", may read this as a call for world conquest, now.

America has experienced waves of evangelical fervor in several "Awakenings". The "Second Great Awakening" is considered to have extended from 1800-1860 and included the evangelism of Charles Grandison Finney and such concomitants as an imperialist war on Mexico, the ethnic cleansing of indigenous peoples, and talk of a "Manifest Destiny".

Prior to invading an oil-rich Iraq, a "born again" American president declared it a "Crusade" and averred that he thought the Nation to be experiencing a "Third Great Awakening". Such an evangelistic millenarian enthusiasm must seek to convert and dominate the World. It characterized Marxist-Leninism and Nazism (to a more limited degree), and is also evident in radical Islam and in Israel's Gush Emunim.

Islamic Fundamentalism

Islamic fundamentalism, like all fundamentalisms, holds up an idealized "Golden Age". For Islam, the imagined Golden Age is the rule of the Caliphs. This was the model advocated by Hassan al-Banna in founding the Muslim Brotherhood. According to Ben-Dor and Pedahzur (2003), key characteristics of Islam are said to be *jiahad* (struggle for the faith), *ishtishad* (among Shiites, the immediacy of action or martyrdom), a totalitarian world view, the identity of religion and state, a belief that the ruler must be a godly man capable of quickly effecting solutions to problems and, since there is no hierarchy, the existence of an open path for radical Islamist movements. Islam is generally fundamentalist and there can be no separation of church and state, for Islam is the way of life of the faithful. Islamic Fundamentalism

What is called "Resurgent Islam" seems to be more political and social than religious. Globalization, development, and commercial-military imperialism have disrupted traditional life, impoverishing peasants and the lower middle classes. There is movement to the cities. The concomitant changes have elevated new elites whose reputed lifestyle may be seen on television. This creates insecurity, jealousy and a feeling of injustice among the displaced. globalization

Such displacements involve feelings of insecurity, fostering the desire to find social support and stable ideological explanations. A perceived threat of Western military aggression intensifies the feeling of threat and the need to unify against it. General anti-Islamic feeling rose as a result of the terrorist attacks of radical Islamists. As a reaction, the religious activity of Muslims further increased. In a media-saturated world, talk of a "War of Civilizations" can easily become self-fulfilling prophesy.

Socio-political estrangement also underlies much Islamic radicalism. Oppressive regimes have denied justice, equality and opportunity to the less fortunate. Many of the oppressed were said to be hoping for liberation by socialist revolution. The collapse of the Soviet Union may have removed this hope and served as an impetus to action. Sayyid Qutb recommended action against all infidel regimes, "whether they call themselves Islamic or not".

The mosque is a political venue. The World-community of Islam, the *umma*, believes that the Koran expresses the social values and ideals of God. Values related to justice and human dignity are paramount. Government has historically been authoritarian and opposition parties have not flourished. Expression in public media is controlled. Religious places offer more opportunity for the communication of anti-government ideas and the local religious leader is usually free to urge his personal views. Thus, the mosque serves as a magnet for those who feel threatened and oppressed.

Fundamentalism in Iran under the Revolutionary government is taking a special form. In Shiía Islam, there is thought to be but one dominant interpretation of Koranic law. However, a disorganized body of clerics (the *ulama*) can routinely produce diverse rulings. Iranian Shiítes developed the view that one religious leader should be the guide for other clergy in matters of interpretation. The Ayatollah Khomeini declared his position as authoritative under the Koran (4:59, 4:62), combining religious and political rule in his person.

The Iranian Constitution established a dictatorship. That rule envisions the "New Islamic Person", calling for the public to inform upon each other, etc. This rule is enforced by an extensive secret police and by ubiquitous religious police. Molding the minds of the youth is deemed essential.

Jalal al-Ahmad talked of "intoxication" with Western things and urged a return to the "Iranian self". The educated and university students do not seem to take the religious government to heart. The consensus appears to be to adopt Western science and technology, framing them in an Islamic ideological context while trying to reject materialist aspects of Western culture.

There is room for creative scriptural interpretation. Abdolkarim Soroush emphasizes that one should distinguish "fact from value", "the end from the means", "is from ought to be" and even seek to "separate religion from the understanding of religion".

Popular social action is scripturally countenanced. One may remember al-Afghani's quote from the Koran: "God will never change the condition of the people until they change it themselves" (13:11). The idea that an unjust or "un-Islamic" ruler may be deposed is common.

Fundamentalism among the Sunni recognizes that submission to the roots of Islam is an essential aspect of being a Muslim. Islam provides a description of reality and an ideal towards which society should be molded. The Koran, being the perfect revelation of God's word, cannot be the subject of doubt, especially concerning social behavior. Since God is seen as the source of all knowledge, human reason cannot exist without God's guidance. From this, Sayyid Qutb saw a binary world where the forces of God were at war with the forces of "ignorance" (*jahiliyya*). The Wahhabi and Salafi sects have always been very fundamentalist and rather xenophobic.

Militant fundamentalist groups generally are political in nature. They claim a religious justification for their acts and accuse their opponents of "ignorance". Such groups assert a strong distinction between secular law and the divine (Sharia) law of Islam. As Yusuf al-Qaredwi said: "either the rulers get Islamic belief in their hearts or political rule moves into the hands of the believers".

The characteristics of Jewish fundamentalism depend on the sect. Certain basics are common in the teaching. It is assumed that God's design is for the world to be "good". If one lives in accordance with the Torah as interpreted by religious authorities, then he can be within the Covenant even while living among gentiles (in *Galut*). The hope is of a heavenly order descending among the faithful, rather than of one ascending to a Heaven. In addition to individual responsibility, the people of Israel must be a holy people. If they are not, they may find themselves in *Galut*. The individual who sins against the Torah may find himself so alienated.

Zionism

The concept of an isolated people in special and particular covenant with God is pervasive in Jewish culture. Thus, the idea of assimilation with gentile society, an idea common after the Enlightenment in Germany and elsewhere, was of special significance. Herzl, in Austria, sought and failed to assimilate.

Conceived by Herzl in 1898, Zionism was a Jewish nationalism. It arose as the colonial drive of industrialized nation-states for the land and resources of the less developed had been accomplished. Herzl saw a Jewish state as a refuge for those Jews "unable or unwilling to assimilate" in other nations. Less developed lands were thought to be void of worthy people. The early Zionists deemed a Jewish state less desirable than assimilation in bringing Jews out of apartheid. This was heresy to religious conservatives who saw a Biblical requirement for a people who lived apart.

The Zionist movement had strong socialist overtones and the New Jew of the kibbutz would be a pioneer, a citizen, and a Torah scholar. Even though the Zionists sought to acquire and never relinquish land in Palestine, Ben-Gurion, in 1924, said "we have no right to deprive a single Arab child, despite our aims". With further Jewish immigration, this attitude changed.

Zionism thus introduced a different outlook. The very fundamentalist *Haredin* consider the State of Israel to be but a continuation of *Galut* and seek to isolate themselves from modern and secular influences. The old yeshiva worldview emphasized the inferiority of women, distained physical labor, celebrated the study and debate of the Torah, and did not envision remaking the World. This was in sharp contrast to the activist views of the Zionists.

Several political events did much to create an activist Jewish fundamentalism: The Holocaust (*Shoa*) threatened the continued existence of Jews as a people and convinced many of the evil nature of gentiles. Safety could only be had in a militarily strong Jewish state. The fragmented nature of Israeli politics resulted in special benefits being given to fundamentalist religious schools. This fostered the rise of reactionary and politically active fundamentalism, especially evident among the ubiquitous "knitted skullcaps".

Fundamentalist indoctrination begets extremism. Ben-Yaakov. a well-known educator, said that, when young people think in a binary fashion and are trained to uncritically accept the views of authority, they will react to problems in an extreme way. Simplistic and violent solutions will be attempted.

The success in the 1967 Six Day War created a sense of messianism. Were the End Times being realized? Nationalist objectives and religious fundamentalism became triumphalist. Bronze Age religious ideas of a Greater Israel (*Eretz Yisreal*) extending from the Nile to the Euphrates and beyond suddenly became a *sine qua non* of Orthodox Judaism. The Talmud required that gentiles within Greater Israel be eliminated.

Sharon called illegal settlement and annexation of additional territory the "Zionist answer". Military leaders saw no obstacles to holding what they had seized and perpetrating further aggressions. A tacit alliance with the ultra conservative Likud Party existed. United Nations resolutions and international law were ignored. The belief that force could eliminate the Palestinians was widespread and persistent.

From a financial point of view, the Occupation was a success. Very little capital was expended on infrastructure. Israelis got markets, very cheap labor, and suppressed Palestinian agriculture, development and production.

Gentiles must either be servants or be eliminated from Greater Israel. The Talmud, or Oral Torah, is the highest form of Torah learning. The message is clear concerning gentiles: they can only exist within greater Israel as daily humiliated servants or slaves. Otherwise, gentiles within Greater Israel are to be killed. What is the Greater Israel of the Bible? Opinions differ, certainly, it is said to include all the West Bank. Many claim it extends from "the Nile to the Euphrates". Still others would also include Iran and Saudi Arabia. The large, government-sponsored terrorist Gush Emunim have World messianic ambitions.

It is clear that Ben-Gurion's vision of a Zion where "no Arab child would be deprived" does not exist. Nor does idealistic socialist Zionism survive. What, today, is "religious Zionism"? Today, Israel is beset by corruption, even among famous religious and political leaders. Liberal attitudes cannot survive well in an atmosphere of selfishness and ideological extremism. Perhaps "politico-religious fundamentalism" better describes the state of affairs.

The Israeli religious fanatic resembles the fanatics of other religions. The Premier of Israel, Rabin, a former general, had concluded peace accords calling for the withdrawal from territory occupied in 1967. This resulted in vitriolic denunciations from the religious Orthodox, from military figures and from the Likud. In 1995, he was assassinated by a conservative religious ideologue.

Rabin had been born in Israel, and, along with his new country, had been formed in an era of mass media saturation. Such an atmosphere potentiates the effects of canned ideology and encourages the formation of mental stereotypes and the absorption of slogans.

Messianic religious Zionism postulated a God-given tribally exclusive right to the land of a Greater Israel as a principal article of faith. This unleashed forces of ethnic hate focused on the possession of land. According to the Third Century religious law (*haskala*), a Jew who gives his land to the enemy must be killed. The same law posits the right of a citizen to kill someone (*rodef*) he sees committing a crime, and says that God's law takes precedence over man's law (*memshelet sadon*).

Judaism is highly decentralized (as is Islam) and much depends upon the interpretation of the local rabbi. Rabin's killer was a third-year law student at a right-wing Orthodox university. The campus rabbi cited the rule that those (Amalekites) who warred with "God's People" were, to the last child, to be exterminated.

The killer was also associated with the Gush Emunim settler-terrorist organization and had obtained his pistol permit by falsely claiming residence among them. It is routine for Gush Emunim terrorists to obtain rabbinical authorization before their acts. The killer's speech included Talmudic and military phrasings. At his trial, he was fully sane and convinced that he had acted properly according to the will of God.

Orthodox rabbi David Hartmann, who headed an institute that sought to update the *haskala*, explained that the killer was young and had taken his religious mentors seriously and literally, finding identity with that tradition. Rabin's assassin, Yigal Amir, cited "God's law" (the *Haskala* interpretations) as requiring the murder of the Israeli Prime Minister. The claim that "God's law" takes precedence over state law is often advanced (as by the Catholic Church) when a religious group does not agree with the policy of the state.

In Jewish culture, legalism appears to be of primary importance. Yeshiva education emphasizes legal interpretations of holy text by authorities. In practice, such legalism is more honored than Rabbi Hillel's general admonition to not treat others as you would not like to be treated. In contrast, Muslim Koranic interpretation puts great emphasis on the *intent* behind an action. American fundamentalists appear to favor literal interpretations as a guide to action.

India

Indian Fundamentalism is more an artificially developed ideology facilitating what is essentially Hindu nationalism. As early as 3,000 B.C., there was a relatively advanced Indus Valley civilization. In the following millennia, Iranians, Aryans, Greeks, Muslims, and others entered India. The inevitable geographic, ethnic and religious pluralism should argue for tolerance and secularism across the land. Could the resulting conglomerate become a nation?

The emperor Ashoka (300 B.C.) made much progress toward creating a great and tolerant India. The Muslim ruler Akbar (1591) legislated religious freedom and tolerance and even attempted to establish a new religion (Din Ilahi) that would incorporate what he considered the best features of the prevailing religions.

Akbar's attempt at creating a new religion did not encounter success because identity comes mostly from one's existing culture. A prophet would have appealed more to the emotions than to reason and would have exploited dissatisfaction. Akbar was a good and popular a ruler. Later rulers were often less benign. Potential hostility between Hindu and Muslim persisted.

Development in India is diversified and complex. The dominant Hindu nationalist party, the BJP, is associated with an intolerant ideology. The related Association of National Volunteers (RSS) is a uniformed rightist wing that follows a violent anti-Muslim line that admires the Nazi treatment of the Jews and copies many aspects of the Nazi organization. At the same time, rapid development is creating a burgeoning middle class while displacing many others.

Hinduism lacks the idea of an intervening God with revealed salvation eschatology and the prescriptions of the Semitic religions, yet ideology seems to have an important place. The fostering of the Hindi language and literature and the extolling of legendary Hindu heroes and gods has been going on for generations.

The fundamental goal of the Hindutva ideology is to unify India's Hindus. Sangh Parivar is an almalgam of groups seeking this end. It includes the BJP (Bharatiya Janata Party); the RSS (Rashtriya Swayamevak Sang); VHP (Vishwa Hindu Parishad) and the Bajrang Dal. The BJP, at the national level, seeks to maintain international and business respectability. The VHP has international representation and raises funds abroad. The RSS is essentially a fascist youth organization with an international wing, the HSS. The Bajrang Dal is a strong-arm organization for street fighting and terrorism.

The BJP took a mythical hero, the Lord Rama, gave him a birthplace and, with a television series, turned him into a patron saint. The BJP provided new and biased history texts for the schools and countenanced violence against Muslims. When the second most populous country in the World, and one possessing atomic weapons, exhibits such intolerant practices, it must be a cause for concern. John Keay's *India: a History* provides a summary to the year 1999. This Hindu revivalist ideology seems to be concentrated in North-Central part of the country and must develop in a culture that recognizes many different gods.

The Hindu RSS party took its lead from the Nazis and urged racial purity in India (see Jaffrelot, 1993). The BJP party was formed as the political wing of the neo-fascist RSS (Rashtriya Swayamsevar Sangh), the "Saffron Brotherhood", their rallying cry is "Land of the Hindus".

Godse, a former RSS member, assassinated Mahatma Gandhi for being too sympathetic toward Muslims. Once in government, the BJP party had millions of textbooks rewritten, deleting any mention of Gandhi's assassination and expanded therein claims of Muslim abuse of Hindus throughout Indian history.

In 2002, in the State of Gujarat, an organized slaughter and burning of Muslims took place under the eyes of the police. Some five years later, court cases awarded compensation to the victims. The complicity of government officials in these atrocities raises serious questions.

In 2004, twenty carloads of thugs attacked a library where a staff member had helped the research of an American author. The BJP Prime Minister threatened the author, saying that the government was prepared to take action against any author who "played with our national pride".

"Militant obscurantism" is defined by Amartya Sen as "the political use of people's credulity in unreasoned and archaic beliefs in order to generate fierce extremism". In northwest India, where the educational level is particularly low, the BJP party has the greatest support. It is suspected that low education is a major factor in gullibility.

The key features of Hinduism are said to be acceptance of the Vedic scriptures as revelation and participation in the caste system. Of the many world views (or *darsana*), only those groupings within the *mimamsa* tend to be literalist and fundamentalist. The coming of the British and their Christianity to India induced a reactive revival of Hinduism. Although there might be some truth in all religions, one could claim that Hinduism represented the best synthesis. By 1300, much of India was ruled by Muslims. The conquest and conversions engendered long-term religious/nationalist enmity.

Indian fundamentalism is being promoted despite a native pluralism. Fundamentalism may be inimical to the historical ethos of India with its pluralist religious and cultural identities. Secularism and tolerance are implied by pluralism.

Secularism is, of course, totally inimical to a nation defined by religious affiliation. It is paradoxical that Pakistan and Bangladesh should have been created in a nation that claimed to be secular.

Factors now favoring fundamentalism in India include: Rapid change in social and economic structures with concomitant insecurity; the effect of mass media in creating and manipulating mass opinion; and the fascist policies of the BJP government. One observer has also suggested that the desire of many newly prosperous middle class people to find social status has prompted them to become active in organized Hindu religious affairs.

Hindu and Israeli nationalism and fundamentalism have some factors in common. The right-wing fundamentalist who assassinated Israel's Prime Minister Rabin cited "God's law" (the *Haskala*) in justification. Those inspired by the Torah/Talmud have the idea that an expanded "Greater Israel" will be an exclusively Jewish state where non-Jews will be permitted only as humiliated menials. Armed strength is required for defense and expansion against surrounding enemies and the millennia-old hostility of gentiles.

Reviewing his clinical practice, the Tel Aviv psychologist Grosbard (2003) likened the collective attitude of Israel to that of an adolescent. The attitudes of the Hindu nationalists are in some ways similar to those of the Israelis, the Hindus believing that the Muslims are a threat and Hindus being in the adolescence of widespread political participation.

In India, certain historical attitudes blend with an insecure psychology. Promises of the neo-fascists and the BJP nationalists respond to and excite a spirit of insecurity. These ideas and promises blended in the mind of one young man and caused him to assassinate Mahatma Gandhi. Individual insecurity is seen by Bhargava (2003) as an Indian characteristic potentiated by changing conditions. This insecurity is seen as a major impulse toward acceptance of the Hindu nationalist ideology among the influential middle class of India.

The large Indian middle class contains disparate groups, including those displaced by globalization, as well as those in the Indian Diaspora now seeking a prideful identity. Flailing at the "other", e.g. Muslims, Christians, secular Hindus and the casteless, can help to establish a feeling of identity. The castes and duties imposed by the ancient "Code of Manu" (a sort of Hindu Torah/Talmud) are useful to exalt and preserve the old social order. Tradition and identity are both served thereby.

Other common attitudes among Hindu nationalists Bhargava (2003) claims, include: opposition to the socialist left, to liberalism, to secularism and to welfare benefits. (These attitudes are also prevalent today in the formerly Democrat-party "Bible Belt" of the United States as this area is ideologically influenced by right-wing manipulation). Support for the program of the BJP Party grew as the hold of the formerly ruling Congress Party declined. The Hindu nationalist focus is now shifting from regional and local collectives to the vision of an exclusively Hindu nationhood.

Being uncertain of themselves in a modernizing world, says Bhargava, nationalists seek a "New India" and a "New Hindu". A national identity is also seen a way to achieve the strength advantage that such identity appears to give other nations. The cultural commonality of Islam is also seen by the Hindus as a source of Muslim strength. Violent conflict with the "other" is imagined as a demonstration of strength and assertiveness. Negative stereotypes and a focus on revenge for real or imagined past wrongs excite passions and ideas of "honor".

M. S. Golwalkar (b. 1906) led the neo-fascist RSS (the parent organization of the BJP) for thirty years. His views are expressed in his *Book of Thoughts*. The basic tenets include the idea that Hindus alone have a privileged position in India.

Parsis and Jews have lesser status, while Muslims, Christians and Communists constituted an internal threat. Democracy he saw as alien to the Hindu ethos. The Code of Manu with its caste system and duties would be an authentic guide for India. Force could be used, said Golwalkar, "we have the means by which our opponents could be immediately silenced".

Nathuram Godse, the man who assassinated Mahatma Gandhi, was a former member of the RSS. At his trial http://ngodse.tripod.com/defense.htm), he unrepentantly expressed his motivations: (1)"[To begin with], I was opposed to the cast system and was a political and religious free thinker"; (2) The writings of Veer Savarkar and Mahatma Gandhi were great inspirations; (3) "All this thinking led me to believe that my first duty was to serve Hindus and Hinduism"; (4) "The Sanghtanist ideology and programme alone could win and preserve that national independence of Hindustan, my Motherland"; (5) Honor may require the use of force; (6) The Hindu holy stories show that killings of leaders may be endorsed for political purposes; (7) Indian politics would be powerful, with armed forces able to retaliate, in the absence of Gandhi; (8) There was no legal mechanism by which an offender such as Gandhi could be removed: (9) "The accumulated provocation of thirty-two years, culminating in his last pro-Muslim fast, at last goaded me to the conclusion that the existence of Gandhi should be brought to an end immediately."

The statement of Godse shows a young man seeking an ideology to give meaning to his life. He seems to blend his personal identity with that of his race and religion and adopts a fictive Motherland. The exclusive framework for realizing this identity he believes to be that of a particular Party. The psychic effect of this belief system grows within him and distorts his reason. His former ideal, Gandhi, becomes an "offender" who must be eliminated "immediately".

Muslims comprise some ten percent of the Indian population. Yet, in a seeming projection of his personal weakness, Godse perceives them as an existential threat to the Motherland in which he has invested his identity. His personal weakness must be compensated for by national strength. Said his brother "from Pakistan and Bangladesh, every Muslim is a converted Hindu" and "we killed Gandhi [because] our love for the Motherland made us do it."

As with Hitlerian Germany and in Israel, there is talk of a "Greater India" to include Kashmir and irredentist claims to all Southeast Asia. The hatred fostered toward Muslims is paralleled by similar communal conflict fostered against Sikhs, Dalits, Parsis, etc., when political groups seek electoral advantage. In cities where there are symbiotic cooperative efforts, Hindu-Muslim relations seem tranquil.

The coming of the Nazi-oriented BJP to India's national government in 1998-2004 was helped by the support of the elite who saw such a strong government as aiding in the exploitation of the lower classes. The lower classes were simultaneously told that Hindu nationalism was egalitarian. Highly negative attitudes towards Muslims were fostered. Globalization brought wealth to technical and business elites, but severely impoverished farmers and rural tradesmen. In 2004, the Congress Party returned to power and the Communist Party received unprecedented support, especially from the landless poor (Nussbaum, 2007).

Hinduism has a long tradition of minimizing desire. Gandhi spoke of the need for the individual control his desire for domination and to accept the equality of others. The new elites in India may live isolated, gated communities and respond to the desire-promoting culture of capitalism. The new Prime Minister, Mannohan Singh, announced that it was necessary for India to forego the Western model of consumerism and learn from the ways of Gandhi.

8

THE IDEOLOGUE

A shamed, unsure child becomes authoritarian. The first experiences of infancy will shape a person's basic attitude of trust or mistrust toward the world, thinks Erickson. Other early character sets will be autonomy vs. shame and doubt; initiative vs. guilt; and the attitudes derived from initial training. Most children also learn "hope" in the first year of life, (an attitude almost as useful to manipulators as guilt). If early training has established attitudes of mistrust, shame, doubt and guilt, then the ground for the authoritarian personality is established and the individual will seek the integration offered by totalitarian religion and ideology, says Erickson.

Shame in subsequent development and behavior plays an important role. George Lakoff, Silvan Tomkins, James Gilligan, Alan Cienki and others have seen the strict father as contributing to the sensitive-to-shame right-wing ideologue, and the nurturing parent as creating the liberal personality.

Gilligan says that shame places a premium on self-love and downgrades love of others. The contrary (the guilt ethics of the liberal) reverses these values. This suggests a simple organon for predicting subsequent behavior, meaning that a shamed person will seek to hurt and devalue others, while a guilty liberal will seek to show love for others. As we shall later see, shame and humiliation are major factors in inducing terrorism.

Seeking an identity implies finding a place. After the shaping period of infancy, one must still find a place in the world. The individual must seek an identity. The young and the weak look for a ready-made worldview in religion and in other ideologies. The ideology should appear consistent with available knowledge, promise a better world, and cover nearly all questions.

There is both an individual and a collective sense of identity. Truth gets altered to appear consistent with these identities. In shaping this identity, one repudiates the unwanted and adores the ideal. An individual also has multiple identities.

Adolescents seek an identity and to be reborn with an ideology. The adolescent is a good target for an ideology. As with geese and primates, the first system a young being encounters is likely to be the one he identifies with. Others may feel the need to be "born again", to shed their previous identity. Constriction by parents, rejection by parents, irrational punishment or a sense of being unworthy can all cause the desire to be "born again". From his work with young people, Erickson observed that, in a regression from an identity crisis, "a young patient will seek to be reborn with a mother substitute".

The dissolved and projected self is then worshipped. An identity can be found by dissolving the self in something else. The individual, formed by society, may not be able to distinguish himself from the society that surrounds him or feel unworthy in comparison to it. He then dissolves himself in some organization, projects it (perhaps in a religion) and worships it. Alternatively, there may be an abnegation of self in a father-substitute and its projection as an ego ideal, etc.

The adored ideal completes the ego. What one feels to be lacking in oneself becomes loved. A group will have a common ego ideal and a common ego identification. Self-love is diminished in a group and libidinal ties are induced among group members.

Finding an identity in a group is thus quite similar to personal integration. It is possible that Arabs, confused by the rapidly engulfing modern world, or Jews who feel out of place and seek to integrate with Israel, are like adolescents in their seeking of integration. The Tel-Aviv clinical psychologist Ofer Grosbard develops this idea further in his *Israel on the Couch.*

Embracing an ideology is a way to put together a weak ego. Most cases of religious conversion occur during adolescence. Factors leading to religious conversion have been found similar to those in the acute confusional state.

Religious Style Conversion

Sudden (as opposed to gradual) converts were more authoritarian and more conservative in religion and politics. They also showed less personality control and intellect. Rapid converts had greater preconversion stress and perceived personal inadequacy (Zinnbauer & Pargament (1998)). Insecure women were more likely to find a "new relationship with God" (Kirkpatrick, 1998).

Conversion makes him feel ill and then cures him. The convert experiences the etiology of the confusional reaction (Carlson, 1961) until he "hears the word", "sees the light", and accepts the ideology and obtains relief. The distinguishing feature of religious conversion (and of Chinese communist thought reform) is that ideology both precipitates the acute reaction and provides the framework for the solution. Ideology seeks to provide a framework for integration. The system makes one feel bad and then offers to make one well.

The overall acute confusional reaction pattern (Christensen, 1963) includes: a predisposing psychological environment; conditions of frustration which produce great pressure; a pre-confusional state of angst; feelings of worthlessness and listless conformity; a confusional phase of helpless loneliness followed by a desperate search for a love object to adore and from which to get help; a reaction formation of affect reversal wherein one seeks to serve a cause or loved one; and reintegration by "going home" to an authoritarian womb substitute. During the reintegration phase, the subject may have various dreams relating to the theme of "going home". This may represent a mental reversion to childhood in order to begin again to orient himself to the world.

Anomie can be cured by surrender and dedication. Embracing an ideology has been analyzed as a reaction to an acute confusional state. In the pre-confusional state, a person feels worthless, believes in nothing and exhibits lifeless conformity. He gives up trying to solve his problems and surrenders to an authoritarian parental image.

The subsequent embracing of an ideology may see him seeking to serve mankind or the state. In the successful resolution phase, the individual has found something to love and a purpose in life. Getting outside himself brought relief. The institution and its ideology provide him with a satisfying place in the world.

Wish fulfillment and salvation are promised. Erickson feels that, if the primitive id controls, then perception will be bent toward wish fulfillment. Religion and ideology usually promise the equivalent of the Kingdom of God, either in this world or the next. Salvation is typically a matter of relief from psychic distress. For the poor, it may be relief from poverty and oppression. For many, it is the hope for a life after death.

Completion, unity and strength are sought. The search to find meaning and to relieve the sense of nothingness may focus on religion. Religious theology offers a way to respond to individual nothingness by postulating a sort of allness, noted Ruben Alves. A sense of allness, unity and strength were also offered to the individual by Fascism and by National Socialism.

To know who one is and where one is going is to have a solid sense of identity, to have an "integrated ego". Many adolescents lack this sense of integration. Embracing a religion or an ideology (or joining the Marine Corps) will allow an integration of the personality. A full set of beliefs is offered.

The dull and frustrated more easily accept ideology. Maranell (1968) found a negative correlation between religious belief and intelligence. Perhaps this implies that those less able to think for themselves will more readily accept canned ideologies. "I sensed I would have to live a leaderless and difficult life. I would receive no directives from anybody, no orders and commands could be issued by me, and no pertinent regulations would be there to consult. In brief, a life never before known faced me", said Adolf Eichmann, on the day of Germany's defeat. A caution is here in order- intellectuals are more easily inclined to believe in imaginary systems.

Adolph Eichmann

Eichmann illustrates the true-believing follower. If Hitler offers us the archetype of the prophet messiah, then Eichmann offers us a caricature of the true-believing follower. Hanna Arendt's *Eichmann in Jerusalem: a Report on the Banality of Evil* (Viking, N.Y., 1963) is our principal source for the following observations about Eichmann. For a different view, one might consult *Eichmann Interrogated* (Lang, 1983), a book by the Israeli police officer who interrogated Eichmann.

"Eichmann was an ordinary man who loved his family, friends, and animals. He cherished loyalty, appreciated art, and even helped Jews wherever he could", said Hanna Arendt. A panel of psychiatrists found him "normal". Of the five Eichmann children, only Adolf was unable to finish high school. He then failed vocational school. Bragging was always one of his vices.

The Jews on his mother's side, as well as his mistress, were among Eichmann's "private reasons" for not hating Jews. He was easily suggestible. Upon reading Theodor Herzl's *Der Judenstaat,* Eichmann became a convert to Zionism. Never very good with language, Eichmann defined himself as an "idealist". He explained that an "idealist" was a man who lived totally for his idea and was prepared to sacrifice everything and everybody for his idea. Such a person, said Eichmann, could never be a businessman.

Eichmann was thought to be almost totally incapable of seeing something from the other fellow's point of view. (We may recall a definition of an ideologue as "a person who sees the world from a principal frame of reference". He was also a bit of a prude. While in prison, he returned the book *Lolita*, saying that it was "quite unwholesome". Of Hitler, "his success alone (in rising from corporal) proved to me that I should subordinate myself to him.".

Eichmann claimed that he would have had a guilty conscience only if he had not done what he was ordered to do. Obsessive compulsive behavior is a way of reacting to doubt about one's own abilities. "Obsessive compensation is often evidenced by fanatical work which compensates for the lack of inner direction", says Erickson. (One is reminded of Nietzsche's view that dutifulness is a transposed form of vengeance.)

Eichmann agreed with Kant that a man should identify his own will with the will behind the law. In Germany, that will behind the law was the will of the Fuhrer.

Eichmann usually read nothing but newspapers. In his work he saw and talked with no one who was against the "final solution" for the Jews. Hanna Arendt's *Eichmann in Jerusalem* presents a valuable study of the true-believing follower. Eichmann's school and work histories showed that he was a loser. He always wanted to be important and he talked big. The dominant Party line could quickly change Eichmann's opinion. He seemed incapable of uttering anything that was not a cliché Canned ideology was especially useful to him. Arendt judged that Eichmann could not, in fact, *think*.

Inconsistencies are not recognized by true believers. It is typical of those who accept the views of authority without integrating such views that inconsistencies are not recognized. If such an individual attends a parochial school, he will be indoctrinated to avoid forming independent views- this being the sin of *propium concilium*. He will also learn to project his conscience onto priest, leader or other authority and will be trained to follow the directions of his betters in a God-ordained social hierarchy. He will view as sinful those who do not behave in a similar fashion. This described Eichmann.

The "house-servant", or "good boy", mentality is common to authoritarian followers. Another sort of follower will be resentful of his inferior position in the social order. Since he dares not cross his betters, who are in power, he seeks to identify with them. Within his limited capabilities, he will echo their views and statements. Beyond this, he will loudly denounce any who may voice views different from those of his masters. In his motives: he is supporting his masters; he is repressing those who rise above him by daring to be independent and he is guarding his worldview against elements that would threaten it and force him to think.

How would Eichmann have scored on Adorno's authoritarian personality scale? Some matching characteristics:

(*a*) Mechanically accepting conventional values;
(*b*) Unreservedly hating all opponents;
c) Being suspicious and disdainful of all outsiders;
(*d*) Abjectly surrendering to authority;
(*e*) Not being introspective;
(*f*) Having stereotyped and rigid thinking;
(*g*) Being superstitious;
(*h*) Being suspicious of self and of others;
(*i*) Projecting.

Those who want to try Adorno's F scale online can try to access www.anesi.com/fscale.htm

9

THE CULT

Potential converts to cults often (a) Feel psychological tension, have problems and are dissatisfied (b) Are at a turning point in life (c) Form ties with cult members (d) Do not have close ties with people outside the cult. Brainwashing and other tricks are not essential in cult recruiting. Commonly, the cult appeals as a surrogate "family", offering intimacy and uncritical support. Deutsch (1980) observed complete submission of cult members without special techniques.-

Micro millenarians commonly form cults. Lofland and Stark (1965) studied a very small California cult. It offers an example of the millenarian cult in microcosm. It was founded by a man in the Orient who claimed to have a revelation that the world would be returned to the Lost Paradise.

With the cult, one gains identity and status in the elect. The leader explained all events in the world in terms of the struggle between good and evil. The potential convert would be at the center of this struggle and, by getting in on the ground floor, would become a member of the elect and have an important place in the world. Many converts to that particular cult were lower middle class persons who had recently moved to the city from the country. By joining, they could regain some identity and status.

The cult leader and the group are more important than the ideology. In this, the cult differs from a movement or a sect. It is necessary to consider the influence of one group upon another. Most individuals adopt an ideology without critical thought. This applies both to the convert who starts to see the world the way the cult does and to the person who gets his ideology because he was born in the culture. Festinger et al. (1956) found that group-shared belief enabled continued support for prophesy that had obviously failed.

A person can behave as a fanatic because this is what the people around him expect. Some experiments have shown that conformists torture more than extremists. Conformists also let their minds be changed more easily (Cox and Bauer, 1964).

Extremists can resist, but conformists cannot. An individual who independently arrives at and defends an extreme position against prevailing popular opinion has greater ego strength and tolerance for stress (See Allen and Levine, 1969). Perhaps the key difference is the personal integration of an ideology rather than its absorption or wholesale acceptance.

The attitude or philosophy with which one views a situation can be strongly influenced by indoctrination and is probably more significant than the situation itself (Ross & Nisbett 1991).

A changing environment influences the cult. Since the ideology is weak or non-existent, the environment in which the cult finds itself is important. In his *Cities on a Hill*, Frances Fitzgerald reports that a cult, in India, displayed spontaneity, openness and a chaotic dissolving of self into the group. When transported to a hostile environment in Oregon, the cult closed in upon itself and became "rigid, controlling and compulsive. The general American ideological environment has little place for the collective expression of man, or for wide deviation in religion. This repressive environment may explain the apparently exaggerated behavior often observed in American cults isolated from the mainstream.

Jonestown shows the primitive workings of an isolated totalitarian psyche, as did the experience of the Munster Anabaptists. Jonestown was the site of a cult like many others- until more than 900 of its members committed joint suicide. The experience of extremist Jews at Masada has many parallels to Jonestown. Jonestown.

The cult leader at Jonestown was the Reverend Jim Jones. "It seems very evident that one person's narcissism has a great attraction for those who renounced part of their own narcissism and are seeking an object to love" said Sigmund Freud. Thus, a narcissistic leader is supplying something for cultists who lack it.

Father Jim Jones came from a working class family. His father was an invalid. His mother, a very strong personality, worked to support the family. He attended many churches as he grew up. He was usually a loner. As did Dollfuss, the Jones boy would play at being a preacher. In a group, he always insisted on being the leader.

A poor scholar, Jones was nonetheless an energetic opportunist and manipulator. Jones had an active bi-sexual life. Within the cult, he promoted himself as being the dominant male. Some thought his paranoia began by being a manipulative technique and ended by being real. A drive for total power appeared to be his primary motivation.

One can join a cult to serve, find purpose, and have security. One well-bred young woman who joined the cult explained that she did so in order to be of service and to introduce some order and purpose into her life. In what was an era of uncertainty, the cult offered a special sort of security.

Cult management is partly effected by peer pressure. Peer pressure was applied in contrived ways. Members were examined in public meetings, and felt compelled to confess in such meetings to flaws of attitude and character. Members were shamed, all good was focused on the leader. Beatings and threats were common. Sleep deprivation and malnourishment reduced the judgment. Terror and total dependency were fostered. Religious feeling, generally, is often defined as a feeling of "dependency".

Identification with the leader is important in the cult. To identify with a symbolically powerful self, or father-image, the personality of a leader is required. Surrender, dissolution of self or dependency- all require a perceived superior entity. Jones promoted the title and image of "Father". Perhaps one can dissolve oneself in the organization, but identification and dependency would seem to require a more personal symbol.

Max Weber thought a highly emotional devotion to and trust in the leader to be characteristic of "people's democracy". This attitude makes the personality of the leader critical. It does not auger well for rationality in the administration of democracies.

The unloved, the alienated, the frightened and the frustrated may all welcome the prophet. One sort of follower, says Rebhan, feels a void and seeks, unconsciously perhaps, to fill it by devotion to, or through the projection of love for the leader. If the projection is unconscious, the desire to love the self is met in the ostensible attraction of the leader. The clinical picture, says Rebhan (in Halperin, 1983), is one of object loss, depression, projection and a hope for fulfillment. By attributing omnipotence to the leader, the follower may abdicate ego and superego responsibilities.

Submission and identification with the aggressor is a potential aspect of dependency. To escape the criticism of the outside world, Jones took most of his followers to the jungle of Guinea. When the mass suicide occurred, only a few objected. Most members died with a smile on their faces. How could it happen? There were, as at Masada, armed police around the faithful to make sure no one escaped, but psychology also played a part. In isolation, the group's ideas define reality. We can speculate that paranoia increased the effect of group-think. There was also the matter of habit- the mass suicide had often been enacted as a drill.

The oppressed can translate their feelings of aggression by displaying unnatural passivity. Suicide can be a way for the overwhelmed ego to identify with the aggressor. It has also been observed that the mass suicide can be seen as an ideological solution: it took the faithful beyond political persecution and it promised them religious salvation.

The mental state of the leader, Jones, may have been of more significance than that of the cult members. It is thought that Jones' paranoiac claims began by being a manipulative device and eventually became real in his mind.

The mental effects of a cult may be beneficial. Brock Kilbourne (1978) presents statistical data to suggest that chanting, ritual and altered states of consciousness resulting from participation in a cult may aid the mental health of the convert.

Regression is a potential adverse effect of membership in a cult. Professionals who have treated people leaving cults claim to have found considerable constriction of cognition. Spero (in Halperin, 1983) performed extensive testing on ex-cultists and sees the cult experience as essentially regressive. Primary, infantile, process tends to replace secondary, evaluative process. Among the symptoms: wide-eyed single-mindedness, use of cliché, great cautiousness or paranoia, phobias, black and white thinking, polarization, a denigrated former self-image, denial, projection, externalization and mood swings.

Disintegration may occur on withdrawal. If much of the self has been transferred to the leader or to the organization, then withdrawal from the group must result in a fragmented personality and a sense of void.

10

AUTHORITARIANISM

Does the child become intrinsic or extrinsic? Many think that the first years of life are decisive in determining the character of a child. Is the child brought up in fear, learning to doubt himself and the world about him? Must he constantly respond to parental reproach? Such an upbringing implies extrinsic authority orientation and an especial susceptibility to canned ideologies. We find that anxiety, neuroticism and strength of expressed opinion group together, as do conservatism and authoritarianism. We shall see that more than eighty percent of us are comfortable with authoritarianism.

A scale was developed by Adorno and others in an attempt to measure patterns of submission and dominance, of rigidity, of paranoia, etc. It sought to show the contribution of such factors to the authoritarian personality. Adorno's scale was thought valid for rightist authoritarianism. Extremists, whether of the right or left, are rather similar.

Aspects of the authoritarian personality profile include:

(*a*) Conventionalism- rigid conventionality.
(*b*) Submission- regularly bows to authority.
(*c*) Conforming.
(*d*) Represses thoughts.
(*e*) Not introspective- does not analyze self.
(*f*) Projects extensively.
(*g*) Thinks in stereotypes.
(*h*) Is aggressive toward out-groups.
(*i*) Vilifies human nature.
(*j*) Awed by power and uses it.
(*k*) Is superstitious.

Subsequent papers have reduced the description to aggression, submission and conventionalism.

Right Wing Authoritarian Scale. The RWA Scale (Altemeyer & Hunsberger, 1992) was a thirty item questionnaire designed to identify those evidencing authoritarian aggression, authoritarian submission, and conventionalism (Altemeyer, 1981). In the North American context, it is a right-wing phenomenon and was associated with the acceptance of double standards and illegal acts by government officials. Since "conventionalism" is not necessarily a right-wing phenomenon, the name of the scale may be a misnomer.

In Manitoba, the correlation between the RFA Scale and Religious Fundamentalism response was 0.66. In Michigan, it was 0.77. RFAs are quite hostile to homosexuals (0.64), score highly on prejudice (0.53) and would like to join posses (.51).

One may speculate that authoritarians habitually showed submission to family, to religious authorities and to their surrounding peer group and this may have contributed to their correlation with religious fundamentalism. The religious fundamentalists tested were less pronounced in their prejudices (.030), less anti-homosexual (0.41) and less inclined to join posses (.34).

People will follow authority's evil orders. Whether of a liberal or of a conservative disposition, more than eighty-five percent of mankind will go along with authority without making a fuss. At Yale, Stanley Milgram found that 93% of normal people would torture a fellow human if told to do so by someone in authority. Both in Nazi Germany and at Berkeley, 87% of faculty members signed loyalty oaths. In Red China, fewer than 15% were deemed politically "backward". While it is not certain that this means that 85% are "authoritarians", it is evident that those who will follow an independent course are in a small minority.

The Nazi Adolf Eichmann showed traits that would match high on the Adorno authoritarian personality profile. Among Eichmann's matching characteristics: accepting authority, completely adopting conventional values and clichés, lacking introspection, being superstitious, projecting his own weaknesses and vilifying human nature, and blindly hating the opponents of the regime.

As an authoritarian personality, Eichmann's conscience would have bothered him only if he had not done the duty assigned to him. A panel of psychiatrists found Adolf Eichmann to be a perfectly normal individual. Now, if Eichmann was "perfectly normal", then it would appear that authoritarianism is normal, and psychological testing among university students seems to confirm this.

The psychologist Rokeach says that the authoritarian personality will be more rigid in behavior and more concrete and narrow in thought. Viewing things as black or white, authoritarians tend toward premature closure of perception and to distortion of memory. The authoritarian personality does not like or trust itself or others. It represses its own unacceptable impulses and projects them onto others, especially on others who are thought to represent a threat.

Authoritarian personalities are more concerned with relations of power and control than with love and affection. The authoritarian is quite willing to submit to external authority. To him, God, (the projected superego), is seen as forbidding and powerful. Authoritarians can project the superego onto God, a hierarchy or a superior officer.

The authoritarian personality grouped conservation, rigidity, conscientiousness, and obsession ("anality"), according to a study by Klein & Cooper (1984). The authoritarian mind is thus closed to the new and different. "Openness to experience" includes values, ideas, actions, feelings, esthetics and fantasy. Butler (2000) found authoritarians conservative/conventional (.56), with minds closed to different values (-.40), courses of action (-.36), feelings

(-.34), new ideas (-.29) and aesthetics (-.28). Submissive to authority, the authoritarian is easily dominated by one who has the charisma, trappings of authority, or is conventionally sanctioned. A group of authoritarians studied by Crowson et al. (2005) got the following correlations: Biblical literalism (.69); need for closure (.39); closed mindedness (.33); preference for order (.27); discomfort with ambiguity (.26); preference for predictability (.22); decisiveness (.18).

Altemeyer (1981) reduced Adorno's nine factors to aggression, conventionalism and "authoritarian submission". Friedrich Funke, in his 2002 dissertation, performed extensive factor analyses that confirmed the importance of the aggression dimension.

Authoritarianism and fundamentalist religion are correlated. The typical man, according to St. Benedict, is weak and needs habits and rules of life sanctioned and maintained by authority. Anxiety and responsibility go along with freedom, so, where there is less freedom, there is less tension. The monastic existence offers less tension. There appears to be an intercorrelation of about 0.70 between religious fundamentalism and authoritarian views.

The authoritarianism of Lutherans is greatest. Those who reject organized religion seem to be less prejudiced and authoritarian. On the ethnocentric-authoritarian scale, the Lutherans are the most authoritarian. (Fromm suggests that the Lutheran quest for certainty is rooted in bothersome doubt). The following were among the scores that Adorno found relating church attendance and rightist authoritarianism Lutherans 4.38; Catholics 4.21; Regular Go 3.79; Anglicans 3.58; Never Go 2.87; No religion 2.71.

In half a century since Adorno, the "authoritarian personality" has been reduced to dimensions of aggression, conservatism or conventionality, closed-mindedness and submission to authority. The correlation with aspects of religion persists, such as Biblical literalism at 0.70, persists (Crowson et al. 2005).

The socially dominant personality is exploitive. Altemeyer (2004) found that some seven percent of authoritarians sought to be socially dominant and scored weakly in several other traits of the usual authoritarian. He sees these socially dominant high authoritarians, when they assume domination over other authoritarians, to pose a major threat to society

Pleonexia is the insatiable hunger for domination. In 313, Constantine had issued the Edict of Milan: "Everyone has the right to worship whatever he pleases". Later, the Christian Church, given more power by Constantine, sought to consolidate that power by enforcing unity, which brought it again more power. The drive for total dominion is unending, a pleonexia.

Authoritarianism may be necessary. As a practical matter, an underdeveloped nation seeking to provide infrastructure may have to act in an authoritarian way. By comparing China and Singapore, one may form an idea of whether the authoritarian elite will wither away.

The archetypical conservative: In his *Psychology of Conservatism*, Glen D. Wilson characterizes the archetypal conservative:

(*a*) Expressing religious fundamentalism.
(*b*) Being thoroughly pro-establishment.
(*c*) Favoring strict rules and punishments.
(*d*) Advocating militarism.
(*e*) Exhibiting ethnocentrism and intolerance
(*f*) Being very conventional.
(*g*) Being against hedonism, especially re sex.
(*h*) Being hostile to scientific progress.
(*i*) Being superstitious.

Conservative and liberal Baptist ministers are easily distinguished. Stewart and Webster (1970) distinguished between theologically conservative and liberal Baptist ministers. They then applied various personality tests. Two distinctive patterns emerged. The terms are further defined in the personality tests used: the *Edwards Personal Preference Schedule* and *Shostrum's Personal Orientation Inventory*.

Personality characteristics of theological conservatives:

(*a*) General conservatism .75
(*b*) Dogmatism .62
(*c*) Ethnocentrism .58
(*d*) Dependence .56
(*e*) Rigidity .56
(*f*) Negative view of man .42
(*g*) Insensitivity .41
(*h*) Low intimacy .38
(*i*) Craving for order .30
(*j*) Getting values from outside .30
(*k*) Rejecting aggression .30
(*l*) Not accepting self .28

Theologically liberal Baptist ministers exhibited the following personal characteristics (factor loadings):

(*a*) Having liberal attitudes (.72)
(*b*) Not being ethnocentric (.55)
(*c*) Inner sufficiency (.49)
(*d*) Positive view of man (.46)
(*e*) Existential attitude (.44)
(*f*) Sensitivity (.41)
(*g*) Self-Determined Values (.39)

The Five Factor Model of Personality is approaching paradigm status. One of the distinctions between liberals and conservatives is the willingness to reexamine social, political and religious values. Less emphatic criteria are derived from Goldberg's (1982) commonly applied terms: "puritanical", "religious", "traditional", "moralistic", "law-abiding", "chaste", "straight-laced", "moral", "respectful", "strict", "prudish". Conservatives were thought *not* to be: "unconventional", "irreverent", "disrespectful", "unchaste", "rebellious", "unethical", "and lawless". In general terms the concept of "open hearts and minds" is said distinguish liberals from conservatives.

Authoritarians are obedient torturers. Stanley Milgram's experiments at Yale show the pervasiveness of obedience to authority among normal people. For example, 37 out of 40 normal subjects were willing to follow orders and assist in the torture of a fellow human.

Moderates are the worst torturers. When Bock (1972) replicated Milgram's experiments, he found that religious moderate believers administered more shocks than did extreme believers. The extremist can think and has courage enough to follow his conscience against authority or the crowd. The conforming moderate, however, can easily act fanatically if the situation seems to demand it. Note that those who felt "nearest to God delivered the highest shocks.

If the victim is male and of a different race, if the leader is high status, if the torturer is (like most of us) authoritarian, if there is hostility and group pressure- these factors potentiate the likelihood of torture. A high status victim, or feelings of personal and social responsibility, militate against performing torture.

Stages of moral development are evident in children. Kay, in his *Moral Development* (1969), cites various investigations to indicate the following stages of moral development in children: a) prudential morality-fear of natural consequences; b) authoritarian control- reward and punishment; c) social control- the idea of reciprocity and community; d) moral autonomy.

Moral action requires that one recognize the existence of moral choices, determine which is the most ethical and act upon it. The spectrum of choice appears to be largely a matter of education. Kohlberg saw the following progressive stages:

(1) Obedience to avoid punishment.
(2) Seeking the best deal for oneself.
(3) Seeking the approval of others.
(4) Obey the law and maintain the social order.
(5) Observe contractual morality, keep agreements.
(6) Use universal ethical principles.

Most people are said to live at stages (3) and (4), where they seek to please others and are obedient authoritarians. The Defining Issues Test assigns a score based on the number of responses invoking levels
(5) and (6). Typical scores were: for twelve and thirteen year old students, 22; secondary students, aged 14-19, 32; adults, 40; university level 42; law students, 52; political science students, 65. http:/edpsy.coled.umn.edu/PSYCHF/CSED/default.html.

There seem to be three overall stages: (1) the authoritarian, (2) the reciprocal and (3) the principled. Kohlberg suggested that only twenty percent of mankind progresses beyond the authoritarian stage. Nonetheless, even pre-adolescents used contractual or general principles twenty-two percent of the time. Adults can be fixed at any of the stages or can regress.

Does society, like the individual, go through evolutionary stages of ethical control? Reisman, in The Lonely Crowd (1964) saw: (a) medieval man as under the control of tradition imposed by social sanctions. (b) Industrial man as controlled by conscience, the superego of society. (c) "Ad-mass" man ruled by public opinion.

Less than 20% of people are independently principled. In Nazi Germany and in Berkeley, California, 87% of the university professors signed loyalty oaths. According to Lawrence Kohlberg, 80% of people are unable to behave according to internal values and require an externally imposed authoritarian system. Chou En-lai reported that, after thought reform, 40% were "progressive", 40% were middle of the road, 15% were backward, and 5% were reactionary. Again, it appears that only about twenty percent fail to fully conform to authority.

These studies suggest that five to eight percent of people will resist and say "no" to authority; fifteen percent may be a little reluctant and eighty percent are obediently content with authoritarianism.

The ad-mass man is selfish. Reisman speculated that laissez faire capitalism resulted in an "inner-directed" man, whereas the mass age will exhibit an "other- directed" man. Of course, ad-mass man is created by paid media spots and these are not calculated to create "other directedness". Today, those with a political agenda are aware of the tremendous influence of media and have bought control.

Children are always the pliable target. "Young people can hardly avoid accepting whatever version of the facts is presented to them. Public instruction should be the first object of government" said Napoleon. Dewey saw the function of education as imprinting children with the group habits of the society. The influence of Dewey and others has served to make "adjustment" or "adaptation" among the highest goals of education. Children as Targets.

The schools and the Hitler Youth were particularly important to the Nazis. Soviet young people were organized into the Octobrists (ages 811), the Pioneers (ages 10-16), and the Komosols (ages 15-26). We must cultivate in our youth the ability to recognize a class enemy, no matter what image it assumes", said a leading Soviet.

Until 1983, Canon law made it a mortal sin for a Catholic child to attend a public school unless he had special permission from a priest. The Roman Catholic Church has been most insistent in maintaining control of schools, even to the point of fomenting civil disobedience and revolution, as in Mexico. In the United States, the movement to free public education began about 1825. Before that, nearly all schools were church schools.

In the U.S., it is now generally accepted that that there should be local control of schools and that the public schools should be free of sectarian doctrine. Such freedom from sectarian doctrine is not universally thought desirable. The Canadian prime minister, Wilfrid Laurier, (a Catholic from Quebec) considered religious teaching in the schools to be a source of social stability.

In Fascist Italy, Gentile let the Church control the elementary schools and reserved control of the secondary schools for the Party. The Jesuit educators Ryan and Boland make the point: "It is plainly the duty of all who teach to banish error from the mind and to close the entry to all false convictions." Pius XI announced that, even in the public schools, Catholic teachers were obliged to represent the Pope in censoring all public instruction.

Legalism is amoral. If a legalistic interpretation of virtue is taught by authoritarian conservatives, A. W. Kay predicted that the future would become amoral. This seems to have happened. From Plato to the present day, schools have been viewed as instruments to imprint children with the worldview of the establishment. Rousseau believed that society, through the schools, could develop a "new man" who would have no inclination to disagree with the general will. .

Argentine authoritarianism forced rural values. The psyche of Argentina, as Crassweller (1987) saw it, reflects a polarization between the values of the city and those of the interior. The interior valued tradition, authority and individual dignity. If those were the values of the majority, then a reformer could be seen as "undemocratic".

Latin corporatism was Catholic and Fascist. Mediterranean corporatism, described by Wiarda (1980) as "hierarchical, elitist, authoritarian, bureaucratic, Catholic and patrimonialist", was an important anti-democratic factor in Argentina. Peron's *justicialismo* was informed by the papal encyclicals *Rerum Novarum* and *Quadragesimo anno*, as had been Fascism in Italy and Austria. Peron sought to redress the social balance by helping the city workers who had recently immigrated from the countryside. The labor movement would be Peron's power base.

The active drive of the Catholic Church for control in Argentina was also a factor in Peron's rise. Peron had introduced compulsory religious education in the public school system in 1943. By 1954, however, the political activities of Catholic Action proved too troublesome and Peron repealed the law requiring religious education, also expelling two bishops. The Church influence continued, however, for even in 1986 the state paid bishops the salaries of lieutenant generals and the Constitution required that the President of the Republic be a Catholic.

Argentine fanaticism had religious roots. Crassweller reports that the Montonero revolutionaries had their origins in conservative and traditional Catholicism and in the right-wing Falangist Tacuara organization. There was a psychological commitment to violent and direct action. The Montoneros, after receiving indoctrination from left-wing priests, saw themselves as revolutionary

Peron's 1952 *Political Plan* called for the creation of a "hit list" of political opponents. When the usual police methods proved inadequate to contain the Montoneros, each army district undertook special action to suppress revolutionaries. The groundwork for the next three decades of government assassinations was laid.

Was Argentina authoritarian or totalitarian? The Argentine experience of the 1970's may serve to mark the boundary between the very authoritarian and the totalitarian. The emphasis was on the negative, on eliminating that which was undesirable, rather than on creating a new order.

Post-Peron Argentina was also different from most totalitarianisms in that it had no missionary component. It did not seek to implement its ideas on an international, global scale. The Videla regime tried to eliminate aspects of Argentine society that it thought did not comport with the conservative Catholic worldview. It imposed censorship on films, theatre and books; it modified university curricula, eliminating majors in sociology, philosophy and psychology. It forbid the use of Freudian techniques in state hospitals, and imposed Catholic education on pupils in the secondary schools. The books of Freud and of materialist philosophers were removed from libraries, reported Jacobo Timmerman in the *Reader's Digest* of January 1982.

Argentina had totalitarian aspects. In *The Carnivorous Power*, Alvaro Abos provides an analysis of the Argentine military regime in terms that can apply generally to totalitarian systems. He notes the special use of words to negate, alter and manipulate reality. Particularly, there is the "process" of national reorganization, which becomes synonymous with "progress".

"Subversion" is anything inconsistent with the official line of the dictatorship. The official actions constituting the true process, all else being foreign and hostile. Heresies, views that praise similar but different values, were especially hated. Thus, Peronism saw social democracy as the Devil.

The economy and social life of Argentina are dominated by polarization of the classes and the ever-present threat of general strikes and class warfare. Vestiges of Catholic medievalism are evident in a Manichean view of the world, a dogmatic need for certainty and absolutes, and an appreciation of messianic martyrdom and the survival of great landholdings. The voices of reason at the center are little heeded. In Argentina, the alternative is always military rule.

Through time, socio-economic class interests will prevail over ethnic and racial concerns. In hard times, people join authoritarian churches. In good times, they seek the non-authoritarian churches. So it is with government. As the 20th Century began, states that were Protestant, industrial and scientific showed progress.

The authoritarian ruler is more concerned with outward order and conformity than with the inner man. He is also more concerned with today's world than with a world of the future. People feel comfortable in an authoritarian society.

Obedience to authority is the norm. Some think that basic attitudes of trust or mistrust are formed before the third year of life. Some eighty percent of us wind up mistrustful and more comfortable with the security of authoritarianism. Few of us are so disturbed as to consciously seek totalitarianism, but there is little to resist the slide from authoritarianism to totalitarianism.

The pliable minds of children, and therefore the schools, are particular targets of both authoritarian and totalitarian groups. The objectives differ, however, in that authoritarianism seeks docile compliance and order, while totalitarians seek to create dedicated true believers. Authoritarianism is pragmatic. Totalitarianism is doctrinaire.

General aspects of authoritarianism

There is a top-down flow of ideas.
One-man or oligarchic rule prevails.
Rule is centralized.
Dictatorship is legitimized.
No effective opposition is permitted.
No attention is paid to human rights.
There are understood limits to power.
There is no real separation of governmental powers.
A limited pluralism is permitted.
The government is anti-democratic.
Stability and immobilization, not mobilization.
Maintains old values rather than instill new values.

The closed society is sought by both authoritarians and totalitarians, but the totalitarian feels driven to extend his ideology toward universal world dominion. The supernatural is psychological projection primarily concerned with ego integration and societal idealization. Theology becomes political ideology when the active emphasis is on man in society. Here, religion assumes practical relevance and here conflict with the state arises. If there is insufficient promise in the society, a religious call to movement may arise.

11

MILLENARIAN MOVEMENTS

When there seems little hope of sufficient improvement, men may dream of a past "golden age" or move out in search of a new "Promised Land". A religious ideology often inspires such movements. Organized religion is integral to the relations of men. If it cannot be totalitarian, then it will try to be authoritarian. Religion is always responding to human needs on psychological, philosophical and socio-economic levels. The supernatural is psychological projection, primarily concerned with ego integration and societal idealization. Stripped of the supernatural, religion is principally concerned with man and society.-

A "golden age" is a time when men are said to be satisfied with the world that they have inherited. "Golden ages" may also be the imagined state of things at some time in the past. Unsatisfactory conditions must exist before a new ideology can flourish. Inconsistencies between cultural expectations and social reality can cause important dissatisfaction.

Times of crisis may welcome new ideologies. The demand for change grows and the establishment will organize resistance to change. Articulating an idcology provides a cognitive map and sets the stage for new actions. Trends of change are voiced in popular songs and in religious movements. Through such expressions people seek to restructure, at least mentally, their world. New philosophies are formulated justifying a change.

The response to change can be accommodation or movement. As change increases, individual stress mounts, some anti-social behaviors become common, and prophets with their followers emerge. Either the new movement takes over the culture or the culture accommodates the new views, but an accommodation with the establishment is effected. The movement then itself becomes institutionalized. The rate at which change takes place has been said to depend on receptivity, the presence of competing ideas, how much intellectual freedom there is, how diverse and dense the population is, and how much contact there is with other cultures. (When these factors are considered, the effectiveness of an isolationist censorship becomes evident.).

Luther's message of the equality of men before God and before each other potentiated the spirit of independence fostered by the Renaissance. Ideas that all property should be held in common and that all should work for their bread were asserted and backed by revolutionary action. The peasant revolts were crushed but the ideas persisted among many Protestants.

The Anabaptists took over Munster in 1534 for a year. As they became more powerful, they progressed from allowing liberty of conscience to creating a community "purified of all uncleanness".

All Lutherans and Roman Catholics were expelled and their property confiscated. Not to be an Anabaptist then became a capital offense. A man who complained was arrested and killed at a public meeting. The terror had begun. All money was to be handed over to the government.

The terror increased, and there were a few more executions. All books except the Bible were burned. Meetings of even a few individuals were banned. Plotting to escape, or criticizing the government, was punishable with death. District guard captains were set up. They were forbidden to communicate with each other, and could only talk with the leader. Although it was supposed to be a communistic society, the leader and his gang lived well.

The Book of a Hundred Chapters (1510) presaged Hitler. Norman Cohn cites this text as being prepared by someone known to us only as the "Revolutionary of the Upper Rhine". The same prejudices appeared to exist four hundred and twenty years later. The pure and married were to form the Brotherhood of the Yellow Cross. St. Michael was to aid the "Emperor of the Black Forest", who would establish a vast empire and reign for a thousand years. The Emperor would "smash Babylon in the name of God and bring the whole world under his own rule, so that there will be one shepherd, one sheepfold and one faith throughout the whole world". "Soon we will drink blood for wine".

The Revolutionary of the Upper Rhine combined socialist and nationalist ideas. He believed that there had been a time when Germans had "lived together like brothers", holding all things in common. The Romans, followed by the Church of Rome, had destroyed this. Roman law and Cannon law brought selfish ideas of private property. It was not the Jews, but rather the Germans who were the Chosen people, the descendants of Japhet. The Italians were the descendants of serfs who had been banished from the lands of the Germans. "The Germans once held the whole world in their hands and they will do so again, and with even more power."

Millenarian movements have common factors. Norman Cohn derived certain common factors for millenarian movements: (a) The objectives of the movement have no limit. (b) Followers come from the marginal, and under-employed. (c) The followers felt alienated from the established Church. (d) Followers could ease their anxieties by participating.

The miserable and alienated join: "The young movement is not meant to constitute an organization of the contented and satisfied but to embrace those tormented by suffering, those without peace, the unhappy and the discontented," said Hitler.

A movement can be distinguished from a "cause". The cause seems to provide a redeeming mission. A movement is less focused than a cause. It is more of a mass in motion. As a movement, early Christianity offered the masses hope for peace, justice, equality and possible immortality. The uncertainty of the times caused many to seize upon the hopeful promises and join the movement.

Mass migrations and mass movements convey a sense of rebirth. Total absorption in a cause would convey the same feeling. Eric Hoffer suggests that new birth really means to become like a child, to be credulous, to join a pack and to follow a leader. Thus regressed to childlike status, would a population tend to become a plastic mass?

Mass man and the totalitarian movement are controlled. Structurally, modern movements are more than a mass in motion. There is usually a hard core of members separated from the outside, real, world by a ring of insiders. The insiders will control the direction of the movement. The control of media becomes critical in this effort. As the mass public, via manipulation by the media, becomes ostensibly more important, government will increasingly seek to present its policies in ideological terms.

12

NATIONALISM

The usual motivations of tribalism are transmuted in nationalism. Linguistic, ethnic and cultural factors are still present, but the primary focus comes within the territory of the state. It is not certain that nationalism is at all compatible with a universal evangel.

Anti-democratic idealism and violence: From the early 19th Century onwards, idealism, as expressed by Kant, Fichte, Schelling and Hegel, dominated German thought. Bismark built a nation without the benefit of liberal democracy. Sorel's syndicalism blended political myth and violence.

Insecurity and self-doubt: By the 1930's, inflation caused panic in the middle class, and the Red revolution increased the feeling of insecurity. Bracker (1982) sees chauvinism and imperialism as a response to that insecurity and self-doubt. Nationalism, anti-parliamentary feeling and the discontent of youth all sought a new set of unifying values. The nation was ready for Hitler.

Romantic mysticism fills the void. Just before World War I the German youth movement expressed a longing for a feeling of community and a mystical revival of Romanticism. Nietzsche and the poet Stephan George were important influences. As had the reaction to the Napoleonic occupation, Germany's defeat in World War I created an inferiority complex. Hitler's claim of racial superiority offered an antidote to that inferiority complex. Anti-capitalist pronouncements furthered his appeal. The black swastika and white circle reflected the colors of Imperial Germany, but they were symbolically set in the red field of revolution.

Self-sufficiency is a common goal of nationalisms. A maximum effort to achieve national self- sufficiency was called "war economy", and was accompanied by cultural self-sufficiency and hostility to liberal thought.

A master race of leaders was needed. Arendt asserts that the Nazis did not think that they were a master race, but rather that they should be led by a master race. In the Nazi view, the state was a "means for preserving the racial nation". The state was defined as the "sovereign manifestation of the racial nation's instinct and common will for self preservation". Racism was more important than the state under National Socialism.

In his *Critique of Judgment*, Kant spoke of an "enlarged mentality", able to think for everyone. This philosophy became broadly accepted. Also present was the *furor teutonicus*, the drive to excess that has been attributed to Germans for two thousand years. The claim was made that total personal submission to state authority was voluntary.

Hitler organized a civil religion. Hitler had been raised as a Catholic. Forty percent of the German population was Catholic. Under National Socialism, says Mosse, political acts were really dramatizations of new myths and cults. Hitler seemed to combine the functions of god and priest-king.

Hegel drew on Machiavelli, Hobbes, Rousseau and Kant, finding the state "the march of God through the world", superior to human life. War was glorified as the ethic of world history. Pietism romanticism, Fichte, Schleiermacher, Schelling, Comte, Nietzsche, and imperialism, all implicated the right brain and articulated a mystical and altruistic unity as the philosophical basis for the German ideology.

Rationality is uncommon. Is Hitler to be regarded as a madman or merely an extremist, as an aberration or merely a point in the continuum of German history? "Rationality" often refers to objective problem solving. This ignores the subjective and the right hemisphere. The human attention span can accommodate at most five or six items at a time. The ordinary person can give only one or two reasons for a decision. Faced with uncertainty, we delve into the unconscious and accept the guidance of the supernatural, the simplistic and the right brain. It thus is an error to claim that Hitler and the Germans were mad.

The Emerging Nation

For colonial peoples, self-determination might require revolution. After the revolution, would the democratic model be parliamentarian, Marxist-totalitarian, or something of each? The first party to take power may feel that it alone has the capacity to lead. If there is substantially no middle class and few technical or administrative personnel, a centralized authoritarian form of government is likely. Local culture and history will influence the choice.

The Latin American ethos until recently was thought to be essentially feudal. Admiring the aristocratic spirit and rural simplicity. In the countryside, the heritage of the *latifundista* (large landholder) is still important. The economics are mercantilist (governmental monopolies) and pre-capitalist, and influenced by Catholic corporatism. The dominant Latin American classes are government officials, landholders, and the military. The culture is family-centered and social organization outside the family is uncommon. Internal exploitation, cash-cropping and investing abroad have been the norm since early colonial times.

The Church is sometime a revolutionary vector. In 1968, Pope Paul VI opened a conference of Latin American Bishops at Medellin, Columbia by criticizing "external neo-colonialism, international monopolies and the international imperialism of money". The theme was continued by the *Priests for the Third World* at Buenos Aires in 1970: "private ownership of capital leads to exploitation". A "liberation" theology developed that extolled Marxian principles. The 1985 Synod of Bishops mentioned the "preferential option for the poor", while those representing Argentina, Mexico and Venezuela opposed it. The Vatican position under John Paul II seemed to favor local communes while condemning both capitalism and socialism.

In Latin America, half the people live below the poverty line and a third are said to have no access to health care. As rural people are displaced toward the cities, the structures of their lives are destroyed. Unemployed males become alcoholic and abuse or abandon their families. Even where social assistance exists, there is scant dignity.

The Liberation theologians attempted to answer this situation by organizing "base communities" that included Bible reading and various economic initiatives. The Vatican has discouraged these developments and it is now the Evangelical Lutherans and other Protestant groups who are in the vanguard.

The evangelical vector is growing in Latin America. The noteworthy inroads made by evangelicals in Latin America may reflect the acceptance of participation and hope in preference to the passive social compliance expected of "minores" (the little people) in traditional Catholicism. Along with a message of salvation, the Protestant evangelical missionaries brought an ethos of voluntary participation by ordinary folk and a hope of improvement in economic and family life and are especially effective in reducing male alcoholism.

The Pentecostal evangelical message is directed toward creating a family of love, marital fidelity and responsibility with emphasis on the education of children and avoidance of alcohol. The ethos is one of economic self-improvement, rather than dependency. Community solidarity offers healing and economic support. Religious symbols are refocused toward non-hierarchical, non-sacramental expression.

The Pentecostals seem especially effective in recruiting former Catholics among the urban poor and middle classes. In Guatemala, however, evangelical Protestantism exists among the elite and Catholicism now has leftist connotations. An anti-communist, pro-capitalist, American influence is present and the Pentecostal appeal is said to be strong among the middle and well-to-do classes, whereas the lower urban classes are more fundamentalist.

In Brazil, the evangelical pastor Rinaldo Pereira combines rock music, hypnotism, and self-improvement messages in creating a very popular and expanding god business. His primary audience is among those with money to spend on the articles he sells along with his services. He is said to be considering bringing his program to North America.

Cuba offers an example of a small group of revolutionaries taking over a largely apathetic population. Recall that personal ideology, and perhaps the modal personality, of the nation are greatly influenced by the tradition and the culture. World-sweeping ideology tends to fail against local culture. In his *Fidel y la Religion*, Castro emerges, despite the revolutionary rhetoric, as rather the paternalistic *buen patron* of the Cuban hacienda.

Fidel Castro

As a child, Fidel Castro was violent, manipulative and defiant of authority, exhibiting much indignation, anger and fury" (Szulc, 1987). He attended private Roman Catholic schools, but felt that "society people" had made him suffer as a child because of his social origins. Other Castro characteristics were extensive reading, an addiction to words, and a need for being constantly on the move. He was an accomplished dissimulator. With time, he seemed increasingly lonely, impatient with democratic liberalism, intolerant of dissent and showed an increasing appetite for total power.

Castro liked Che's phrase: "the love of humanity must be daily transformed into concrete acts that serve as examples". Castro declared revolution necessary because the "interests of the exploiters and the exploited are irreconcilable". "We have no elections" said Castro, "because Marxist truths are irrefutable, but the people have to be educated to understand them. Once people understand them, why bother with elections?"

"I believe the Revolution is eternal...when human society has been revolutionized, there must be a struggle to perfect it. And, when it has been perfected, then we must revolutionize nature". It was Castro's opinion that equality was more important than the overall standard of living.

Other nationalisms are discussed under imperialism, national character, political creeds and ideologies.

13

THE SEEDS OF TOTALITARIANISM

Egypt and Mesopotamia were totalitarian. Around 2300 B.C., Sumeria tried to reconstruct its ancient history. Legends of creation, original paradise, forbidden fruit and a great punishing flood were produced. In Babylonia, Hammurabi (2,100 B.C.) claimed to have received a code of laws from Shamash, the Sun god. The king was, technically, merely the agent of the local god.

The Egyptian pharaoh was the chief priest of the faith and descended of the gods. The priests were the "secret police of the social order". The pharaoh Ikhnaton (1370 B.C.) had a vision of a universal religion and thereupon had the names of all other gods but his erased. He declared all other creeds illegal and closed their temples. After Ikhnaton's early death, the unemployed priests regained power and thereafter referred to him only as "The Great Criminal", erasing *his* records.

Through temple offerings, the priests in Sumeria became kings. In Egypt, the priests also accumulated great wealth. After Ramses III, the high priest took over the government and Egypt became a stagnant theocracy.

The Old Testament Heritage

Out of the violent and intolerant furnace of the Near East arose Zoroastrianism. Zoroastrianism proclaimed a jealous God and introduced concepts of Hell, the Promised Land and the Chosen People. In contrast to the ever-cycling universe of the Greeks, Indians and most Chinese, Zoroastrian eschatology saw a linear movement of history progressing toward a consummation. The world was a struggle between good and evil, and one should wage war on the side of the good (Ahura Mazda) and await the Messiah.

As Zorastrians, the Persians contributed many ideas to the Hebrews including. Concepts of heaven, hell, demons, a Last Judgment and an intolerant god, and the myth of being a chosen people. The Persian prophet Zarathustra spoke of one supreme god, Ahura Mazda, who, alone among all the gods, was deemed uniquely right. By the 8th Century B.C., the Hebrews had incorporated the idea of this intolerant god and other aspects of Zorastrianism into their religion.

Armageddon precedes the Kingdom of God. The Jews passed on to the Christians the idea that a moral god required the destruction of present conditions and the installation of the Kingdom of God on Earth. The essence of the idea is the rule of God mediated by his prophets. This arose again as a promise of redemption from oppressive alien domination.

Nationalism began among the Chosen. The pagans thought the universe immortal. The Christians claimed that the individual was immortal. The Jews claimed the immortality of a people. Is the immortality of a people the beginning of the *volkgeist* concept? Is nationalism a modern version of the claim to be a chosen people? Are revolutionary movements a way of seeking the Promised Land? It can be argued that Christianity, Islam, Marxist-Leninism and Nazism are but reprises of the Hebrew (Zoroastrian) ideology. To explore this further, let us a look a little more closely at certain aspects of the Old Testament legacy.

Intolerance characterizes the Old Testament jealous God. The Jewish *Exodus* has Yahweh say: "I am a jealous god". Competing rivals were to be overthrown and their images destroyed. The belief that any god but theirs was false was a major contribution of the Hebrews to our history said Northrup Frye. This ideological legacy made an attitude of compromise impossible for Judaism, Christianity, Islam and Marxism. By contrast, one should note that compromise is a major requirement in Chinese Confucianism.

Must intolerance and uniformity characterize the racial state? The *Gleichschaltung* of Hitler's Germany was the attempt to achieve unity and uniformity by eliminating all distinctions and all competing forms of social and cultural life. When does uniformity become intolerance? In Israel, said Hanna Arendt, at first, no Jew could marry a non-Jew, children of mixed marriages were legally bastards and a non-Jew could be neither married nor buried.

"The people at all times see proof of their own right in a ruthless attack upon a foe" (Hitler). When Moses encountered the burning bush, said Northrup Frye, Western culture received such concepts as a belief in historical revelation, the historical integrity of scripture and an attitude of dialectical intolerance. As with the Persian Zarathustra, so the Hebrew prophets proclaimed divine revelation as the source of their message. When written, these messages came to be regarded as sacred texts, scripture that could not be challenged.

The Hebrews became "peoples of the Book", with great rigidity in scriptural interpretation. Prophecy yielded to scripture. This legalistic approach tended to frustrate man's expression. Pressures thus created might find a partial release in increased scapegoating and in demonstrative behavior. In China, legalism has been a recurring counter to the individual responsibility and perfection exhorted by Confucianism. "legalism leaves people no sense of honor" said Confucius (500 B.C.) in the *Analects* II, 3.

The Mosaic myth: Feuer outlines the essence of the Mosaic myth: (1) A people is oppressed. (2) A young man appears and intervenes. (3) The people are liberated. (4) The leader articulates a new doctrine. (5) The people depart from the doctrine. (6) The leader imposes new moral discipline. (7) A false prophet arises and is defeated. (8) The people move toward a vision of a better life.

Bad times bring out prophets and their psychopathy. As Moses told it, Yahweh would protect his people as long as they were faithful to Yahweh. This was a social contract with the god for the benefit of a chosen people. After Jerusalem was captured, things seemed to be bad and the prophets emerged, trying to introduce a social consciousness into religion. Amos (760 B.C.)

seems like a forerunner of Jesus. Isaiah speaks of hope for a leader who will bring on the millennium.

Sheldon Cohen saw the following psychopathy in the Biblical prophets: (1) strong personal anxiety and guilt (2) hallucinations (3) preoccupation with the intervention of spirits (4) oedipal attachment to father (5) passive feminine identification (6) concern with castration (7) birth and womb fantasy (8) primitive, oral mode thinking (9) analóral associations (10) obsession (11) pathological spacetime distortion and (12) mood swings. Cohen asserted that concern over others, rather than with self, distinguishes the prophets from the mentally ill.

The Sicarii fanatics were early terrorists. Hellenization and Roman domination represented the main threats for the Jews at the time of Christ. In response, pietistic Hassidists became prominent, promising immortality to those who would die resisting the Romans. The Sicarii zealots would assassinate Jews who did not share their anti-Roman views. (At Masada, these fanatics were harangued by their leader and his guards into a mass suicide more extensive than that at Jonestown.)

The Old Testament is a scripture of revenge. The "Day of the Lord" symbolized revolution against oppressors. It would destroy the existing world order and establish the Kingdom of God on Earth, directed by the prophets. Such a day would be a sort of revenge.

From his experience in teaching the Hebrew scriptures, Theodore White found the *Old Testament* themes primitive. They conveyed, above everything else, the idea of revenge, of a need for vengeance on the part of a people, he said.

"In no other religion in the world do we find a universal deity possessing the unparalleled desire for vengeance manifested by Yahweh. The Jewish religion became a notable religion of retribution", said Max Weber. A contrary view is expressed in Rabbi H. H. Donin's *To Be a Jew*: He mentions the Torah commandments: "You shall not take revenge" (Lev. 19:18) and "It is forbidden to carry a grudge" (Lev. 19:18).

The worldview of the Old Testament assumes: (a) That the present times are lamentable. (b) That history ends with a return of the Kingdom of God on Earth. (c) That the course of history is a progress of redemption. (d) The Chosen People are the instrument of God. (e) Salvation and responsibility are collective. (f) The goal is the creation of a new world.

With the Hebrew diaspora, people started thinking in terms of individual, rather than collective, salvation. Others have noted that, in translating the "Kingdom of God" as: the "New Order", or the "millennium"; the "Chosen People" as the "Party" or "priesthood"; "progress" as "process", etc., one may claim Zoroastrianism, (via Judaism, Christianity, and Islam) as the fundament of Marxist-Leninism, National-Socialism and Christian totalitarianisms.

The Zoroastrian message is an intolerant, patriarchal, ideology that divides the world into the enlightened and the unenlightened on the basis of a unique and exclusive revealed truth. That "truth" claims that its believers are a chosen people, destined to fulfill a divinely ordained mission. This is the basic ideology that informs the West. It might sometimes be useful to interpret Christianity as a more superficial layer that seeks to repress and sublimate the Old Testament legacy.

The Greeks did not share the near-Eastern linear view of history, but saw things as moving in great circles. Ideology is also a reaction to social conditions. Good times encouraged confidence, rationality and liberalism. Hard times brought out superstition and thought control. Plato spoke for totalitarianism and Aristotle for the individual conscience.

Heracleitus of Ephesus (500 B.C.) spoke of a *logos*, a universal law of nature that united apparent opposites and explained the functioning of the universe. All was in flux. All emerged from and dissolved into a universal fire. He claimed no difference between Greek and non-Greek, man and woman, or freeman and slave. The idea of a universal principle (*t'ien li*) and a normalization of activity toward a golden mean were also known in China at the same time. (*T'ien* suggests "Heaven").

The Hellenistic Age

With the death of Alexander in 323 B.C., the Hellenistic Age began. Some fifty years of struggle among his generals and their successors in the initial period resulted in three empires: the Seleucids in the East, Ptolemies in Egypt and the Levant and the Macedonians in Greece and Asia Minor. A creative middle phase (from 280-160 B.C.) gave way to decline and Roman influence in the period 160-30 B.C.

The educated classes across this great area communicated in the Greek koine language, adapting a common Greek culture to their local conditions. High levels of trade fostered wealth and cultural dissemination. Such trade and communication cut many loose from their roots and promoted a selfish individualism, rather than the civic spirit that had formerly been evident in the Greek city-state. Larger cities were built, again favoring cosmopolitan commerce and personal alienation.

There was a fusion of eastern and western ideas. From the East came the idea of ruler-worship. The Greeks already thought of the political and religious community as being the same. The idea of a powerful and remote ruler taking on aspects of Zeus fit with this view. Great power did inhere in the ruler, who owned vast lands and his subjects. The word *soter* (Savior) was used for him, as it would be for Jesus several centuries later.

The Middle Period (280-160 B.C.) was prosperous from trade and was stimulated by the communication that went with it.

The prevailing attitude has been described as a restless optimism dominated by realism, rationalism and science. Such was the culture of the Hellenized elite. Most of the population, uneducated, could not share in this attitude.

Eastern softness weakened the Greeks, as did the availability of slave labor. Philosophies fitting the new circumstances developed. Cynicism, Epicureanism, and, especially, Stoicism, developed. Cynicism urged a cosmopolitan independence. Epicureanism sought a peaceful life away from political involvement. Stoicism urged following the laws of nature and would have its adherents act to promote such an ordered world.

Heraclitus indicates some of the thinking that was to be embraced by the Stoics. Zeno of Citium (c. 300 B.C.) founded the Stoic school. Time was a dimension in a cyclical, repeating, universe (although a utopia was described, the linear progress of humanity to such a Paradise was not eschatologically envisioned).

Many were the names of God. Reason was seen as a creative fire (*pneuma*) within the individual and within the universe. *Logos* was the primary symbol for God, but Zeus, creative fire, ether, reason of the world, providence, deity, order and law of nature all meant the same thing. Among educated people, some Epicureans said that gods existed, but that they did not involve themselves in the affairs of men.

In the later Hellenistic Age, the individual felt alone and helpless. Men lived for themselves. Demagogues pandered to the mob and Greece was conquered. Arbitrary chance seemed to rule. People first tried magic and then leaned to fatalism. There was a search for both realism and magic, coupled with a desire to withdraw from the world. Materialism became important. Some then found joy and the hope of an afterlife in Dionysus.

Although the elites became Hellenized, there was a strong tendency for local ways to prevail. In Egypt, Ptolemy I sought to unify the Hellenic outlook with the native religion and identified Serapis with Zeus. Later this became Osiris. (Some suggest that Osiris became merged with Jesus and Isis with

Mary).

The large Jewish population of Alexandria had lost their Hebrew language by 250 B.C. and scholars were brought in from Judea to translate the Bible into Greek for them. This was the Bible used by St. Paul and by Philo. To overcome the evident superstition, Philo used allegorical interpretations.

The distance of the ruler and the reduced civic spirit, let the poor approach subsistence levels. The disadvantaged increasingly sought hope in chance and in mystery religions, blaming their troubles on fate.

Optimism and science yielded to pessimism and superstition in the final Hellenistic period (160-30 B.C.). It is possible that the void of such alienation could make welcome a doctrine of universal brotherhood. The Stoics talked egalitarianism, were solicitous of the downtrodden and preached reform to leaders. Will Durant assures us that, after Zeno of Tarsus, Stoicism became a theology, rather than a philosophy. We may suspect that a dominant philosophy represents the worldview of the times.

Is our age Hellenistic? The Judeo-Christian teleology envisions continually ascending progress toward a Kingdom of God on Earth, but the Stoics of ancient Greece and most oriental cosmologies view the universe as an ever-cycling repetition. The Greek experience shows us how changes in religion and philosophy reflected changes in the world.

To imagine an analogy between the development of Ancient Greece and the development of the West, one could compare the Roman Empire to the Mycenaean Age, find a similar 400 year Dark Age, note a recovery and revival marked by cathedral building, see a redevelopment of trade, towns and middle class, observe a similar Renaissance, note a rationalist Enlightenment, see the cultural pride of empire followed by the failing of old gods and the prevalence of opportunistic individualism. The parallels are interesting, but we are too close to say with certainty that our period corresponds to the Hellenistic Age.

The Judeo-Christian tradition projected a universe ruled by a stern father, mediated by prophets and leading to a Kingdom of God on Earth. Plato described a controlled collective and his ideas were adopted by St. Augustine, who contrasted the "City of God" with the "City of Man". From these beginnings, one can find the genesis of National Socialism and Marxist-Leninism- the principal secular, political, religions of the Twentieth Century.

In Iran, Zoroastrianism announced that Good would ultimately triumph over Evil. (The development of Christian mythology from these and other roots is well traced in W. R. Halliday's *The Pagan Background of Early Christianity* and in Northrup Frye's *The Great Code: the Bible as Literature*. M. A. Larson's *Story of Christian Origins* offers some different views.) With the Council of Nicaea (325 AD), a stern, authoritarian and Trinitarian father-god became fixed in Christianity.

Promising universal salvation and equality helped Christianity. In the 2nd Century, men believed in predestined fate. To provide hope, redemptive salvation was promised. Salvation (escape from fate and sin) was possible if one adopted the Christian belief system. Jesus was the activist leader of a group of Palestinian Jewish heretics. The Greekspeaking Paul, however, saw Christianity as a salvation religion for the world, not just for Israel.

Cynicism, confusion, and despair encouraged Christianity. In the First Century B.C., the Greek confidence in reason had degenerated to cynicism and a popular search for magic. Romans were confused about religion and the state. Hebrews saw their legalistic culture being overwhelmed by the Romans and foreign ways. Greek salvation doctrines appeared with Neo-Platonism, the Manicheans and the Gnostics. The time was right for a simplistic ideology of revolution and of hope. Christianity was the sequel, with its magic of miracles and proffered hope of conquering death.

Philo blends a divine order and a personal God. The mental expositions of the Greeks contrasted with the revealed prophetic voluntarism of Moses. Is impersonal law consistent with the will of a leader? Prophetic religion assumes a prophet-lawgiver. The Greeks would imagine an impersonal law, while Jews would look for the will of a living god. Philo (c. 30 AD) attempted a synthesis by identifying the personal God of the Jews with the divine order *(logos)* of the Greeks. Western development has been reflecting this mix ever since.

By the time of Marcus Aurelius (d.180 A.D.), the Stoic ideal of the brotherhood of man had become a general philosophy of the times. Since freedmen were becoming numerous, the worth of labor was more valued. In the temple, members of the popular mystery religions were an egalitarian group. Christianity was thus a symptom of a greater era of change.

To perfect man and unite with the absolute: As an idealized projection of man, God must be defined before the perfection of man can be attempted. Yet, we find that even the most ostensibly religious have difficulty defining "God". For Anaximander (546 B.C.), deity was the "boundless". Plato (340 B.C.), spoke of "perfect righteousness", the "One", or "beauty", and St. Augustine later claimed that by this Plato meant "God". Aristotle (322 B.C.) called the infinite "divine".

For the Stoics becoming like god meant becoming one with the universe, for god was seen as immanent and not transcendent. For all, the idea was to unite with the absolute. With Pythagoras (530 B.C.), man, the measure of all things, could seek perfection through philosophic contemplation. For Epicurius, the utility of religious contemplation lay in its ability to *free* man from a belief in the gods.

Materialism brings on superstition. In the First Century, B.C., the High Priest of the Romans explained that there were three sorts of religion: (a) The fictions of the poets (b) Philosophy (c) Materialism. The religion of the state (materialism) pervaded Roman society. Money made the man. This created a void and a desire for spiritual values. Paganism did not value irrational belief, but Christianity did. Today, again, cyclical reappearance of superstition could be the compensation for materialism.

Reincarnation is identification with the people. The reincarnation of the god might be seen as the only way of establishing a connection between the god and the people. This line of reasoning leads to the "living god" or "Christ preached" of the liberation theologians. Mao explained: "My God is the Chinese People".

By 1964, Pope Paul VI defined the Church not as the "Kingdom of God, but as the "people of God". "In Latin America, the overall problem is moving from an abstract and inherited faith to a more concrete and activist praxis. The relationship God is changing from a relationship to God to a relationship to the Kingdom of God" said Jon Sobrino, S.J., a Liberation Theologian.

Where is the Kingdom of God? Irenaeus, in the late Second Century, claimed that believing in an *earthly* paradise was a part of Christian belief. Paradise would be found in this world. The Church tried to destroy the writings of Irenaeus. Augustine announced that the Church, itself, constituted the millennium.

The Christian division of the world between God and Caesar had introduced a political source of friction that presaged centuries of conflict in Western society. The Patriarch of Constantinople, even concerning religious issues, obeyed the Emperor. This has been styled "caesaropapism". A clerical state is one in which the religion and the state are inseparable. This is found in Israel, some Muslim states, and, formerly, in Italy and Japan.

The Eastern and Anglican churches would subordinate themselves to the state. The Roman Church, on the other hand, would claim independence from and dominance of the government.

Eastern teleology is subjective while Western teleology is reformative. In Hindu and Buddhist belief, the worldview of the individual is considered to be a projection of his own feelings. One should strive to dissolve oneself in the ever-cycling universe. By contrast, the Judeo-Christian drive is to confront and reform society according to a revealed plan.

Greek thought influenced Islam. An effort was made to merge the ancient Persian writings with the tradition of Greek philosophy. In the Islamic view, knowledge is more important than love in perceiving the divine. By the 8th Century, Islam had become a closed theological society. Averroes (1150) said that a man ought never to attempt beyond his powers to comprehend scripture and that a philosopher ought never divulge to the masses his interpretation of truth. Some Moslems assert that Islam has stayed at the early medieval level, whereas Judaism and Christianity have experienced periods of self-examination and progress.

Christianity was initially revolutionary. The communist message appeared early in Christianity: "not a man among them claimed any of his possessions as his own, but everything was held in common... all who had property sold it and lay the money at the feet of the apostles; it was then distributed to any who stood in need". We are told that the Lord struck dead Ananias and his wife who withheld their portion. For Jesus, faith was linked to action: "I come to bring not peace". As Celsius noted, by denying the divinity of the emperor and of the local gods, the Christians coupled religion with political revolt.

After the Third Century, Christianity started to obtain government recognition and became concerned with suppressing heretical sects. A Christian basis for political revolt never disappeared. "True religion and undefiled is this, to make restitution of the Earth which hath been taken and held from the common people. I tell you Jesus Christ was the head Leveler" said Gerrard Winstanley, 1650.

Deism, Methodism and moderation prevailed in Britain. Thomas Jefferson, Benjamin Franklin and Thomas Paine were notable deists. Deism included a message of simple equality, optimism and reason. In Britain, Methodism coupled compassion with a moderate political outlook. Perhaps this helped Britain avoid the excesses of the French Revolution.

The universal church had discrepant praxis. The discrepancy between morality and practice was a significant factor leading to the Reformation in Germany. In 1838, the German, Strauss, spoke of changing history by deliberate deeds. Moving people together on a broad basis would change the ordinary secular community into a universal church. The world would be made divine through such "praxis". Thus were presaged the totalitarian civil religions.

Some Catholic Latin American clergymen called for revolution, rather than development. Operating from premises that were, for the most part, Marxian, theological arguments were phrased which showed Jesus as a revolutionary seeking to bring about a Kingdom of God in this world. The Resurrection is then preached as a symbol of "transforming oppression into the possibility of freedom".

If the Church were a revolutionary party, one could follow it through the successive stages of: adaptation and compromise; political promises and recruiting, repression of competing parties; co-opting competing ideologies; censorship; ideology changing with circumstances; intolerance; terror and totalitarianism. In the ontogeny of missionary activity among native peoples, one can see this phylogeny recapitulated.

The Roman Church gives us the history of a "party" that sought to dominate society and the state. The Eastern, Anglican and Lutheran churches and most non-fundamentalist religions of the world do not share this pretension. The important Church history of the West relates to the exercise of power concerning societal or institutional objectives.

The developments of revolutionary theology and of liberation theology show a religious movement as popular philosophy with an ideological framework for political action. As loyalty to the state increasingly becomes a secular or civic religion, dissent may increasingly find a non-secular religious expression. Similarly, insecurity may find compensatory expression in the expansion of fundamentalist religions.

Alliance with the establishment is frequent. "The powers that be are ordained of God and whosoever resisteth that power, resisteth the will of God" (*Romans* 13:1). In 311, Galerius granted religious toleration to the Christians. In 313, Constantine made Christianity an officially authorized religion. By 380, Theodosius had made Christianity the sole official religion of the Empire. Christian leaders then found scriptural reasons for supporting the government. "Render unto Caesar those things which are Caesar's" (*Matt*. 12:21). "The authorities are in God's service" (*Romans* 13:6).

As civil government disintegrated, the bishops took over some administration and fostered loyalty to the local leaders. Much later, the encyclicals of Leo XIII made it clear that the form of government was of little moral consequence to the Church, but that Christians must support the authority of government.

Medieval Christian doctrine was a fundamental aspect of feudalism. This implied a great landowner as boss of everything within a large area- the *oikos*, or *latifundia*. Catholic tradition split society into leaders ("*maiores*") and those whose duty was to obey ("*minores*"). Priesthoods favored patriarchal organization because they hoped to influence the human leader. For similar reasons, social systems that transcend the economic are favored by priesthoods today, and the Catholic hierarchy is suspicious of capitalism.

In *The Protestant Ethic and the Spirit of Capitalism*, Max Weber said that **Calvinism in Geneva sought to control the individual not merely in matters of religion but in all aspects of private and public life**. The Puritans began by seeking to "purify" the Church of England, then became more revolutionary and suggested that their government should rule as "Christ's officers". When the Pilgrim Fathers went to America, they signed a "covenant" in which they constituted themselves an ecclesiastical state.

The Church asserted temporal power. Constantine let the Church have some power. By the time of Theodosius I (d. 395), Catholicism was established as the sole religion, paganism was forbidden and the government was employed to persecute heretics. Augustine made some pronouncements about the state being subject to the Church and the state being obligated to persecute the enemies of the Church. Fifty years later, Leo I was asserting the supremacy of the papacy over all rulers.

Since the relations of men in society have been defined as "moral questions" by the popes, it follows that politics and economics are within the purview claimed by the popes. Pius XI (d.1939), in his encyclical *Restructuring the Social Order*, asserted: "it is our right and our duty to deal authoritatively with social and economic problems... our weighty office of propagating... the entire moral law demands that both social and economic questions be brought within our supreme jurisdiction in so far as they relate to moral issues".

God (says the church) is over the state. "Under the Paje there is no difference between religious and political matters. I am the representative of God and your commander on Earth" said Iran's Ayatollah Khomeini. (As such, Khomeini later edicted that the rules of the Koran were subject to the interests of the Iranian state). "The state, as a creature of God, cannot determine the extent of its power, but must accept the limitations imposed by God" said *The Catholic Almanac*, 1950.

Leo XIII (1888) thought separation of church and state a "fatal principle". In 1948, U.S. Archbishop McNichols explained the desirability of a union of Church and state, with the state serving the Church as needed. During Vatican II, the Pope repeated to the assembly that every priest has three roles within his community, those of king, of teacher and of priest.

The Confucian Sazan Kan put it plainly: "there are many religions with many norms, but they all practice the trick of setting the priest above the ruler. It is most apparent that this is harmful to our political ideology."

God gives the right to revolt, when the priest says so. It is the priestly hierarchy who announce to the faithful that the state is the creature of God and who then interpret God's will to the faithful. "The right to command is required by the moral order and has its source in God. If the civil authorities legislate or allow anything that is contrary to that order and therefore contrary to the will of God, the laws cannot be binding, for we must obey God rather than men." Pope John XXIII, *Pacem in Terris*, 1963.

A similar rationale has been advanced in China, where the ruler was long called the Son of Heaven. The Heavens warned him with natural calamities if he was not doing as he should. "The ruler of the Hsia has committed innumerable crimes and it is the will of Heaven to slay him, as I fear God, I do not hesitate" said T'ang (1752 B.C.). The T'angs were later disposed of with similar reasoning.

"Worldview" has been defined as "faith". The Roman Catholic Church claims infallible "knowledge" within the realm of faith and "morals". "Faith" is defined as man's worldview ("perception of God") and "morals" are defined as "relations with man and with God" (all social and political conduct). "What the Catholic Church teaches and declares regarding the social life and relationships of men is beyond question for all time valid" John XXIII, *Mater & Magister*, 1961.

In *Reconstructing the Social Order* (1931), Pius XI claimed that **all social and economic questions were moral matters** and "it is our right and our duty to deal authoritatively with them". Pius IX, in *Pastor Aeternus* (1870) claimed that the faithful, separately as well as collectively, were subject to the Pope, not only in faith and morals, but also in matters of government everywhere in the world.

The Secretary of the Pontifical Justice and Peace Commission, Msgr. Gremillion, summed up the current state of affairs: "Natural law" is postulated as the essential nature of the human person, especially as reflected in social relationships. "Principal among these relationships are marriage, economics and politics."

If the ruler cooperates, the priests will keep the faithful in line. For an unfriendly ruler, this pressure is exerted as opposition, including mass demonstrations, boycott and the absolution to revolt. Pope Gregory and the German emperor Henry IV, quarreled. Gregory declared Henry deposed and absolved Henry's subjects of their allegiance to Henry. Pope Paul III announced that all Englishmen who sided with Henry VIII were slaves and were to be free booty to any Crusader who could capture them. Papal action declared Queen Elizabeth I excommunicated and dethroned. The "authorization" to revolt appears to convey the suggestion and authority to do so.

In his *Chief Duties of Christian Citizens* (1890), Leo XIII claimed that a citizen who obeyed a law that the clergy opposed was guilty of a crime. If the clergy opposed it, said the Pope, the Christian had a positive duty to resist the law of the state. Paul VI, in his *Populorum Progressio* (1967) explained that revolution was to be avoided, "except where there is a manifest, long-standing tyranny which would do great damage to fundamental personal rights". The Catholic Church was very recently successful in deposing the government of the Philippines.

In the *Instruction on Christian Freedom and Liberation* (Mar. 22, 1986), the Vatican drew nearer to the position of the Liberation Theologians: "one cannot passively accept... groups that take over the state apparatus... and impose an imported ideology contrary to the culture of the people." Thus, it is "perfectly legitimate" that those oppressed by the "wealthy or politically powerful" take action through "morally licit means", even using armed struggle as a last resort. In February of 1986, the Catholic bishops of the Philippines called for the peaceful disobedience of the people, saying "a government which uses fraud to gain power has no moral basis... thus the people have a serious moral obligation... to actively resist." In a few days, the President fled and a revolutionary government was proclaimed.

The Church again as revolutionary: "Action on behalf of justice and participation in the transformation of the world seem to us a necessary part of preaching the Gospel of the Church's mission for the redemption of the human race and its liberation from every oppressive situation" (Synod of Bishops, *Justice in the World*, 1971).

Politics are morals. In the United States, Cardinal Manning said "politics are morals on the largest scale". The special significance of this statement lies in the hierarchy's claim of obedience from the faithful even unto civil revolt, should the state act in a fashion the hierarchy considers "immoral". When there is irreconcilable conflict between Church and state, according to the *Catholic Encyclopedia*, the decision of the Church must prevail among the faithful.

The attempt to exercise temporal power through the control of legislators customarily takes two forms: indoctrination and pressure. Indoctrination takes place in the schools and institutions of higher learning run by religious orders. Activation of mental connections formed in the previous indoctrination effects the control. There is also the handle of guilt, wherein a legislator tormented by a sin may become over-anxious to implement Church policies. For example, Cannon 1118 made it compulsory for Catholic legislators to oppose divorce laws. Special claims are made on judges; see, for example, Msgr. Francis Connell's book, *Morals in Politics and the Professions*, or Father John D. Davis' book, *The Moral Obligations of Catholic Civil Judges*.

The proclamation of holy war is the last resort of the pretension to priestly power. In fundamentalist Moslem nations, the potential for armed *jihad* is always present. In the modern West, it may be masked as a "just war", or as a campaign for something calling for the repression of something else.

Power is a major issue in such "religious" exercises. The Crusades, for example, have to be assessed in relation to Rome's desire to subjugate the Eastern Church, the financial aggrandizement of the Church, and the weakening of princes thus deprived of their knights. The faithful are motivated by ideology and their elites by the prospect of profit and participation in power.

Uniformity is useful. "God wishes that one should put aside all humanity when it is a question of striving for his glory", said Calvin. After the St. Bartholomew's massacre of Protestants in France, Catherine Medici of France proposed that Elizabeth do the same thing to Catholics in England, uniformity of belief and control being useful to monarchs.

Independent thinkers disturb uniformity. Meister Eckhart (c.1300) announced an independent spiritualism. His views presaged the German mysticism that would alienate many from the Roman Church and from the Holy Roman Empire. The year 1325 saw Marsilius of Padua publish his *Defensor Pacis*, which claimed liberty of conscience. Marsilius further asserted that the source and ultimate residence of all power lay in the people. Pope Clement VI called him "the greatest heretic of the age".

Independence was Repressed

Bible and king replaced a universal church. In England, John Wycliffe spoke (1325) of the primacy of scripture, of the primacy of the monarch, and of the likelihood of predestination. These three theses directly challenged papal power, which relied on priesthood, pope and personal behavior. Luther advocated monarchial, as opposed to papal, supremacy. (In the Soviet Union, in the 1980's, Wycliffe's *Bible Commentaries* were seized as "anti-Soviet").

The Parlement of Paris, in 1334, announced that, even in spiritual matters, the Pope was not the superior of the King. In England, later in the same century, John Wycliffe began to preach against the wealth of the Church and in favor of the right of the Crown to redistribute such wealth. In an interesting German variant, Luther is said to have declared that, since the power of the King was given to him by God, the King was excused from usual Christian ethical obligations defined by the Church.

In the early 16th Century, control by the Roman Catholic Church was variously challenged. The most serious of these was Luther's Reformation. With the *Act of Supremacy*, Henry VIII declared the English Church to be a part of the political structure of the English state. And, in 1543, Copernicus published his findings concerning the revolution of the planets.

In Naples, in 1775, the administration took over for itself the appointment of clerics and determined the curriculum of the schools. In France, Church property was nationalized. Many religious orders were dissolved. The state decided to take over the payment of clerical salaries. The Civil Constitution of 1790 provided that bishops and clergy were to be popularly elected.

The Catholic Church advocated Fascism. Pius XI thought Communism a grave danger and allied himself with Fascism, which, in part, sought to implement Papal social encyclicals. He publicly expressed hope for "the new order of Europe being founded by Herr Hitler and Signor Mussolini". He congratulated Franco: "Raising our hearts to God, we thank him and your Excellency for the desired victory of Catholic Spain".

Support was given Hitler government by the Catholic Church, particularly in the Fulda statement of 1935. Wherein the combined German hierarchy announced support for Hitler. Upon learning of Hitler's death, the primate ordered solemn requiem masses throughout Germany. In the Catholic system, the maintenance of the social and political order is deemed necessary for the common good. Performance of civic duty thus becomes a moral obligation. In Germany, the Lutheran north and center were more active in support of Hitler than the Catholic south.

Modernism sought to reconcile modern scientific and historical knowledge with the traditional Catholic worldview. Loisy, for example, rejected the supernatural and sought to explain religion in a personal, rather than in a transcendental, manner. Loisy was excommunicated and all clerics were required to take an anti-modernist oath. Much of the modern world was strange to the worldview of the Catholic hierarchy.

Problems included: Protestantism and scientific thought, the secular national state, and the changed class structure of industrial society. This reality contrasted with the ideological view that Catholicism was a closed and perfect system.

Scripture allows interpretation, but dogma does not. Canonical scriptures contain revelations and traditions, whereas dogmas are priestly interpretations of their meaning. Would literacy and metaphysics be reserved to the priesthood? Protestants have allowed more independent possession and interpretation of scripture than have Catholics.

Disloyalty was sedition and heresy for National Socialism, since only the statement of the Fuhrer mattered. His latest words became the official orthodoxy. Scriptures are useful, for they provide a basis from which deviations can be measured. Deviation from sacred text, as decided by the establishment, is one measure of heresy. When one has only the latest words of the leader as dogma, then disloyalty takes the place of heresy.

Heresy can also be sedition. If a religious system includes a total worldview including politics, heresy becomes also seditious and treasonable. Heresy is a useful instrument for effecting control through terror for publicizing the correct official view and for removing political challengers. It allows establishment officials to protect their position and to increase their power.

The guilt ridden or insecure may relieve their angst by projecting their guilt onto the heretic. The insecure population at large may find some satisfaction in the berating of those who dare to question and threaten beliefs that make up the accepted world-view.

The concept of heresy is said not exist in the East Indian religions, for they feel that there must be some basis of truth in every heretical view. By contrast, Aquinas urged death for heretics who could not be made to recant. "It is much worse to corrupt the faith than to counterfeit money". Bonaventura helped to incorporate this idea of "convert or kill" into Cannon Law and the practices of the Inquisition. Orleans, in 1022, was first to smell the burning flesh of heretics.

"Opposition to this government will be considered opposition to Islamic laws and regulations. Therefore, I am warning those that may take action against this government that the punishment for them will be very harsh according to Islamic jurisprudence. Any action against this government will be considered blasphemy" said the Ayatollah Khomeini.

In his *Constitutions of Melfi* (1231), Frederick II said that, in a model state, "it was sacrilege to discuss the judgments, decisions and edicts of the Emperor." Frederick II considered revolt against his reign to be heresy, because he was appointed by God's will. Burning of heretics became law in the Papal territories in 1231. The Empire started burning heretics in 1233.

***Atwood's Case* held blasphemy to be sedition.** Prior to 1382, English common law was not concerned with religious opinion. By the time of *Atwood's Case* (1616), it was held indictable for a man to say "your religion is a new religion, preaching is but prattling- prayer once a day would be more edifying". Such words as those uttered by Atwood were considered seditious as an attack upon the King as head of the established Church.

Such an utterance was also seen as soliciting a breach of the peace. The Star Chamber, in *Traske's Case* (1618) found the heretic guilty "not for his gross and superstitious opinions... but for making factions which tend to sedition and commotion and for open scandalizing of King and clergy."

Taylor's Case (1676) provided: "to say that religion is a cheat is to dissolve all those obligations whereby civil societies are preserved... the Christian religion is part of the law itself." *Regina v. Woolston* (1729) held "to say that an attempt to subvert the established religion is not punishable by those laws upon which it is established is an absurdity."

As the power of the Church declined and the power of the state increased, there was a need to make blasphemy punishable by the state rather than the Church. Thus, the emphasis would shift from heresy to breach of the peace. By 1981, the applicable Canadian criminal statute provided that there would be no offense of blasphemy "if the publication were made "in good faith" and "with decent language". In 1984, the operative statute dealt with "hate propaganda", but the Blasphemous Libel section remained on the books.

Tolerance is not freedom. Vatican II was to focus on the Church, on its renewal and on ecumenism. The Eastern Orthodox churches refused to attend. An argument developed over the question of religious liberty. Seventeen cardinals favored the general freedom of religious expression, excepting only the right to proselytize. The official position finally adopted was that the goal of ecumenical discussion required tolerance, not liberty. Paul VI proposed a "dialogue of the Church with the contemporary world" as an additional goal for Vatican II. John XXIII wanted to open dialogue with all levels of the Marxist world.

The Vatican returned to socialism. "The right to private property is subordinate to the right to common use, to the fact that goods are meant for everyone" John Paul II, *Laborem Exorcens*. "John Paul II may be described as the first socialist pope", said Newsweek on June 20, 1983. He advocated the virtues of planned economies and the priority of labor over capital. This was followed in 1988 by *Sollictudo rei socialis* and, in 1991, by *Cestesimus annus* and, most recently, by the Council for Justice and Peace. The problem became how to secure justice and social security for workers in the capitalist countries with their varied stages of development.

John Paul II was said to agree with Marx and to break with Catholic doctrine in that "through labor, man creates his own history and becomes the person he ought to be". John Paul II was a Polish worker and identified with workers. His encyclical *Laborem Exorcens* instructs that all capital is to be controlled by and used for the benefit of workers. It also calls for local community ownership of capital and centralized economic planning. The encyclical *Populorum Progressio* (People's Progress, 1967) says no one has a right to anything he does not personally need for his family, when there are others in need. Paul VI sought to apply that principle to economics and the relations of nations.

John Paul II firmly believed in the Marxian view that capitalism alienates man. Man ought to be the *subject* of work, rather than only the *instrument*. When man is only the instrument, then this should properly be called "capitalism", says the Pope. As John Paul saw it, there is a real conflict between labor and capital, but Marxism transformed this real conflict into a class struggle.

Max Scheler claimed that pre-existing ideas must be received by a social movement that needs an ideology. Myth must be followed by movement. Thus, the thinker must, to "think", join a movement. Since all men share in the divine nature, they achieve union through action reflecting sympathy and love with the oneness of the universe. Here, we have a double dissolution of self: into the movement to obtain the thought, and from the thought to the unity of the universe. Max Scheler influenced papal thinking.

Bishop Lafleche, in 1866, outlined Quebec ultramontanism. He saw the Church, the family and the state as all being of divine origin. Since the Church spoke for God, it was superior to the state and to the family. The nation, Lafleche claimed, was formed by language, tradition and faith. Since faith was the most important component, the nation had to be supervised by the Church. Lafleche also said that, through its priests, the Church must help the people choose the right candidates. Supervision required control of education, to insure continuance of the faith. As a symptom of growing clerical power, the Quebec Ministry of Education was abolished in 1875. The Ministry was not restored until 1964.

By the mid-1960's, poets and politicians had taken the lead in expressing the feeling of the Quebec people. Priests no longer led. A quiet Revolution had taken place.

State vs. Church

In 1837, the Prussian King imprisoned the Archbishop of Cologne and other Catholic bishops for their refusal to compromise on the question of mixed marriages. In reaction, there developed an ultramontane movement with loyalty to Rome rather than to the state.

Bismarck, in 1872, launched his "cultural struggle" against the influence of the Catholic Church. School inspectors were created, seminaries were placed under state control, the Catholic Bureau in the Ministry of Education was abolished and some recalcitrant bishops were imprisoned.

The bishops of France recommended, in 1925, that Catholics unite, emulate Communist methods, and go on strike to ruin the economy of the country. Later, when the Third Republic collapsed and Marshal Petain, a Catholic, took over the government: (a) Priests were allowed to teach in the schools. (b) Religious instruction compulsory in schools. (c) Laws against abortion were passed. (d) Freemasons were outlawed.

Mexico warred against the Church. In Mexico, the clergy were the major opposition to the government. All Church property except the Church buildings themselves were ordered confiscated by Juarez. Article 130 of the 1917 Mexican Constitution provided: (a) Ministers shall be licensed as are other professions. (b) Only native born Mexicans can serve as ministers. (c) No ministers may engage in political activities. (d) Degrees from religious institutions shall not be recognized. (e) Church premises shall not be used for political purposes.

The early reaction of the hierarchy was to call on the faithful to "obey God rather than man" (i.e., to revolt). The hierarchy then decided to mobilize public opinion by forbidding priests to conduct religious services. These efforts by the Church to overturn the Constitution were not successful.

As after the Revolution in France, the anti-clerical government in Mexico offered little economic opportunity to aspiring young educated Catholics. In France, the Wars of the Vendee sought to advance the interests of the Catholic bourgeoisie. In Mexico, after WWI, physical revolution by the Cristeros was next. A member of the British Foreign Office reported that the Cristeros were especially intolerant of school mistresses, whom, they were told, taught "socialism and sex education".

In 1937, Pius XI issued his Catholic Action Plan for Mexico as the encyclical *Firmissimum Constantium*. Agents were enjoined to work in silence. Parents were told to keep children away from school. Catholics were enjoined to vote in blocs. Catholic Action is officially defined as: "the cooperation of the laity in the apostolate of the hierarchy." Today, Opus Dei is said to perform in a similar, but more clandestine fashion.

Vigilante action is envisioned. "Law in a pluralistic society must not penalize one minority group in order to please another. It is because courts are slow and lax that the 'social dynamism' of the Legion of Decency and the National Organization for Decent Literature is necessary", said Father Gardiner in his *Catholic View of Censorship*

"The unchecked development of false theories results in ethical aberration... Catholic patriots, entrusted with the government of a Catholic state, will not shrink even from repressive measures in order to secure the domination of Catholic principles among their countrymen", said Father R. A. Knox in *The Belief of Catholics* (Sheed & Ward, 1943).

Since the late 1800's, papal encyclicals have advocated the use of government to achieve "social justice". Pius XI organized Catholic Action to effect his social and political programs. The organization taught that party politics were unclean, that it was necessary to take action to change society, and that governments would later adjust to the new social order achieved.

Catholic Action was described as a "lay apostolate" working for a totally Catholic civilization in which the Church will be "the mistress and guide of all other societies", said Father J. J. O'Toole in *What is Catholic Action* (Paulist Press, 1940). For Luigi Civardi, in the *Catholic Action Manual*, it is an "army involved in a holy war for religion".

Today, it is Opus Dei that is described as a "lay apostolate" on the road to sanctity. J. J. Thierry explained that key posts in society should be in the hands of Opus Dei members, a "White Masonry", rather than be in the hands of "opportunists, communists or Masons". In 1985 it was said to have 85,000 members, to control 479 universities, 694 newspapers, 52 radio and television stations, 78 publicity agencies, etc.

The Jesuit magazine *America*, in 1928, published a step-by-step example of how, with one priest, a letterhead, and a couple of laymen, the business department and the managing editor of a publication could be forced into cooperation. There is a difference between censorship, which is done legally, and "control" which is effected otherwise. Pius XII, in a 1957 encyclical, assigned to the bishops the responsibility for "supervising radio and television, as well as films".

"The very root of philosophical liberalism is an erroneous affirmation of the autonomy of the individual in his activity, his motivation and the exercise of his liberty" (Paul VI, *Octogesima Adveniens*, 1971) "The unchecked liberalism of capitalism leads to a dictatorship rightly denounced by Pius XI as the "international imperialism of money".

The main argument used to support Church power is common to totalitarianisms. The institution of the party and the hierarchy must be preserved. In doing this, we are serving "god", whether "god" is the Chinese people, the revealed ends of the historical process, the Revolution, or the God of a church.

The Eastern Orthodox rationale would say that with Christ becoming man (John 1:14) all life became a striving for the sacred and that secularism ceased to exist. The state would then exist to preserve law and order, to defend the Faith and the homeland with the Faith shaping and guiding society.

14

TOTALITARIANISM

There are clerical and secular "political religions". Emilio Gentile notes that a political movement tends to make politics sacred. The totalitarian movement becomes the main source of values for individual and mass behavior. The movement and its values are then exalted as the supreme ethic.

The sacralization of politics (variously defined as civil religion, civic religion, and political religion) is an element of the totalitarian phenomenon. This process takes place when a political movement claims a sacred status for an earthly entity (the nation, the country, the state, humanity, society, race, proletariat, history, liberty, or revolution) and renders it an absolute principle of collective existence, considers it the main source of values for individual and mass behavior, and exalts it as the supreme ethical precept of public life. It thus becomes an object for veneration and dedication, even to the point of self-sacrifice" (Gentile, 2000).

Totalitarianism has irrational aspects. Totalitarian ideology may call for actions that are irrational according to practical standards. Hitler's claim that Germany deserved to be destroyed if its war did not succeed, or the Soviet desire to prove the validity of environmental heredity (Lysenkoism) are examples of such irrationality. "The greatness of every mighty organization embodying an idea in this world lies in the religious fanaticism and intolerance with which, fanatically convinced of its own right, it intolerantly imposes its will against all others," said Adolf Hitler.

Totalitarianism seeks complete, total, control of the individual and of society. Since this can never be achieved, there can be no limit to the demands of totalitarianism, and it must exhibit pleonexia, a continuing search for greater power and control. In this, totalitarianism differs from authoritarianism and from simple tyranny.

Mind control is an aspect of both supernatural and secular religions. The Jesuits Ryan and Boland gave examples of this in their books written in the 1950s concerning Catholic education. Coercion and repetition were said to lead to belief and compliance. *The Captive Mind* of C. Milosz (1953) shows how the repetition of slogans penetrates the consciousness until the individual is no longer sure whether he really believes what he was once feigning. The "World of the party" has become his reality.

Operating upon and on behalf of the mass, totalitarians can claim to be democratic. An identity is claimed between leader and people, between party and nation. The attempt to effect moral education and to coerce conscience is an early indication of totalitarianism.

Ideology outweighs economics. Party leaders must be ahead of changes in policy, and this puts more stress on them than on the general public. To the totalitarian state, the principles of the ideology are more important than economics.

Total control of the individual is sought. Authoritarianism requires only political passivity, while totalitarianism forces pretended enthusiasm. In China, even control of popular music was sought. Stalin, also, was concerned with the moods generated by Soviet classical music. Music is symbolic, non-verbal communication involving the right brain. It tends to escape totalitarian control.

http://www.cerebromente.org.br/n15/mente/musica.html.

Totalitarian rule promotes regression to perpetual childhood. In 1835, Tocqueville speculated that democracy in America might lead to a form of government that would offer an "escape from freedom" into a perpetual childhood. Talk about a "Good Shepherd" suggests that the masses are like sheep. The shepherds, Hitler and Stalin, eliminated choice and made things simple for the masses. The letter of a German soldier shortly before World War II expressed the poignant thought: "We Germans are so happy- we are free of freedom". Relieving and avoiding mental tension is a fundamental human drive.

Total control is sought. Totalitarianism must eliminate, rather than merely restrict, freedom. Liberalism is more of a threat to totalitarianism than is mass democracy. For the individual would have the responsibility of choice. No uncontrolled organizations can be allowed. The individual must be convinced of the hopelessness of independence or resistance.

Individuals must be isolated from independent thought. Except in mass meetings, the individual is to feel isolated from others and from the government. Through indoctrination, external repression will eventually be supplanted by an induced internal repression. The oppressed person may begin to view himself as a child. Perhaps a repressed rage will develop. Will he identify with the system or seek to circumvent it?

Totalitarianism requires terror. "We have never rejected terror in principle, and, indeed, we cannot do so," said Lenin. Utility is sacrificed to ideology, so political compromise and dialogue are viewed with contempt. An impatient and intolerant attitude may welcome terror as a rapid way to eliminate a danger. A system of terror, however, generates anxiety and threat. Thus, a regenerative system producing ever-greater excesses is launched. An American Communist leader testified that there was one characteristic that all the party leaders shared: *a feeling of fright.*

Random terror makes one feel helpless. Does the logic of terror require that it be applied only to specific targets? Or, is terror most effective when used randomly, against the population at large? Random terror is best for bringing on a feeling of helplessness, for there is nothing one can do to avoid a random threat. The lack of any law other than the leader's whim also leaves one helpless.

Unlimited pleonexia is invoked in striving for unattainable goals. The feeling of helplessness and futility extends even to Party members. Political police and concentration camps were common to Hitler's Germany and to Stalin's Russia. Conformity, coordination and sequencing characterized the state. Totalitarian ideology is more interested in changing human nature than in changing the physical world. Since it seeks to control man's total personality, it can never fully achieve its ends. There can, therefore, be no limit to the means employed to strive for total domination.

Totalitarianism requires surrender and dissolution of self. One can voluntarily accept slavery. Rousseau advocated this in theory. Hitler demonstrated it by inviting voluntary submission to absolute authority. The phenomenon is also evidenced in certain religious orders. Such voluntary submission lets the authorities experiment. The Sanskrit word "Sraddha" is said to mean giving oneself wholeheartedly to the direction of a man of superior wisdom. This is the nature of the surrender expected under totalitarianism. The stress of choice is removed and the superego is vested in the leader. If one joins a well-organized group, the dissolution of self and the absolution of conscience is effected. The Party knows the "true interests" of the citizen.

The born-again New Man realizes himself by becoming a part of the teleology of history. History is seen as the culmination of the ideology, leading to a realization of the Millennium or the Rapture. By joining the movement or embracing the ideology one receives an identity, but the individual also seeks to forge a significant new identity while meeting the criteria of the ideology. Thus, there is an impetus to strive for the perfection of the ideal "New Man".

The ego investment in the new ideology requires one to ignore or to deny unfavorable facts. History can move in mysterious ways its wonders to achieve. Teleological ends can justify unpleasant means. The commitment to ego preservation can become so great that one may interpret disasters as favorable developments. The Great Purge of 1934 was celebrated by some of its victims as the realization of the teleology (Hellbeck, 2006) as, today, many Christian fundamentalists welcome Armageddon as a condition immediately precedent to being swept to heaven by the Rapture.

Totalitarianism uses the leader as priest-king. The totalitarian leader leads ceremonies in the manner of a priest. Thus, the form of the priest-king is recalled. Jung suggests that society needs the "magically effective figure" to channel its energy. As symbol, father, and surrogate self, the leader manipulates the will to power and the will to submit of the individual.

Masses need a supreme leader, classes do not. Ritual and ceremony provide the appearance of mass consent. Totalitarian movements are of masses, rather than of classes with specific interests. The leader appears to express the desire of the mass. If belief wanes, then the mechanics of terror and repression replace voluntarism. A movement has then become a totalitarian dictatorship.

The will of the leader becomes the law of the moment. "The Fuhrer himself alone is today and in the future the German reality and its law," said Martin Heidegger, Rector of Freiburg University, in 1934. In 1943: "the command of the Fuhrer is the absolute center of the present legal order". Can there be a totalitarian system that does not express the will of one man, the leader? Can a committee really rule?

The totalitarian state can function with normal law, adjusting when the leader makes decisions. "Dictatorship", said Lenin, is "unlimited power resting on force and unrestricted by laws". Modern totalitarianism has technology and a rootless mass on which to use it.

The elite- the Party, the priesthood, or the elect- form the vanguard in implementing the leader's worldview. Non-party leadership is denigrated. Competition is not welcome, for theoretical and for selfish reasons. Said one refugee from Communist China: "I realized that the Communists had no sense of fairness or justice. They insisted on beating down any person who was looked up to outside party circles." Nor is it welcome to note that having an elite is inconsistent with egalitarian democracy.

Can the cell replace the movement? Benhabib asserts that "the new unit of totalitarianism is the terrorist cell, not the Party or the Movement". This is a particularly disconcerting insight.

The mass lives in a world of organized ideology. When full control is achieved, propaganda can be replaced by indoctrination. The party line now offers a total explanation of history. The controllers will censor or reinterpret uncomfortable facts. The new technology makes possible more complete indoctrination, and achieves faster creation of mass opinion. But, newer technology, may make it more difficult to keep out unwanted information.

The Roman Church as totalitarian. Bertrand Russell, in the New York Times of Nov. 17, 1950, characterized a totalitarian system:

(1) Adherence to a rigid and static system of doctrine, part of which is doubtful and part of which is demonstrably false.
(2) Use of persecution as a means of enforcing orthodoxy.
(3) Believing that salvation can be found only within the faith.
(4) The true faith must be spread throughout the world- by force if necessary.
(5) The priesthood alone has the right to interpret the scriptures.

Russell was speaking of the Roman Catholic Church, but his criteria could be applied to totalitarianism generally. The indoctrinated totalitarian cannot tolerate a contrary opinion. The source of contrary opinion must be personally reviled if it cannot be refuted. Totalitarians make unpleasant neighbors

Totalitarianism defined. Gentile suggests (2000) that 'totalitarianism' can be taken as meaning: a process in political domination undertaken by a revolutionary movement, with an integralist conception of politics, that aspires toward a monopoly of power and constructs a new state based on a single-party regime, with the chief objective of conquering society. Aiming to regenerate the human being and create the new man, dedicated to the realization of the policies of the totalitarian party. The ultimate goal is to create a new civilization beyond the Nation-State.

The revolutionary party is organized for hierarchy and obedience. It has a complex of beliefs, dogmas, myths, rituals and symbols that define the meaning and purpose of existence in this world. Good and evil are defined in keeping with the goals of the Party and no other ideologies or parties are tolerated. Power is concentrated in the Party and the charismatic leader and the indoctrinated masses are used to effect the goals of the Party. Coercion, demagoguery, pedagogy and elimination of unwanted ideas and individuals is practiced.

Establishing totalitarianism under Hitler and Stalin:

(1) A minority seizes power by force or constitutional fraud.
(2) The minority party ultimately takes over complete control.
(3) The party constitutes the social elite.
(4) Economic planning and control is centrally exercised.
(5) A massive military establishment is created.
(6) All competing organizations are rendered impotent.
(7) Massive propaganda efforts are undertaken.
(8) The party seeks to make a "new man" and a new society.
(9) Censorship is imposed in all fields.
(10) Terror is instituted.
(11) There is no legal limit to the demands that can be imposed.
(12) Independent organizations are suppressed.

There is a general etiology of totalitarianism. (1) Rootless and isolated individuals join a mass movement. (2) The bureaucracy controls the economy. (3) Ideology, rather than power, motivates. (4) There is full control of communications. (5) An official ideology, millenarian and intolerant, is fostered. (6) The short term is sacrificed for the long term. (7) The rulers have unlimited coercive power. (8) A future order of society is defined. (9) Parties with competing ideologies are not allowed. (10) An individual is not offered free choices. (11) A closed and integrated society is established. (12) Supreme rulers are created and deemed infallible. (13) The leader is venerated and deemed to act for all.

Totalitarianism a Checklist

(1) Leader, party, people said to have same interest?
(2) No limits to government power?
(3) Is an overall worldview articulated?
(4) Is the worldview total and complete?
(5) Is principle more important than the concrete?
(6) Is dogmatic principle applied to daily living?
(7) Is the future emphasized more than the present?
(8) Is a revolutionary change of values proposed?
(9) Are all resources of society mobilized?
(10) Are inquiries made into the minds of people?
(11) Are uncontrolled organizations repressed?
(12) Can the party or the leader overrule the law?
(13) Is terror characteristic of the government?
(14) Is making a "new kind of man" a public goal?
(15) Is a surrender of self to the collective sought?
(16) Is the society closed to outside information?
(17) Are there big attempts at social engineering?
(18) Is there a myth of historical necessity?
(19) Is there a supra-national missionary sense?
(20) Is there a vanguard that must decide for all?
(21) Is individualism condemned?
(22) Is the revolutionary change demanded?
(23) Are policies implemented to extremes?

Totalitarianism-general summary: Totalitarianism claims the identity of leader and people, of party and nation. Since economic concerns are essential to all social life, they are not discarded, but merely subordinated. Historicism, a mythical worldview, the "new man", the closed society and utopian attempts at social engineering characterize totalitarianism.

The claim of historical necessity ("God is on our side") is paramount. Totalitarians of the left look forward to a future utopia. Totalitarians of the right look back to an imagined golden age. Those of the left are more likely to have a grander ideology.

With a totalitarian ideology, the logic of an idea is carried to extremes. Thus, a totalitarian movement cannot rest content with the achievement of power in only one country. World domination must be sought.

Faced with historical determinism there is little room for individual human will. Mass society isolates the individual. Does totalitarian society then seek to destroy the individual? "You must think of all humanity-past, present and future- as one great body requiring surgery. All acts that further history and socialism are moral acts", said a Soviet instructor, indoctrinating agents.

Liquidation, terror, and pleonexia are common aspects of totalitarianism. The concept of liquidating class enemies was not new to Russia. But, can totalitarian power stop at this, or must terror become ever more pervasive? Between nine and twelve million people were destroyed within the Soviet Union in the years 1928 through 1933. For the most part, these were people who were considered class enemies. The purge of 1938 took three million victims. Were the latter objective enemies, or just victims of general terror? "We have never rejected terror in principle", said Lenin, "nor can we do so".

Revisionism is Marxist heresy. Lenin's *Materialism and Empirio-Criticism*, written in 1909, was a measure of orthodoxy in the Soviet Union. "Marxist-Leninism" was the term used by Stalin to label his own version of Marxism. In 1957, heresies of major concern to the Soviet hierarchy were said to be:

(*a*) Minimizing the threat of imperialist aggression.
(*b*) Denial of the leadership position of the Party.
(*c*) Rejecting the concept of the class struggle.
(*d*) Fostering collaboration between classes.
(*e*) Supporting social democratic parties.
(*f*) Rejecting the power of the Central Committee.
(*g*) Denying the dictatorship of the proletariat.
(*h*) Adopting national Communism.

Although these are not called "sins" or "heresies", the close analogy to the "errors" specified in the *Syllabus of Errors* of Pius IX is evident. In Soviet jargon, these were sins of "Revisionism".

Liberation theology is Marxian. Important similarities between former totalitarian movements and the position of some leftist churchmen arise in these areas: (a) The people are told that they are victimized and oppressed. (b) There must be a revolution and power must be exercised to bring about the Kingdom of God on Earth. (c) All are to be absorbed in the local collectivity; and, in service to the collectivity, a "new man" will be formed. (d) A total worldview is required, with involvement of all aspects of life: political, economic, social and cultural. (e) All institutions are to be subordinate to the movement. (f) There is to be no fixed structure of legality, all is to be based on situational ethics.

There is a demonology. The villains are the Western capitalist oppressors and international capital. Liberation theology as a movement seems now to have been "contained" by Vatican policies. Protestant Evangelical churches are attracting many in the Third World now, offering a more personal salvation and a sense of group involvement.

Evangelicals are unsuspecting totalitarians. Largely in the rural South and Midwest, white evangelical Protestants comprise some 23% of the population in the United States. With a belief system obtained whole from authority and reinforced by such evangelists as Jerry Falwell, Pat Robertson and Tim LaHaye, they respond to media-orchestrated calls. Their unthinking belief set has included total acceptance of and support for anything that Israel does. These primitive voters enabled a clique to direct the foreign policy of the United States.

Armageddon is a mass fantasy. Politico-religious delusions of Biblical prophesy are said to be held by a third of Americans. Typical is the belief in "The Rapture". This scenario holds that, once Israel has regained its "Biblical lands", legions of the Anti-Christ will attack it in the Valley of Armageddon. The Messiah will then return for The Rapture, raising true believers to sit at the right hand of God and watch those left on Earth writhe in pain. Such a fantasy may represent a desire for revenge on the part of those who consider themselves looked down upon. According to the *Washington Post,* American President Ronald

Regan repeatedly referred to his belief that "Armageddon may well occur during this generation and could come in the Middle East". Regan had frequent contacts with evangelicals.

With American evangelicals so moved by media techniques, change can come quickly. The mass may be easily redirected. In the United States, Rick Warner, a new popular evangelist has emerged. In addition to his media-driven Saddleback Church, Warner has two thousand other churches on his internet mailing list. He seems to be advocating more concern for social betterment than for the repression of "sin". About a third of the US population is said to be evangelical and the number of megachurches doubled (to twelve hundred) in six years. The megachurch, with more than 2,000 members, is an example of mediatized manipulation.

The Israeli Likud government-sponsored Gush Emunim extremist movement promulgates views based on the belief that End of Days has begun and that Jews will reclaim (*Genesis* 15:17 and 17:18) the entire Mid-East and, they claim, the World. The Gush Emunim are well organized, armed and fanatical. The Israeli government has financed their movement into illegal settlements in occupied Palestine.

By Israelis and many evangelicals, Muslims are especially viewed as evil beings and holy war against them is seen as welcome and leading to the inevitable destruction of the World and heavenly rapture. A "Rapture Index" is said to be maintained that predicts this Doomsday scenario by 2040. Although many believe in the Biblical *Revelations*, it is not certain how many accept the foregoing extreme views.

The indoctrinated worldview of the evangelicals is essentially pre-Enlightenment and anti-Enlightenment, and thus incompatible with the organic constitutional law of the United States. Repercussions are experienced in medicine, science and education. This situation is analyzed in detail in Anatol Lieven's *Extreme Makeover* (Oxford, 2005). See also his *Rapture Exposed*.

Holy War and Totalitarianism

The Crusades introduced in Western civilization the concept of ideological total war. Augustine spoke of the "just war". A just war was one with a just cause, such as self-defense, declared by proper authority (such as Pope or Emperor) and not motivated by gain or grudge. A "holy war" differs significantly from a Crusade, for it includes Old Testament totalitarian and apocalyptic attitudes that can be used as a rationale for ethnic cleansing and genocide. Holy war also includes an admixture of intolerant and messianic ideology.

Religion, greed and politics are crusade motives. The First Crusade (1066-1069) illustrated religious enthusiasm, greed for land and money, and the politics of empire. Politically, the *de facto* leader of the West, the Pope, was most interested in bringing the Eastern Church back under the hegemony of Rome. A crusade toward the capture of Jerusalem seemed to offer such a potential for reunification as well as ideological and material inducements for crusaders.

The Pope offered members of the fighting nobility something that they all needed- an indulgence freeing them from the burdens of sin. In addition, everyone saw the prospect of loot and younger sons of the nobility could obtain lands and even principalities.

Pope Urban II talked with the ideological nomenclatura of the Church at Cluny before announcing, in a great outdoor revival meeting at Claremont, his proposed Crusade. The Eastern Church needed help, and pilgrims in the Holy Land were being abused by the Muslims, he said. Here, men were poor and unhappy. There, they would be prosperous and true friends of God. Cries (in Latin) of "God wills it!" came from the crowd. As he finished, certain of his friends quickly came forward to publicly volunteer. Many others joined in. Letters went out to all the bishops of Christendom, calling for the encouragement of volunteers.

The unstable times favored movements. The Muslims were advancing toward the West, and Jerusalem and Antioch had fallen. There was increased economic activity, increased population pressure, and railing by iterant preachers who called for Church reforms and who inveighed against Muslims and Jews. Peter the Hermit and others quickly recruited tens of thousands who swarmed after them. (Tyerman 2006, Wakefield 1970, Runciman 1951)

The evangelical and ideological aspect had particular potency among the less educated. There was also the influence of the Normans (Douglass, 1970). These Viking descendants, thought to be predatory warriors, formed the staff of the Alsatian Pope Leo IX (1049-1054). Some argue that, with Leo IX, the Church ideal shifted from retreat from the world to converting the world (see Stillman & Pfaff, 1965).

Leaders may easily release the repressed and bottled genie among the demos. Urban II spoke of "rescuing that land from a dreadful race". Iterant preachers also lambasted Jews. Horrible pogroms ensued as these Crusaders began their march within Europe. Once the masses were put in motion, they were not easily controlled. The genie had been let out of the bottle.

With indulgences, and by giving them a portion of the wealth of the victims, the popes also enlisted the services of trained fighters in the quest for hegemony. The means, ideological and physical, were thus at hand to wage extensive crusades within Europe against pagans, infidels and heretics.

The crusades show a prototype of Western colonialist imperialism. Significantly, they also show the use of religious-type ideology to incite and involve the mass. The elites are involved with the prospect of power and profit. The instigators (Church, Party) hope to control it all. The lower level cadres hope to get a smaller piece of the gains. This pattern seems to have obtained for more than nine hundred years, even encompassing the ambitions of America in the Second Iraq War.

Islam

Resurgent Islam looks back to the Golden Age of the Caliphs. Caliphs who succeeded Mohammed were styied "rulers of the faithful", blending political power and religious authority.

Imagination has created that period as a "Golden Age" and modern-day *Salafast* fundamentalists seek a return to that earlier age. Eventually, the learned men or *ulama*' became the definers of the faith and their support was necessary to legitimize the ruler.

The call of Islam had a revolutionary appeal for the oppressed and the faith spread rapidly for the next hundred years. By 1000, the *ulama* were generally apologists for the ruling power. Violent dissent existed, however, as with the Kha'rijites who used assassination against those who evidently did not conform to the ideals of the faith.

In an authoritarian society, religion may be the only practical way to express dissent. Thus, the Mosque is particular forum for political activity. Islam is viewed as a way of life and a culture by its adherents. Therefore, political expression may be deemed to be religious expression. al-Turabi asserts (1992) that the Islamic resurgence is an attempt to completely restructure society. Although some hope for a return to the imagined Golden Age, the principal goal is to restructure Islamic society (the *umma*) according to the principles of sacred text and to eliminate poisonous Western influences.

Local autonomy is part of a common Islamic culture: The Arabs originally were loosely organized tribes with certain leading families. These provided the leadership for the Umayyad dynasty in the 7th and 8th Centuries. The succeeding Abbasaid dynasty was more imperialist and was influenced by the peoples conquered and by Greek neo-Platonists. The subsequent and long-enduring Ottoman dynasty practiced great local autonomy. This heritage, together with the common culture (*umma*) of Islam, set the tone of that part of the World. This common culture or worldview, *umma*, underlies Geertz's suggestion that Islam is not a Church, but rather is society itself. Geertz highlights this by contrasting Morroco's effort to return to pure, scripturally -based life with Indonesia's syncretism.

The clerical scholar is intermediary between people and ruler. A specific characteristic of that culture was the idea of the learned Koranic scholar being an intermediary between the people and the ruler. There was also the obligation of the landholder to care for those who worked for him. Albert Hourani's *A History of the Arab Peoples* emphasizes especially the culture of the cities, wherein the burghers lacked charters.

The Shi'ia' early on became the party of the lower class. Shi'ia' Islam gave the religious leader, the Imam, much more authority than did the majority Sunni Islam. In the Twentieth century, the failure of Islam to prosper in competition with the Christian West was evident.

The encounter with Western imperialism was traumatic for Islamic countries. As commercial agriculture developed for export, the bond of loyalty between landowner and laborer dissolved. The initial desire to copy the ways of the conqueror yielded to a wistful desire to return to the imagined Golden Age of Islamic rule. Others sought to find in Arab nationalism a response to European nationalism and a reprise of the early Islamic conquests. Today, forces of religion and anti-imperialist nationalism combine among the young populations to create a strong movement potential.

Successful foreign imperialism evoked a fundamentalist response. Was Christianity and Western culture superior or had the faithful not been true to the principles of Islam? An attempted return to true fundamental principles was chosen. Although such a response may be expressed in religious terms, rapid change, loss of traditional social ties, insecurity and a sense of powerlessness cause people to seek a new identity and philosophy or ideology.

In Iran the *ulama* joined with the radical reformers against the Shah, as they would against his son. The Shi'ia Imam Khomeini articulated a pure and fanatical creed, claiming that Islam is a theocratic faith. Implementing it was to be but a return to clearly understood and agreed-upon basic principles. In Islam, the rightness and justice of the principles are accepted. The world is seen in black and white. "Islam does not recognize two deities, the deity of religion and the deity of politics." *Echo of Islam*, June/July 1985.

Classless union in faith is asserted by Islam. "Islamic government is founded upon the sovereignty of the faith... power does not rest with classes or with the dominion of an individual or group, but is the crystallization of a unanimous ideal in the march toward God. The nation has rid itself of the dust and impurities of idolatry and the dregs of foreign mentality, and returns to the ideal worldview of Islam" (Preamble to the *Iranian Constitution*).

Liberation of the oppressed is a tenet. "Our nation prepares a man formed to the high ideals of Islam and applied to the entire world... The Iranian Revolution is a movement for the victory of the disinherited against the powerful... on the road to creating one world community and to liberate the oppressed peoples of the entire world.... the objective of the government is to move man toward the ideal order and cause the divine dimensions of man to appear" (Preamble to the *Iranian Constitution*).

"By the replacement of the decadent American-oriented culture with an Islamic one, Iran has been able to achieve a social consensus among its citizens, while breaking all cultural, economic and political ties with the United States. In this way, it has established a unified body of purposeful people". (Dr. Ahmad Huber).

The Letter of Ali was the first publication produced by the Islam Orientation Office in Tehran. This Seventh Century document "can be considered the principal source for an Islamic political science". The Imam Ali would have the ruler be the true servant of his people. Islam offers justice and care for the oppressed. The individual has dignity, no matter what his station in life. Similarly, his duties are clear. Such is the message of Islam. This is why bureaucracy is rejected in favor of more flexible executive power. The means of communication will be harmonized with the revolutionary movement and will refrain from destructive and anti-Islamic ferments. The basic principle of justice is to prevent any deviation or the development of any deviation from the path of Islam (From the *Preamble*).

Islamic holy war and world revolution is envisioned. "The elite Corps of Revolutionary Guards are not only to preserve the frontiers, but to participate in the Holy War of God to bring divine rule to the entire world. To achieve Islamic goals, the executive power ought not to be hampered.

Rights within conformity are permitted. Individual rights and freedoms are guaranteed by the Iranian Constitution. These rights, always and everywhere, are subject to the condition they be not exercised in a manner contrary to the interests of Islam. Committees of Doctors of the Faith are established throughout government to monitor and interpret activities for conformity to the faith.

Ideology is needed to counteract materialism. "The Marxist philosophy results in materialistic persons rising to positions of power. Such people are devoid of human and moral principles. Although the West does not claim to be materialist, it is so in fact. People without ideologies rise to the top in the West. The worst aspect is capitalism, which makes capital sovereign. Prior to American independence, the capitalists designed plans to rule there forever and they have done so."

"Our system must allow some people to become rich, but without their having any influence on the government. If people in the United States knew their own true interests, and were not swindled by propaganda, then government would be good or bad depending upon the quality and standard of education of the general public" (Hajj Hashemi Rafsanjani).

"The West wants to promote religion-free culture inside Islamic countries. The need to fight this cultural penetration is of the utmost importance". (Dr. Ahmed Huber).

Killing improves humanity. "When you tell people of Islamic injunctions, tell them of the verses of the Quetal (killing). Quetal is a blessing, too, for it seeks to mold and elevate human beings. The Koran says to treat Muslims as brothers, but of the infidel, it says "kill them, hit them and imprison them". Forget kindness. These are not acts of mercy, but of opposition to God. The logic of the prophets is to be severe against infidels and those who are against humanity. That severity is a blessing upon them. (Imam Khomeini *Echo of Islam* Feb/Mar 1985, p. 20).

Uniformity gives security. The unity of the object of worship and the uniformity of the worship provide an inner security which is nowhere to be found outside the framework of faith.... man is bound to revolt against all other false deities that usurp the right of the true deity... [and] search and struggle to establish the Kingdom of God on Earth..." (*Echo of Islam*, June/July 1986).

The goal is to bring in the Kingdom of God on Earth. The establishment of justice is indeed the philosophy behind the Divine Revelation whose ultimate goal is to bring material and eternal prosperity to man. This sublime objective can be fulfilled only through the establishment of divine laws and the sovereignty of God crystallized in the government of the Prophets, Imams and qualified Muslim jurisprudents. Thus, holy war and struggle to bring true this divine objective and to oppose all kinds of anti-human oppressive governments is a divine obligation of all Muslims." (*Resolution*, Third Islamic Conference).

"We must exert efforts and wage holy war for the establishment of an Islamic government in our respective countries. Since the day they abandoned Islamic laws, Muslims have faced many problems" (Egyptian). "God will grant the prayers of those who have been wronged and oppressed, when they curse the oppressor...God has said 'I shall take revenge from the oppressors of the oppressed, sometimes with delay and sometimes not" (The Prophet Mohammed).

Terrorism shows the power of Iran and of Islam. "When people see that the United States puts barriers around the White House to make it safe from Iranian bombing, the people realize the strength of Iran and the power of Islam" (Imam Khomeini *Echo of Islam* Feb/Mar 1985, p. 19).

"When God's orders are taken to heart in America's heartland, the world will understand that His word, and action taken to establish that word, reverberates in such a way that the consequences are incalculable. Had one of our Muslim brothers... [made a suicide attack] he would have struck the most significant blow to date for renascent Islam in a land whose foreign practices are literally awash in Muslim blood" (Editorial, April 14, 1985, *Kayhan International*).

Purification of self and of society is necessary. "If someone is corrupt, he will be unable to express himself. If he is not purified, he cannot purify society. One measure of purification is that, when one takes the name of Islam, no one opposes it. For almost twenty years, the Islamic scholars have been working on the people, on the youth. They have raised their consciousness and changed them. Had it not been for the scholars, the youth would have been taken from us and from Islam" (Imam Khomeini).

"The new Islamic person must be an informer and a martyr", said Golnar Mehran in commenting on the Iranian school program, he "must be ready to become a martyr and must be the eyes and ears of the state."

Crisis begets visions. In Egypt, Arab socialism, pan-Arabism and Americanism have all been at one time exalted and subsequently deemed to have failed. As economic conditions worsened, there was frustration, lack of direction and despair. "We are all looking to the past", said M..H. Heikel, "when you are in crisis, you need a dream". Egyptian university students, in 1985, were reported to be overwhelmingly in favor of a totally Islamic state. In the same year, President Zia of Pakistan moved to establish a fundamentalist Islamic state.

Egyptian Islamist activist groups were mostly young university people in difficult fields of study, coming from small town or rural lower middle-class backgrounds. Supporters were traditional middle-class groups and recent migrants to the city. (al-Turabi, 1992, Lewis, 1988).

Although all Islam may be considered fundamentalist, one should distinguish between the extremist Islamic societies and the conservative fundamentalism of al-Azhar University. The latter supports and is supported by incumbent regimes. For example, al-Azhar endorsed the stationing of American troops in

Saudi Arabia while the most considered it as a crusade against Islam.

The underclass will rise in the Kingdom of God. Shi'ites comprise 95% of Iran's population and are a majority in Iraq and Bahrain. In Lebanon and in the United Arab Emirates they form about 40% of the population. Except in Iran, Shi'tes are in socially and economically less favorable positions. Shi'ia have a religious tradition of being opposed to the ruling state, of suffering and of martyrdom. There is also a tradition of awaiting the Mahdi, who will set things right and establish the Kingdom of God on Earth. Those who seek reform may be losing place to those who seek revolution. In Lebanon, for example, the reformist Amal was challenged by the Party of God (Hezbollah), which was trained by the Iranian Revolutionary Guards.

Since 1979, Iran has had a theocratic government. The Imam Khomeini and the *ulama* had the problem of running a country as well as preaching. Khomeini noted that one should select between facts that represented Islamic values and those that did not; that sometimes it was necessary to choose the lesser evil; that to attain an Islamic end, one might use non-Islamic means; and that the intention counts more than the act. In performing illegal actions, one may also make a distinction between "law" and "divine law". With such rules of interpretation, scripture does not inhibit much government action.

The important sources of current radical Islamic thinking are. Sayyid Qutb, Maulana Maudi, Hasan al-Banna and Khomeini. Kepel sees Islamism (as opposed to Islam) as the creation of a few religious intellectuals. General principles of Islamism include: that, while the West is homocentric, imperialistic and capitalistic, Islam is obedient to God, theocentric, united and comprehensive, subordinating human reason to revelation, honoring the dignity and needs of all Muslims. There can be no separation of the worldly and the religious. The world is divided into the ignorant and those obedient to God. Man cannot know the universe solely through his own reason. Dr. Soroush, Iran's leading theoretician, notes that Islam must distinguish existing fact from "value", the end from the means, and what "is" from what "ought to be". These, and the failure to distinguish ethics from sciences, he considers major Western fallacies. Satanic Western creations include Freud's *id,* Marx's *class* and Hegel's *spirit.*

Yusuf al-Qaradawi claims that either belief must move into the hearts of the rulers or that political rule must move into the hands of the younger generation. One should note that the majorities of most of the populations are under twenty-five years old.

The vast majority of Muslims believe that their faith is good and sufficient. The majority Sunni tend toward a restrictive and fundamentalist canon that admits of little innovation. The reform agenda of bin Ladin and like Salafists envisioned a return to an imagined golden age. A more centralist (and opportunistic) set of agendas talks of putting an Islamic structure on top of existing institutions.

External threat potentiates fundamentalism. The abuse of Muslims in Palestine and Iraq, and the evident imperialism of the Bush administration, together with its Crusading evangelism, were widely perceived as threats to all Muslims. External threat provides an impetus to return to the literal and militant fundamentalist faith. Such militantism was historically successful against Christian Crusaders.

In September of 2001, Wahabis of this fundamentalist line successfully attacked buildings in New York. This may have been done to provoke a counter-attack from Americans and thus stimulate a reactive unity among Muslims. A March 17, 2004 announcement from al-Qaeda seemed to confirm this intent, concluding: "Being targeted by an enemy is what will wake us from our slumber".

Nationalism is often a stimulus to autonomy and local economic development. A considerable middle class is developing and these seem more interested in consumerism than in fundamentalism. The Islamic poor are overwhelmingly conservative. The ideology, which emphasizes justice and dignity rather than democracy, is their natural choice. Thus, a polarization of Islamic society seems likely with globalization.

Another stimulus for change is the general disgust with their governments among the Arab public. Will such change lead to atavistic fundamentalism or to an Islamic "Modernist Crisis" and Enlightenment? Oliver Roy's *The Failure of Political Islam* foresees no Enlightenment. Graham Fuller's *The Future of Political Islam* admits the possibility of a middle course, while for *Islam and Democracy in the Middle East* (Harvard), a modernist revision as a possibility.

15

POLITICAL CREEDS

Priests had, for a long time, a near monopoly on literacy, and thus on the organized and articulated ideology. With printing, many people who were not priests started to read. The rising nation-state let the common folk identify with the nation. With the Enlightenment came talk of a "Social Contract". Balancing class interests became important. Ideas of social contract did not initially include laborers. Only those who usually participated in politics were considered part of the social contract. These were the people who formulated political creeds.

Politics is the struggle for power. Those in power use religion and ideology to manipulate worldviews and stay in power. Hegel (1800) saw life as a struggle both for power and for recognition. Those who risked the least would become the slaves of those who risked the most.

The oligarchy controls the ideology. In 1950, the Soviet Communist Party numbered less than six percent of the Russian population. They ruled. There is always a minority which rules and a majority that is ruled. In politics, in religion, and in the arts, the oligarchy controls the most of the "ideological state apparatus"- the media and symbol system."

Society's view of itself, as mediated by the oligarchy, changes with the era. One scholar has characterized such views as: (a) In the Middle Ages, of the *faithful*. (b) In Locke of *property owners*. (c) With Hobbes, of *acquisitors*. (d) As Marx saw it, of *producers*. (e) In today's common view, of *job holders*. (f) In the Communist world, of *laborers*.

The values of the bourgeoisie became dominant through example, hope, and control of the ideological state apparatus. By accepting bourgeois values and working hard, workers (or their children) believed they could rise in the world. Eric Hoffer, *In Our Time* (1976) said that the disappearance of the middle class that "would sell its soul for cash" would probably mean the end of civility, tolerance and laughter.

The bourgeoisie allows relative freedom to the individual, since it is more interested in the material rather than the social. Says Theodore White: "It came to me slowly that the values liberals cherish are better served in the world of the trader than in the Pharonic world". The "strong man" who can preserve order may be welcomed by the businessman. The merchant is not really interested in politics, he wants to be able to do business in an orderly way. Within media-fostered North American ideology, the selfish, individualistic pursuit of wealth is rationalized as providing more goods and freedom. However, one no longer has the patron, or noble, to care for his people.

Fascism may be a culmination of capitalism. Formerly, the wealthy had only to tax surplus, but now many are concerned with producing surplus. This is seen as requiring increasing discipline and man, himself, becomes an unfinished product, as Zygmont Bauman observed. This logic could explain a progression from patronialism to capitalism and thence to Fascism. The bourgeois worldview often assumes that economics politics and society are all wrapped up together. This is close to Fascist view. W. Schivelbusch suggests that, especially in its economic aspects, Roosevelt's New Deal was the American equivalent of fascism.

Industrial workers seek an identity. The machinery of the industrial revolution resulted in fewer craftsmen and more laborers. Labor, Arendt observes, combines "necessity with futility". Given the right to vote, a laborer still wishes to be recognized as part of society and to think that his role is important. Hanna Arendt saw the mid-Twentieth Century West as a society of laborers about to be liberated from the drudgery of labor. Does mindless television articulate the worldview? Who will lead people toward greater things? Does the society even postulate or articulate greater things?

Nicaragua

Who participates in revolutions? For Vilas (1984), the major factors fostering the Nicaraguan revolution were: (a) Extensive capitalist development dispossessed many people. (b) The government became alienated from the people. (c) The government put wealth in very few hands. (d) The revolutionary group was effective.

The allegiance of the lower middle class was critical. Normally they will support the dominant power. The murder of Nicaraguan opposition leader Chamorro created an apprehension of terror and caused the middle class to feel threatened.

Only a fraction of the population participated in the revolution and these were quite young. Many lacked the schooling that would have fostered an attitude of superiority. Vilas suggests that this tended to create an egalitarian, rather than an authoritarian, attitude among them. The occupations of this small revolutionary group were as follows: (a) Students- 29% (b) Repairmen- 22% (c) Laborers- 16% (e) Farm- 4%. The young repairmen provided leadership. Vilas feels that the driving force of agricultural revolutions comes from those who still have something to lose, rather than from those without hope.

Nicaragua claimed a collective consensus. Committees of Discipline were established to eradicate "attitudes prejudicial to the march of production". Aiding a strike could result in three years in prison. Worker participation could be achieved only through a union organization. Discipline was based on the socio-political advocacy of the proletariat, its class responsibility and its patriotism. Decisions were reached not by vote but by "consensus".

Vilas also claims that the hierarchy and the clergy had preached acceptance of dictatorship as the acceptance of divine will. To "educate", for the clergy, was to give man the form which God conceived for him. The "Christian" whom the bourgeois has in mind is the isolated being, tied down with an individual faith and with a passive attitude toward a severe and dictatorial God, says Vilas. The thing that turns an individual into a citizen is the removal of this individual isolation, claimed the Sandanista author.

Religion, education, civil liberties and conventional political rights became the focus of class conflict. Although people could use the same words, definitions made for disputes. The bourgeois strategy was one of reduction and articulation. The concept of the "Christian father of a family" was introduced by the opposition.

Is Liberalism a political creed? Liberalism is an attitude of live and let live, of seeing both sides to a question. As such, it is the antithesis of totalitarianism. There was also a connotation of magnanimity and generosity. For the English, it meant minimum interference by the state and protection of the individual from the state. The term also became associated with laissez-faire capitalism. In France, liberalism implied opposition to the Church and to the forces of reaction. There, it developed overtones of statism, rather than individualism.

Liberalism and Capitalism

In current use, "liberalism conveys the idea of tolerance, of the protection of individual rights against the state and of magnanimity. Is liberalism but the worldview of those members of the prosperous middle class who are magnanimous?

Liberalism, according to Ortega y Gasset, is that principle which causes public authority, even though it may be all-powerful, to make efforts to protect and give scope to those who neither think nor feel as it does. The antithesis of liberalism, in Ortega's view, is the rule of the mass, which seeks to crush anything different.

After a lifetime of mulling over such questions, the philosopher-stevedore Eric Hoffer pronounced that, as a ruling group, the middle class stands alone in being unwilling to employ magic or naked force to cope with human nature. This implies that only middle class people can be liberals.

For many, capitalism is a political creed. "Everything is for sale. Whatever brings profit is moral. Such is the code of morality cultivated in the American school," said a Soviet Minister of Education. "Capitalism is intrinsically wrong at its base. The basic concept is that man is selfish, and capitalism argues that being realistic, we should accept this and cater to it rather than change it," said the Sandanista Foreign Minister of Nicaragua.

Was Protestantism essential to the rise of capitalism? To start a business requires a surplus of capital. Could such accumulation could arise only after Luther's "anal-retentive" character became widespread? Max Weber saw classes as rooted in production and claimed that only in Europe did the householder evolve into the capitalist. Elsewhere, the *oikos*, or diversified patronial estate, developed. One may ask whether Protestantism generated capitalism or vice-versa. Recalling that the townsman developed capital independent of land and achieved relative independence suggests that capitalism generated Protestantism.

Capitalism may imply liberalism. Psychologically, competitive struggle gives rise to individualism, economic planning produces rationalism, and the need for initiative promotes liberalism, claimed Bukharin. Thus, a developing capitalist state is seen as promoting an individualist, rationalist and liberal ideology. Should the capitalists opt for cartels or Fascism, the attitude changes.

More people may be in favor of "social justice" than are concerned with the system by which it is achieved. Said Lao Tzu (479-438 B.C.): "the way of Heaven is to diminish the superabundant and to supply the needy, while the way of man is to take from the needy to swell the superabundant". Mo Tzu (fl. 400 B.C.) tempered Confucian precepts with a socialist worldview. Socialism.

Socialist government is as old as recorded history. In Sumeria, two thousand years before Christ, the entire economy of the state was controlled by the crown. Not unexpectedly, there was a central administration recording all the transactions on countless thousands of clay tablets.

Egypt, in the three hundred years before Christ, was a totally controlled economy. In China, the abuses of capitalism sometimes brought on vast socialist reforms. In his fifty-year reign (140-87 B.C.), the Emperor Wu Ti stockpiled various commodities to regulate prices, imposed income taxes and undertook vast public works.

Those who paid the taxes in ancient China complained of supporting non-producers. Socialist government entailed bureaucracy and high taxes. Human corruptibility and incompetence made government ownership unworkable, said the conservatives. What was needed was a return to a system that harnessed the natural drives of men- free enterprise. After eighteen years, the Emperor agreed.

"The state should take the entire management of commerce, industry and agriculture into its own hands with a view toward helping the workers and preventing the rich from grinding them into dust," said Wang An-See, Chinese Premier (1068).

In Paraguay, the Jesuits imposed their own theocratic, militarized and socialist society on the Indians. Reportedly, the Indians preferred Jesuit servitude to Spanish slavery. In Peru, for some three hundred years, the Incas ran a fully controlled and socialistic state.

In 1827 Robert Owen suggested "socialism" (social concerns) as preferable to "liberty" (laissez faire) in forming public policy. Socialism could be seen as an attempt of man to achieve transcendence a voluntarist attempt of man to redeem society. Utopias often postulate socialistic systems. Most recognize that "education" is necessary to form the "new type" of person necessary to produce and share in such a society.

Is equality more important than freedom? We may recall that equality and freedom are not the same. In fact, economic freedom, as laissez faire capitalism, must inevitably result in great inequalities. It may be that perceived inequality is a more important source of discontent than is the actual standard of living. Thus, it is not certain that capitalism produces human emotional satisfaction. Might people rather be equal than prosperous?

Egalitarianism requires cooperation. In the cooperative, egalitarian, society says Fischer (1961), both the self-reliant and the overly dominant person are feared, since survival depends on cooperation. Importantly, the lack of hierarchy forces one to be more obedient and responsive to the wishes of others. Perhaps this "internalized coercion" is more oppressive than overtly imposed control.

"Equality", like "justice" is claimed as a restorative value in many national cultures. Like "democracy", it means different things in different nations. The essential claim is for a reduction in disparity. One may speak of differences in treatment or in opportunity- of the rich and the poor; between the Party and the people; between sexes and races.

A system of unbridled competition will assure inequality rather than equality. To what degree should economic inequality be permitted? The effort of a government to achieve "equality" in one domain may conflict with the priority of values in the culture. Tocqueville foresaw that, with too strong a central government, the drive to enforce similar attitudes would result either in poor average performance or in a tyranny of the majority.

Is making a "new man" a futile exercise? If man must be severely corrected for selfishness and vanity, then his basic nature is not accepted. Those who would create a "new man" to populate their social orders see the "good" human being as being different from what he presently is. It would appear better to try to harness and temper the natural selfish urges.

Christian attitudes favor a socialist ideal. "All who had property sold it and brought the money to the feet of the apostles; it was distributed to each according to his need." (Acts 4, 5). "Socialism cannot be brought into harmony with the dogmas of the Catholic Church, for it conceives of human society in a way utterly alien to Christian truth" said Pope Pius XI in

Restructuring the Social Order, 1931. "The Catholic bishops of West Germany have endorsed 'the Christian doctrine of socialism as the popes have so long demanded" reported the New York Times on August 1, 1949. "Although the Pope and the Bishops are agreed on the Marxist social changes to be effected, they have yet to get a majority of the faithful to side with these changes", said Fr. Gregory Baum, Canadian Catholic Theologian, 1983.

Marxism

Marxist-Leninism is a secular religion. In common with the Zoroastrian-derived Abrahamic religions, humanity's teleological ascent to a better World is assumed. Class struggle replaces Hegel's "competition of ideas". Theses of exploitation and alienation are combined with a critique of capitalism and a vision of communism as a final resolution are presented. Marxist ideology requires belief in a simple and closed explanation of society. The promised land of social salvation here on Earth is offered to the true believer. Salvation is within reach. Augustine spoke of God and Marx spoke of history. Both demand that man believe in order to understand.

The collectivity is exalted over the individual. "If man is social by nature, he will develop his true nature only in society, and the power of his nature must be measured not by the individuals, but by the power of society," wrote Karl Marx, in *The Holy Family*. Marxism sees only two classes with a conflict between them.

Marx saw laboring man as alienated in several ways: from his psychological nature, from the natural environment, from his product and by the character of the productive process. Similarly, Marx saw money and the processes of the market as controlling man.

Democracy requires economic equality. Genuine freedom would be possible only when mankind had overcome the constraints of economic scarcity.

There are three main versions of Marxism: the original, or Social Democratic; the dominant Marxist-Leninism; and a sort of personal, existentialist Marxism. In 1909, Bernstein explained the "piecemeal evolution of socialism", wherein increasing state intervention, the formation of trusts and cartels, and the formation of local manufacturing for the benefit of workers would be steps toward the realization of the total socialist state. This is quite close to the program advocated by Pope John Paul II in the encyclical *Laborem exorcens* (1981), and is also a bit like Fascism.

Democracy

Democracy is a disorderly creed. "Democracy is doubtless a doctrine exceedingly well calculated to flatter and to influence many passions, but it lacks all proof of validity and all power of assuring public order", wrote Pope Leo XIII in *Immortale Dei* (1885).

Democracy was a system that encouraged rivalry among cliques, thought Thucydides in 430 B.C. He thought the mob was likely to give authority to a demagogue. Similar misgivings occurred to Tocqueville two millennia later as he studied the emerging American democracy.

People's Democracy" is certainly different from "Western Democracy", although both suggest that the system is for the benefit of the people. Can the majority of the people effectively change the government? That may be the deciding question for Western style democracy. If one claims that the people should have the ability to directly initiate legislation, recall officials, and put policies to referendum, then even most Western democracies would fail to qualify.

Plebiscitary democracies can become dictatorships run by omnipotent leaders. Legitimacy is claimed to come from the will of the people, who demand a dictatorship. Cromwell, the leaders of the French Revolution, Lenin, Hitler, Fidel Castro, etc. took this view.

"Democracy" really means rule of the politician. Democracy requires more maturity from the people than does authoritarianism. What really happens in the Western world, says J. A. Schumpater, is that politicians compete for the people's vote. Afterwards, "democracy" means the rule of the politician. It works because the vast majority of people are used to the institutional structure and do not question it.

"Hyperdemocracy" is mass action. Ortega uses this word to describe the mass acting directly, imposing its will outside the law. To have a social order, it is necessary to have unity. Does such unity require a common set of values? Would that presuppose equality (or indoctrination)? Is the idea of tolerance, of liberalism and of parliamentary democracy consistent with social and psychological reality?

Representative democracy is required for larger groups. "Democracy" implies the real or theoretical participation of the people in the political process. Direct democracy is workable only in small groups. Ordinary folk cannot be expected to maintain an informed and sustained interest in politics. In larger polities some form representative democracy thus becomes necessary. The effective ability of the people to elect and remove such representatives is a key criterion of representative.

The tyranny of the manipulated mass is real. Arguably, if the people are sovereign, individual exceptions or rights cannot be claimed contrary to that general will. The mass can thus become tyrannical. Concepts of "natural law" and political equality are then posited to justify a "constitutional" democracy to limit the general will. Reality may be quite different. In a mass society, where an oligarchy of organization, money and power controls both media and judiciary, who can withstand the manipulated mass? Oakeshott suggests that such concepts as "democracy" and "liberty", have meaning only in the environment that engendered them.

Culture and ideology overlap and interact. The ideology of a government must come to terms with the culture of the people. The traditional culture will affect the ideology. The Great Russian mentality was explored by Inkeles in 1958 in an effort to assess the modal personality. From that study, it would appear that the party rulers, and higher status Russian people generally, have personalities quite different from the mode.

The common Russian is said to value being able to trust his fellow, to affiliate in close groups and to express his feelings freely. He wants to depend on direction from a warm, personal and forgiving leader. How such a modal personality would be comfortable with Marxist-Leninism is not clear, although it appears that many simple folk retained a fond memory of Stalin.

Fascism

Fascism developed over several centuries. Fichte's *Theory of Knowledge* (1794) asserted that the future belongs to those who know how to impose their will on the external world. He claimed that no morality should apply to such men. Unity with the absolute would be achieved through dissolution of the self in a self-sufficient state.

Devotion to an omniscient and omnipotent leader was forseen. The poet Novalis in his *Annals of the Prussian Monarchy* (1798), said that the state would impose itself by creating feelings of devotion, faith, and love. It would make an appeal to the mystic communion of subjects and to common faith in the Leader. Kant (d. 1804) praised an enlarged mentality able to think for everyone.

Acting on feeling and belief could allow the people to participate in a universal church. Freedom, said David Strauss in 1838, would be achieved by being conscious of one's place in history, sweeping away raw facts and acting vigorously on belief. Thus would the secular community become a universal church. The divine mind was represented by the spirit of the Folk and the individual shared it by losing himself in service to the state.

The civilizing evangel was assuming an ethnic/racial character. The rights of pastoral peoples ("barbarians"), said Hegel (d. 1831), are "only a formality". To take their territory would not be "a victory of force, but of reason". J-A Gobineau (d. 1882) articulated a widely accepted racial doctrine.

Wagner (d. 1883) put Romantic ideas into a myth of religious and musical form. Such philosophical and poetic expression laid the groundwork for Fascist and National Socialist ideologies.

Unacceptable reality is rejected by the ideological mind. Reality, after the First World War, was unacceptable. Fascism rejected it and saw a world of ideology. According to the French Fascist Brasillach, Fascism was the spirit of joy. Mosse explains it as a theology that provided the framework for a national worship.

A chance to be somebody under new leadership is offered to the alienated. The old elites had failed. Domestic servants, small farmers, and government clerks hoped for a new leadership in a new social order. Support for fascism gradually spread to the higher levels of society.

Dissatisfaction with materialism called for ideology. As mass opinion became important in politics, dissatisfaction with materialism, French rationalism and positivism, and slow social progress increased. Hedonism, selfishness, the impotent bickering of political parties, foreign laborers and the Marxist threat of class conflict were among the perceived threats. The capitalism of international finance became a special target.

Fascism offered a promise of action and status to the masses. Each citizen would be identified with the greatness of his national heartland. All rules were to be subordinated to what was good for the heartland. Impatience took precedence over reason and duty to the state was more important than freedom. Despite these appeals, political power could only be achieved by alliance with important establishment forces. "Fascism" has today become an unpopular word. Not everybody so regarded it before World War II. For example, there was considerable enthusiasm for Mussolini in America.

Against threat, Fascism offered security. With the old order of society destroyed, with a real threat of Red revolution and Soviet imperialism, with a disintegration of values, people sought economic and emotional security. Fascism appeared to offer both. As a corporatist "third way" between weak and divisive pluralist democracy and godless Marxism, it received the support of the Roman Church, as did Hitler, Mussolini, Tiso, Salazar and Franco.

Fascism offered an important place for misfits in the classless gang. Apart from the theory and ideals of Fascism, one must consider the "elite" who would implement it, the new oligarchy. A significant portion of these seemed to have been unemployed losers and misfits. Hitler's own police, the brown shirt SA, were largely recruited from the unemployed. The motives of leaders, members, sympathizers and mere voters should be considered separately.

Yinger (1976) discusses the attractions of a gang: you "belong", you have a place and a sense of importance, you have a code of values and your life takes on a meaning. You can now assert your worth and the standards of success are redefined to accommodate your type.

"Mankind is tired of freedom", said Mussolini. Fascism began in Italy in the 1920's. The principal slogans were: "have faith, obey, fight" and "Mussolini is always right". Said Mussolini: "many political phenomena in Italy which today are not fully understood are phenomena of a spiritual revival". He claimed that the class system was an invention of the Marxists. Mussolini said that the corporate state was the answer to class differences. Mussolini sought "everything in the state, nothing outside the state, nothing against the state", all to be implemented with a "violent totalitarian will."

Nationalism distinguished Fascism from universalist evangels. Although the supreme leader seems to be a common feature of Fascism, the primacy of the Party may not be. Fascism wants the people to be an enthusiastic mass, authoritarianism wants them to be quiet. Fascism was highly national and particularistic, rather than universal. The economy was to serve the state, rather than vice-versa. Armies and police forces independent of the regular state structure characterized fascism. Rituals and the formation of the "new man" were characteristic. Power was sought to achieve goals other than economic betterment (Paxton 2004).

Roman Catholicism was perceived by many of its adherents to be a perfect and closed system. Alien to the modern world and its economy. The policy of the Papacy and the bishops in economic and social matters has been expressed in encyclicals since the late 1800's. Recurrent themes are: the establishment of fixed occupational classes, central economic planning, and social ownership of industry.

The rationality of the "economic man" is essentially amoral and adaptive. It is thus incompatible with the prescriptive nature of salvation religions. Pope John Paul II and his bishops began, in the early 1980's, to implement the essentially Marxian social plan of the encyclical *Laborem exorcens*.

Pius XI enthusiastically endorsed the "Corporate State", Fascism. The dictator of Austria, Dollfuss, was even more enthusiastic in establishing a fascist Christian state according to the principles laid down by the Pope.

Prior to World War II, Poland, Spain, Portugal, France, Austria, Hungary, Croatia, Romania, Argentina, Bolivia, Brazil and Chile, as well as Italy had large fascist movements. Such broad popular support seems to have been motivated by economic anxiety as well as perceived external threat. To appreciate how easily ordinary people may support fascism, consider how many would respond affirmatively to the following quiz.

Fascist Attitude Quiz

(1) Communists, Muslims and other such foreigners represent a serious threat to our country.
(2) The wealthy got there because they have superior qualities.
(3) People should stay in their own class.
(4) We are in the majority and can move things if we stick together.

(5) Attitudes and principles come in a package. One can't cherry-pick among them.
(6) If people don't want to follow the law, they should be dealt with swiftly.
(7) Don't tie the hands of the police. They know their job.
(8) The legislature is corrupt and inefficient. A fast and effective administration is required.
(9) In the present world situation, democracy gets in the way of effective action.
(10) Individualism corrupts society. We need teamwork. Pluralism and multi-culturalism weaken society.
(11) Our society has decadent values. We need renewal with clear standards.
(12) Those who don't endorse such clear standards are liberals or fellow-travelers.
(13) Moral relativism is a liberal disease in our society.
(14) Godless materialism renders us vulnerable.
(15) Big corporations are essential to our defense and our prosperity, government should help them.
(16) Unions cause trouble. Government can regulate corporations and labor where necessary.
(17) We want to be self-sufficient. If necessary, we can occupy foreign territory for resources.
(18) A strong military is necessary for our defense and moral fiber.
(19) Military virtues are the answer to liberal weakness.
(20) A nation should be like a family.
(21) Mass rallies show our strength and unity.
(22) Attention to values can give us a renewed man.
(23) Tolerance is weakness.
(24) Hatred of evil is good and natural.
(25) Violence is often the most effective way.
(26) Immigrants, Freemasons, Marxists or Jews may be responsible for many of our problems.
(27) Rural and country people understand real life. Cities are dens of corruption.
(28) Woman is subordinate to man. Her place is in the home with children.

(29) Intellectuals are non-productive time-wasters.
(30) Internationalism is unpatriotic and weakens us.
(31) Those who support the United Nations and international law are unpatriotic.
(32) Moral strength means endorsing Christianity.
(33) Christianity should be the official state religion.
(34) Religion should be taught in the public schools.

Italian Fascism differed from National Socialism. Goebbels said that Mussolini was not a revolutionary like Hitler and Stalin. The latter were men of passionate and permanent beliefs. Mussolini's government lacked the viciousness of religious ideology. From 1926 to 1932, the Fascist inquisition in Italy released 12,000 of those arrested. Only seven were executed.

Italy had suffered a million casualties in World War I and did not receive the benefits from it that Britain and France had promised. The government and economy were weak and the international socialist agitation was strong. Mussolini's Black Shirts (Faschi) were financed by local capitalists to attack the Socialists. The country was receptive to the promise of strong government.

Rather than a true-believing fanatic, Mussolini was an illusionist hoping to inspire something of what he promised. "The credo of Fascism is heroism, that of the bourgeoisieis egoism". Here, as in Germany, the talk was of national, rather than class, loyalty. Before World War II, many admiringly said of him: "he made the trains run on time".

Mussolini's deputy, Gentile, handed over the elementary schools to the Catholic Church and reserved teaching in the secondary schools for the Party. Mussolini's *Concordat* with the Vatican provided: (a) Catholicism recognized as the state religion. (b) Full autonomy for Catholic Action groups. (c) Compulsory religious education in the schools. (d) Literature of Freemasons, Methodists and other heretics made a penal offense. (e) Dancing during Lent outlawed, etc.

The Catholic Church supported Mussolini. Pope Pius XI called Mussolini "the man sent by Providence". "The New Constantine", said the Archbishop of Milan. Said Cardinal O'Connell of Boston: "a genius in the field of government, given to us by God. In the 1929 Italian elections, most of the clergy instructed Catholics to vote for Fascist candidates.

Austrian Fascism

Austrian Fascism was subordinate to the Church. In the encyclical *Reconstructing the Social Order* (1931), Pius XI called for the creation of an authoritarian corporate state very similar to that of Fascism. When Engelbert Dollfuss organized his Austrian state according to the ideas of the Pope, some called it a "totalitarian state working within the Church".

Fascism offered to fill a threatening void. The collapse of the Empire at the end of World War I had left Austrians with no focus for feelings of loyalty and with no ready substitute for the symbolic authority of the Monarchy. The feeling of being lost and vulnerable was increased by the perceived threat of Marxist revolution.

The intellectual climate of the time was reflected in Professor Vogelsang's ideas of a "Catholic Corporate State". These same ideas appeared in Leo XIII's encyclical Rerum Novarum (1881). The priest, Seipel, as Chancellor of Austria, planned to impose such a state.

Dollfuss

"The age of the capitalist system and of the capitalist-liberal economic order is past; the days of materialist-Marxist betrayal are also finished. The rule of the parties is over and done with. We reject terror and the concept of total coordination. What we want is the social, Christian, German, state of Austria, built on a cooperative basis and under firm authoritarian leadership" said Engelbert Dollfuss, Austrian Dictator, proclaiming the "German Corporative Christian State" on "Catholic Day", May 1, 1934.

Engelbert Dollfuss came from a poor and very devout Austrian peasant family. As a child, he played at being priest. He was educated in a seminary. There, he failed his first year, eventually graduating twenty-third in a class of twenty-six. Of very short stature, Dollfuss had a compulsion to lead. Despite his size, he managed to talk himself into army and soon became a well-beloved officer. Dollfuss.

As Chancellor, Dollfuss would love to lead parades mounted, like Mussolini, on a white horse. After the war, Dollfuss returned to study law in Vienna. He joined the Catholic Youth Organization and subsequently became a member of the politically powerful Catholic Brotherhood. Dollfuss cooperated with a priest-professor to exclude from the University "all students tainted with Jewish blood".

Dollfuss never held an elective office. He became Chancellor through a series of appointments. His power resulted from his activities in Catholic and agricultural organizations. The rise of the paramilitary Homeguard, the *Heimwehr*, provided some focus for feelings of patriotism and offered some security. "Rooting out Marxism, throwing out the parliamentary system and reorganizing Austria as an authoritarian state", were part of the 1929 program of the *Heimwehr*. Their spokesman, Bardoloff, also saw Austria as the eastern anchor of a new German Empire.

The "Corporate State" of the Heimwehr was indeed the "Catholic Corporate State" of Vogelsang, updated by Professor Otto Spahn and the example of Mussolini. The "horizontal groupings" of the class system were to be replaced by "vertical groupings" according to occupation and profession. This offered a vague reprise of the guild and *oikos*, or patronistic structure, of early medieval times.

Dollfuss often consulted with the Pope and with Mussolini. After resignations had left the Austrian Parliament adjourned and leaderless, Dollfuss was ready to take over. "The leadership of a country does not rest only with the legislative, but equally with the head of state and the government", he announced.

Wounded in an assassination attempt, Dollfuss convinced himself that he had been "given a mission to perform, regardless of whether I should succeed. We are all God's messengers... I feel I must now try and lead this society to Christ. That is my mission." Dollfuss parroted the social teaching of the Roman Catholic Church.

Only the idea of a "German" state was extraneous. There was considerable pan-German sentiment in Austria and Dollfuss shared it: "we believe that it is our duty to preserve the true German culture in these Christian lands of Central Europe".

To "secure law and order in these troubled times", on May 7, 1933: all public meetings were banned; press censorship was installed; and a concentration camp was set up. Dollfuss's dictatorship had begun. That same month, all political parties were banned and merged into the Fatherland Front. The Catholic Youth Organization formed paramilitary "Chancellor's units", loyal to Dollfuss.

On the first of May of 1934, Dollfuss proclaimed his new Constitution for Austria. "In the name of God... the Austrian people receive... this Constitution." The previous September, Dollfuss had given a speech which was nearly a verbatim repetition of Pius XI's *Quadragesimo anno.* His biographer reports that Dollfuss had read and reread the encyclical a hundred times. Now, he announced: "We want to be the first to turn the words of the noble encyclical into reality". "We all go away today in the faith that we are fulfilling a higher mission... just as the Crusaders... we look forward to the future in the conviction- God wills it!"

Brook-Shepherd's well-written *Prelude to Infamy* has been the principal source of the foregoing comments on Dollfuss. He gives no hint of neurosis or evil intent on the part of Dollfuss. Rather, Dollfuss emerges as a well-meaning, devout and energetic peasant. Unreflective, fully accepting the socio-political teaching of the Church, Dollfuss sought to be a leader of men and the instrument of his Church's ideology.

The Jesuit publicist Husslein, writing from Marquette in 1942, called Dollfuss "the greatest European statesman of our age". Under Dollfuss, Austria became the "German Corporative Christian State". The day it was inaugurated was proclaimed "Catholic Day". When Dollfuss promulgated the new Constitution, he sought to give effect to the papal encyclical Quadragesimo anno, and attempted to establish people in permanent classes of work- "occupational estates".

Other Fascisms

Spain and seven other Fascist nations existed in Europe by 1936, including governments also existed in Japan, Greece, Bulgaria, Rumania, Poland, Hungary and Austria. In Spain, Franco was to be responsible "only to God and to History". (In 1947, Franco established in Spain a "Catholic Kingdom". The Church was given control of education and the exclusive public right to religious ceremonies.)

As part of their religious instruction, Spanish children were taught that liberalism claimed freedom of conscience, freedom of worship and freedom of the press. It was explained that these things were bad and that the government had to suppress these freedoms.

In Argentina, Juan Peron's party stood for "government, order and unity". Peron made an appeal to the "shirtless" laboring masses to fight against capitalism and Yankee imperialism. The former Jesuit seminarian, Mende, helped Peron implement *justicialismo*, the Argentine version of the Catholic corporatism that informed Italy's Fascism. In Argentina, as in Europe, Fascism was the making of a revolution for the people before they could make one for themselves (Sebreli, 1985).

Catholicism could be used to rally many people toward a stable society with a stable class structure. Fascism offered to organize and discipline the masses, to secure for them a fairer share of society's wealth, and to make them behave. (In essence, this was a reprise of the Bonapartism that succeeded the French Revolution).

The Fascist leader can be a marginal who appeals to the disenfranchised while promising to keep them in line for the bourgeoisie. During his years of training in Italy, Peron developed an appreciation of Mussolini's system. As did the Church, he sought a third way, national socialism, between "Yankee imperialism" and international socialism. As did the Church, he fought to wipe out the spirit of individualism.

"Proto-Fascism" was illustrated by post-War regimes in Portugal, Greece, Chile and Indonesia. Lawrence W. Britt compared the following regimes: Nazi Germany, Fascist Italy, Franco's Spain, Salazar's Portugal, Papadopoulos's Greece, Pinochet's Chile, and Suharto's Indonesia. He did not review Austria under Dollfuss, which was closest to the Fascism advocated by the Vatican.

The following basic characteristics of proto-fascism are more prevalent and intense in some regimes than in others, but they all are similar.
1) Symbols of nationalism: Displays of flags and bunting and lapel pins.
2) Catchy slogans, exaltation of the military, and calls for unity were usually coupled with a suspicion of things foreign.
3) Disdain for human rights, demonizing those targeted.
4) Covering abuses with secrecy and denial.
5) Unifying against "enemies" or scapegoats. Opponents were labeled as "terrorists".
6) Ruling elites always identified closely with the military and the industrial infrastructure that supported it.
7) The political elite and the national culture were male-dominated. They were anti-abortion and also homophobic.
8) A controlled mass media. The leaders of the mass media were often politically compatible with the power elite.
9) Obsession with national security.
10) Religion and ruling elite tied together.
11) Power of corporations protected.
12) Power of labor suppressed or eliminated.
13) Disdain and suppression of intellectuals.
14) Obsession with crime and punishment.
15) Rampant cronyism and corruption.
16) Fraudulent elections.

S. G. Payne saw pre-World War II fascism as a reaction to liberalism, communism and capitalism. It sought to create an integrated social structure in a new, authoritarian and empire-building nationalist state. The mass was created and manipulated with patriotic quasi-religious symbols, marching and vast meetings. A separate party police or militia was always created.

Hindu Fascism

Hindu fascism began around 1925 and has in recent years been the ideology of the government of India. It is represented by the BJP Party and the related RSS movement. The RSS is modeled on a similar movement in Nazi Germany. The electoral base of the BJP is the middle class in north India.

The rise of Hindu nationalism was facilitated by several factors: the ineffectiveness of Nehru's socialist command economy in the face of globalization; the burgeoning of the middle classes subsequent to the liberalization of the economy; the resort of the Congress Party to majoritarian politics; and the displacement of the caste conflict latent in the Hindu culture onto the Muslim community. The BJP took these factors into consideration and integrated fascist ideas of the RSS organization, together with an artificially constructed Hindu discourse.

The middle classes in north India were mostly upper caste and included shop keepers, petit bourgeoisie and wealthy farmers. These were very concerned with preserving their relative privilege. Quotas and other proposed concessions to the disadvantaged were viewed by the middle classes as a threat to the status quo. The earlier inept response of the Congress government to an invasion from China had already created insecurity. The middle classes wanted a strong government that could deal with threats.

As befits a secular religion, the BJP makes much use of rituals, offers a mythology of "national humiliations", has a constructed dogma of "Hinduism", and concentrates all hate on a single scapegoat (the Muslims). This aspect of the BJP program is explored under

Rights may depend on the context. "A rational ant would find... the very concept of individual freedom intrinsically evil," said socio-biologist Edward O. Wilson. Duties are far more important than "rights" in the Chinese view, one specialist saying "rights are all but unthinkable if they jeopardize society or the state".

Freedom

The concept of freedom poses basic orienting questions. Do men exist to serve themselves, or to serve some "higher" purpose? Is man the measure of all things? The answer to this question determines one's approach to freedom. Is freedom, defined as liberty, more important than equality? For freedom to exist, there must be a choice available among desirable alternatives. Does freedom consist in the ability to do as one desires, or to do as one ought? To think, must people be free to communicate with each other? Locke claimed that this was necessary, but Hobbes and many monastic orders believe that communication and thought should be controlled. The *Catholic Almanac* defined "liberty of thought" as "freedom to think the truth".

The collectivity reduces freedom. Judgment and much of our sense of reality seem to be derived from communication with others. Also, there are psychological and practical benefits to be had from unity and ostensible certainty. For these benefits, one may reject pluralism and its essential freedom of communication. Just as the individual must mentally model his world to define reality, so must the collectivity. That collective perception of reality must be communicated. If the isolated individual receives his views from his leader or from a television screen, what of his sense of reality and his judgment? Is he then free?

The ancient Greek views of freedom included peace. For the Greeks, to be free meant to be without inequality and to move about in the polis. For Aristotle, freedom consisted of status, personal inviolability, freedom of economic activity and freedom of movement. There was also a word, *skhole*, which meant freedom *from* political activity. Epicurius used the word *ataraxia* to describe the happiness of freedom from disturbance.

Can economic freedom be separated from intellectual freedom? Would most people rather be equal than free? Are most people more comfortable with ostensible certainty than with intellectual freedom? Man's place in the world is always perceived relative to other men. To whom, besides a few intellectuals and liberals, is intellectual freedom important? If people are born unequal, then freedom must result in further inequality. A utopia that postulates equality must restrict freedom.

The egalitarian and controlled state is inadequate in providing for the playful man and does not respond well to the needs of the thinking man because leisure, variety, change and intellectual pursuits seem incompatible with achieving equality for everybody. Are not most of us intolerant? Thus, it can be argued that an egalitarian state would be more comfortable to the majority of people than would one that permitted economic and intellectual freedom, in reality only enjoyed by a few.

Can the individual be autonomous? "At the very root of philosophical liberalism is an erroneous affirmation of the autonomy of the individual in his activity, his motivation and the exercise of his liberty," Paul VI, *Octogesima Adveniens* 1971. Said Pope Paul VI: "the Christian cannot adhere to the liberal ideology which believes it exalts individual freedom by withdrawing from it every limitation, by stimulating it through seeking of interest and of power, and which sees social groupings as the natural result of individual initiatives."

Freedom of speech is destabilizing. "It is of paramount interest to the state and to the nation to prevent the masses from falling into the hands of bad...educators. Therefore, the state must exercise strict control over the press ", said Hitler. "In our state, naturally, there can be no place for freedom of the speech, press, etc., for the foes of socialism," said the URSSR's Andre Vishinski. "Rights are merely means to rational ends... the liberty of thinking and of publishing whatsoever one likes is not in itself an advantage. On the contrary, it is the fountainhead and origin of many evils", said Frs. Ryan & Boland, in *Catholic Principles of Politics*.

Censorship is defensive. Does society wait for an offense to be committed, or does it suppress a potential offense? Since action proceeds from opinion, said Hobbes, the sovereign must censor books and decide who will be allowed to speak. Suppressing opinion can thus be seen as a means of preventing unwanted action.

Freedom is only for true and righteous views. "There is no more reason for permitting a man to say or write what he pleases than for permitting him to exercise any other set of muscles... the natural right of freedom of expression extends only to those opinions and doctrines which are true and righteous." Fathers Ryan & Boland, *Catholic Principles of Politics*. "Literature is 'immoral' if it is opposed to Catholic standards, and no one has a 'right' to publish such literature anymore than one has a right to poison wells or to sell tainted food", says Father Heinan in *Priest and Penitent*.

The catechism for Spanish children in 1946 taught that freedom of speech and assembly were not to be permitted because such freedoms taught error, propagated vice and enabled plotting against the Church. Children were told that censorship of the press was necessary to prevent deception, calumny and corruption of people, thus harming the public good.

The attitude toward freedoms varies with the religious denomination. In a Detroit study, 75% of the Protestant clergy thought one should have the right to advocate communism, as did 39% of the Protestant laity, 32% of the Catholic laity and only 16% of the Catholic clergy. Similar ratios obtained for other questions involving the right of free expression.

Hadden and Shupe report that fundamentalist textbook reviewers in Texas oppose modern mathematics textbooks because of an absence of absolutism. They also mention a case in Greenville, Tennessee where a federal judge agreed that parents were justified in changing schools because their children were exposed to teaching concerning Shakespeare, the Renaissance, the Wizard of Oz and other subjects incompatible with their fundamentalist views.

Freedom of religion is prescribed by law but only partially accepted. "No official can prescribe what shall be orthodox in politics, nationalism religion, or other matters of opinion, or force citizens to confess by word or act their faith therein", held the United States Court in *West Virginia Board of Education v. Barnette* (319 U.S. 624; 1943). In *Torcaso vs. Watkins* (1961) the Court held "neither a state nor the U.S. government can constitutionally force a person to profess a belief or disbelief in any religion". Although enlightened leaders may articulate tolerant principles, such principles do not seem to accord with the common desire for the security of the closed society where everyone shares the same values and beliefs.

Freedom is necessary to parliamentary democracy. Since it must always strive for total control, there is no limit to the power or control that will be sought by a totalitarian system. It must, therefore, repress free expression and free association. The logic of parliamentary democracy is the inverse. Without free expression and free association, how can democratic compromise and consent be obtained?

Organized ideology serves several purposes. The subject of organized ideology is human behavior. Achieving social solidarity is one objective. Ideology is also a useful instrument for manipulating the masses. For the individual, accepting an organized ideology may be a way to handle anxiety and tension. It also helps to reconcile the differences between the ideal and the actual and offers a way to form an identity.

Declaring the leader infallible helps control attitudes. According to Hitler, the claim of infallibility made ideological movements more effective. For good order and discipline, it is well to disguise the leader's mistakes, particularly if the organization operates on the "leader principle". The Executive Committee of the Nazi Party never again met after Hitler became its first Chairman in 1921. Wrote Martin Heidegger: "the command of the Fuhrer is the absolute center of the present legal order."

In the 1864 *Syllabus of Errors*, (which was soon to be followed by renewed claims of papal infallibility), Pius IX announced that the separation of church and state would undermine the pope's moral authority and the moral cohesion of society. Freedom of speech was also an error, declared the pope, because it inevitably led to the corruption of minds and morals.

"Our people have decided to remain free, independent, and Islamic and not be fooled by the imperialist myth of human rights." (Iranian Delegate, U.N. Human Rights Committee).

There is no limit to the duty of an individual. The intertwining of totalitarian ideology, the leader principle and the identity of morality and government makes for a most potent suppression of individual freedom. An important aspect of the fuehrer principle is that, without the limits of law, there is no limit to the duty of the individual. Whether the individual has done his duty depends upon what the leader says.

Recalling Loyola's instructions to his Jesuits, we may observe that overcoming one's conscience in order to follow orders may be viewed as a highly moral act. All totalitarian governments will agree that "private judgment" is heresy. In the explanation of the Roman Church, "*proprium concilium*" becomes "willfulness" and the source of all sin. The insistence of Wycliffe and Hus on making scripture available to the laity would have facilitated private judgment of what the scripture intended. Hus was burnt at the stake.

The one-party state, the one true and universal church, "everything in the Revolution, nothing outside the Revolution", insistence on ritual all focus on Party rule. All independence must be eliminated as the sin of pride or deviationism. There must be but one true consciousness, and only one vanguard to guide it- the party or clergy.

16

MIND CONTROL

Censorship is believed necessary. "To prevent the masses from falling into the hands of poor educators, the state must exercise strict control over the press" (Adolf Hitler)."There is no more reason for permitting a man to say or write what he pleases than for exercising any other set of muscles. The natural right of freedom of expression extends only to those doctrines which are true and righteous." Ryan & Boland, *Catholic Principles of Politics.*

Censorship is the negative aspect of indoctrination, the shutting out of all competing ideas and views of reality. Censorship is the very opposite of tolerance. In his classic *On Liberty*, John Stuart Mill advanced arguments in favor of free expression: (a) An opinion might be true. (b) An opinion might be partially true. By contending with other opinions, a fuller truth could develop. (c) Contention makes even the whole truth better understood.

Does "freedom" mean the freedom to do as one ought, or the freedom to follow one's own conscience? Plato, Spinoza, Hegel and Bergson lined up with the restrictive interpretation, as must any totalitarian system. "Since citizens are not equipped to determine for themselves what is socially desirable, competent persons with legitimately delegated power have the duty to impose social 'oughts' on citizens". (Fr. Harold C. Gardiner, S. J. *Catholic Viewpoint on Censorship.*)

In China, in 250 B.C., all books- except those about medicine, husbandry and divination- were burned. In Rome, Caligula burned both a writer and his books. Nero simply deported the writers, but still burned their books. As the laxity of his court increased, Domitian (90 A.D.) not only executed the historian who recorded the fact, but crucified the secretaries of the historian.

Early Christians, such as Hilary, Ambrose and Augustine, favored toleration for the views of individuals. Their attitude was different toward groups or books, since these might lead to the establishment of a counter-Church.

When the Council of Nicaea (325) formally condemned as heretical a book by Arius, Constantine, who was most anxious that there be unity in his realm, thereupon ordered the burning of all books by Arius. Mere possession of such a book was punishable by death. With the baptism of Theodosius in 380, orthodox Christianity was established as the state religion. Publishing Christian heresy then became a crime against the state.

Thought control descended with the Dark Ages. By the time of Theodosius II (445), the state was committed to use its force to coerce compliance with the views of the Pope. Citizens had the duty to seek out, inform upon, and kill heretics. The books of Origen had been condemned in 400. In 496, the Pope issued the first list of prohibited books. The *Index* had begun. Simultaneously, the Dark Ages descended upon Christian Europe.

While Christians wallowed in the Dark Ages, the Moslem world flourished. Tenth Century Cordoba was a center of philosophy, poetry and medicine. The Library at Cordoba had 400,000 volumes at a time when a Christian center might have only a hundred. In 975, a fanatical soldier became Caliph, and the great library was destroyed.

In 1222, the charred flesh of burning heretics could be smelled at Orleans. As of 1229, no one was allowed to have in his possession either an *Old* or a *New Testament*, since independent reading of the Bible could provide the seed of schism. Thomas Aquinas would soon be demanding the death penalty for heresy "because it is so infectious an evil".

Independent religious thinking and the rise of national languages were seen by the Church as major threats. To keep such information in fewer hands, the Pope and the Emperor decided, in 1369, to burn all books and sermons not written in Latin or Greek.

The invention of printing added difficulties for those who wanted to control thoughts. In 1487, the Pope decreed that no new works could be published without prior approval by the Church. Henry VIII burned English language copies of the *New Testament* and persecuted the translator. Henry also established a licensing system for controlling writers and publishers. The law remained in force until 1695.

By 1644, faint breezes of freedom were stirring. Milton's *Aeropagitica* argued for the "liberty to know, to utter and to argue freely according to conscience". The *Toleration Act* of 1689 granted freedom of conscience to several sects. Catholics, Jews and Atheists had to wait until 1888 to achieve full rights.

As the power of the state increased, fear of sedition took priority over fear of blasphemy. As fear of sedition faded, obscenity took over, possibly as the target of necessary psychological projection. *Gulliver's Travels* was, in Ireland, considered obscene and detrimental to both government and morals. In Brooklyn, in 1905, Mark Twain's *Adventures of Huckleberry Finn* was removed from the public library as a bad example for youth, and is suppressed by some local school boards even today.

Film censorship continued in the United States until 1952. It was not until 1952 that the Supreme Court eliminated censorship of films that were "sacrilegious", "immoral", or even "prejudicial to the best interests of the people". In Quebec, in 1953, the Censorship Board banned the film *Martin Luther* on the ground that it would antagonize Roman Catholics. In 1979, charges of blasphemous libel were sought against the presenters of the play *Les fe'es ont soif.*

"Literature is immoral if it is opposed to Catholic standards. No one has a right to publish such literature any more than one has a right to poison wells or to sell tainted food" (Father J. C. Heinan, *Priest & Penitent*). From the first Index in 496, religious censorship by the Holy Office of the Vatican continued into the Twentieth Century. At the close of Vatican II, to celebrate its ecumenical objective, the Pope declared a six month holiday from ecclesiastical punishment for priests who might read schismatic books.

Applying boycott and other extra-legal pressure against booksellers has been a frequent and documented tactic used by religious pressure groups in the United States. This approach was rebuffed by the courts in *New American Library v. Allen* (114 F. Supp. 823) and *Bantam Books v. Medko* (103 A. 2nd 256). In Canada, extra-legal pressure is said to be effected by warning visits from the police. Argentine bishop Derisi, in 1985, called on the faithful to "use all means" to stop the showing of the film *I Hail You, Mary*. The government charged the bishop with public intimidation and inciting violence. "What we want is a declaration on tolerance, not on liberty, for error has no rights" (Cardinal Ruffini, Vatican II).

Personal contacts must also be controlled. Since contaminated ideas must come from other people, one should also control social relations to keep truth pure and the worldview unthreatened. The mental stability of the weak personality is enhanced if nothing is presented to disturb his worldview. Psychological factors of denial and projection are also at work.

Projected guilt influences censorship. The paranoid reaction comes in. The subject denies and projects onto others the impulses he has difficulty repressing. He alters his view of the world so that what really threatens him from inside himself seems to be threatening from the outside. In the American South, for example, the worst abusers of blacks were the lowest classes, the "poor white trash". In a large city, a man was active as president of an organization that sought to remove sex education books from public libraries ("Parents Against Kiddie Porn"). His crusade came to an abrupt halt when he was convicted of sex and perversion charges involving children.

Paranoiac projection cycles with the economy. Tolerance and intolerance seem to come in successive waves with the economy. Worsening conditions make people look for someone to blame and xenophobic paranoia is likely to appear. Leaders can promote such paranoia and even foster it on a long-term basis.

There is a developmental sequence of censorship, coercion and informing. One writer suggests the following: ideally, one begins with the children so that they will act and become as the elite desires. Coercion must next be applied to adults, so that the society may function more smoothly. Sacrifice is then required to defend against external threat. Finally, everyone must watch his neighbor. Lastly, all will be required to be vigilant lest one's neighbor succumb to contamination from evil influences. President Zia of Pakistan seemed sincere in explaining to foreign journalists that his country was too divided to function effectively against perceived foreign threats. A few months later, he arranged a plebiscite to establish a fundamentalist Moslem dictatorship.

Censorship is comfortable to the average man. A great many citizens find censorship natural, fit, and proper. Perhaps a majority of citizens would eagerly censor their fellows if there were not laws, educated people and liberals to prohibit such censorship.

The American Library Association had an exhibit of books that were banned in the period 1976-1980. Included were the *American Heritage Dictionary* and *The Adventures of Huckleberry Finn*. A school committeeman found Huckleberry Finn subversive and anti-American, "working against the melting pot theory of our country...". In 1982, a large majority at the United Nations voted not to allow satellite broadcasting into any country without the permission of the local government.

Peace, order and good government are the ideals of Canada. The fundamental libertarian ethos of Canada must be understood within the ideals of "peace, order, and good government", as contrasted with the American "life, liberty and the pursuit of happiness". Whereas the American Republic was founded under the ideals of the Enlightenment Canada never had an Enlightenment.

The English system places vast powers with the Parliament. In Britain, an ingrained respect for a tradition and fair play serves as a check upon government. Citizens may there confidently believe in the "rights of Englishmen". A different situation obtains in Canada. Early on, the British governor sought to apply the Anglican approach of having the clergy control the common folk. To this end, the Catholic primate of Quebec was put on the British payroll and the British government supported the Catholic religion for the people of Quebec. Later immigration policy sought out European peasants to populate the rail lines leading west. The worldview of these immigrants was not that of the English yeoman.

No criticism of government was allowed. When Canadian wartime censorship was imposed in 1939, to criticize government policy in speeches was forbidden. This was to avoid "arousing passions that... would endanger the national unity of Canada". A politician had said that Canadian judges were "political heelers". Louis St. Laurent, the Justice Minister (and later Prime Minister) cited this as the sort of statement he would ask the censors to suppress.

In February of 1978, the Canadian Library Association warned members of five years in prison and/or a $10,000 fine if they distributed copies of the U. S. Congressional Reports that mentioned an international uranium cartel. The Canadian federal government had passed an Order-In-Council forbidding distribution of such information.

Organized propaganda has a venerable tradition. The Roman Catholic Church established, in 1622, the College for the Propagation of the Faith. From this came the word "propaganda". "Propaganda" can be aseptically defined as "presentation contrived to influence opinion". (Our friends do not engage in "propaganda". The friendly action is known variously as "information", "truth", "education", or "consciousness raising".

Politics requires that ideology be flexible, since politics must appeal to presently felt needs. The propaganda of ideology must show a connection to the needs of daily life.

Prophesy fulfillment is claimed as part of propaganda. The essence of indoctrination is to convince the trainee that the old way is discredited and that the new way is true. Since organized ideology involves an explanation and prediction of events, it becomes a function of propaganda to make it appear that the explanation and prediction were accurate. If necessary, a disaster can be forecast and produced, or "prophecy" can be elicited from statements.

Slogans and the big lie are easily absorbed. How can people be made to believe something other than what they want to believe? If one has a general feeling, rather than an integrated opinion, the words of another may be more easily accepted as one's own idea. Slogans, once ingrained, persist in the culture. There is psychological justification for the "big lie". Within the brain, the most excited elements will dominate the less "excited elements."

Satisfying propaganda must seem to confirm what one already suspects and satisfy id, ego and superego. One seeks confirmation of what one already thinks (Festinger, 1957). The sequences of patterns become established "engrams". Lasswell suggests that propaganda appeal to the ego, to the id, and to the superego. For the ego, it should be rational and expedient. For the id, it should offer pleasure and a sense of power. For the supercgo, it should be morally righteous. The ideology may allege the existence of witches, saboteurs and enemy agents. Propaganda must then expound on the conspiracy it has detected. To the public, propaganda will offer a simple explanation of why things went wrong.

Certain techniques become standard. Bad news is dismissed with humor, with calm and with the aspersion of sources. Aspersion and denigration may be accomplished by using the words "so-called". The qualifier "true" may also be employed to exalt what is proposed and to denigrate what is contrasted, as "true democracy", etc.

Thought control must exclude other views. Although modern technology makes it easy to convey a message, it makes it more difficult to keep competing views away from the public.

Two contrary sets of propaganda may thus reach the individual. If people start to be skeptical about the news, then it becomes harder to engineer a social consensus. A government losing support has to use increasing force or to dissolve.

In general, it is the purpose of indoctrination to condition a person for a predetermined role in society. Myth and fantasy can create a world in the mind of the believer. Television creates views that the individual does not need to integrate-one gets the pictures, words and explanation all together. But, unintegrated views, accepted from authority, can rapidly be replaced by other views provided by authority.

Censorship seeks to keep the worldview undisturbed and the ideology pure. We all try to conserve our worldviews. Since most of us are, it would seem, authoritarians, the prescriptions of fundamentalists and/or intolerant institutions and movements affect a broad audience. The redneck mentality being widespread, it is the appearance of tolerance to which the educated pay lip service. People are not naturally tolerant.

Heresy needs a creed, arbiter and a community. For heresy to exist, there must be an official creed. Heresy needs a heretic, an official set of exclusive ideas, an arbiter and a community of believers. Bernard of Clairvaux thought all heresies had their origin in the presumption and arrogance of human reason. Cardinal Mindszenty of Hungary demonstrated the suppressive attitude: "Darwin", he said, was "a dangerous heretic who ought to have been burned at the stake".

A special situation existed in Nazi Germany. There, Hitler's latest pronouncements formed the only official cannon of ideas. Thus, loyalty and disloyalty took the place normally occupied by orthodoxy and heresy. Under such a regime, guessing the leader's probable party line puts a special strain on spokesmen.

Pope Pius IX, in 1864, issued his Syllabus of Errors outlining major heretical ideas of his time. Although the Devil, (often corresponding to today's "imperialist aggression") was not specified, the Pope found heresies that parallel the errors of Marxist "revisionism":

(1) Minimizing the evils of Protestantism (*Noscitis*).
(2) To deny the temporal sovereignty of the Pope (*Cum Catholica Ecclesia, Maxima quidem*).
(3) To deny. that all but the Catholic religion should be excluded by the state (*Nemo vestrum*).
(4) To admit that Protestantism is just another form of the true Christian religion (*Noscitis*).
(5) To sympathize with clerico-liberal societies (*Quanto Conficiamus*).
(6) To deny that the Church can use force (*Ad Apostolicum.*),or that it is not supreme in deciding its own jurisdiction (*Damnatio, Multiplices inter*).
(7) To suggest that the supreme pontificate can be moved from Rome or vested in another bishop (*Ad Apostololicum.*).
(8) To claim that national, independent churches can be established (*Multis gravibusque*).

In the Soviet Union, heresy was called "revisionism". The seven typical revisionist sins were identified by a Soviet ideologist in 1957:
(1) To minimize the threat of imperialist aggression.
(2) To deny the leadership of the Communist Party.
(3) To reject the doctrine of the class struggle and/or to promote cooperation among the classes.
(4) To support social democrat parties.
(5) To deny Lenin's view of the dictatorship of the proletariat.
(6) To reject a centralized, disciplined Party.
(7) To adopt national, not Moscow directed, socialism.
(8) Another revisionist heresy was to apply Marxist analysis to the condition of a Marxist country.

Thus, loyalty takes precedence over logic. As revolutionary ideology becomes official doctrine, the new establishment will reject those of its own ideas which might be used against it.

Inquisition.

The Inquisition established terror. As the Inquisition began, so did the closed society. In southern France the Albigensians sought to have a more idealistic Christianity. After the army had occupied the area, the Inquisition was set up and continued for a long time. It appears that there is no limit to terror. "

Real enemies give place to "objective", or potential, enemies. Insecurity, pleonexia, hate released from constraint seem to converge.

The witch is the one at whom the others point and the belief in witches is exploited to force conformity (C. McWilliams, in *Witch Hunt: The Revival of Heresy*). Institutional persecution can yield to witch-hunting which spreads like an epidemic, but whose persistence depends on the will of the authorities. "Even when all the counter-revolutionaries in existence have been rooted out, new ones may emerge", said Chairman Mao. Fidel Castro made a similar pronouncement.

One should distinguish the inquisitorial procedure from "scapegoating" and "witch-hunting". Witch-hunting is general, but scapegoating is usually individual. Problems are blamed on a particular individual or group and the scapegoat thus targeted is ritually disposed of. The psychology of projection applies here, for emotional tension is reduced by displacing it onto symbolic enemies.

Pope Leo XII restored the Inquisition and its torture chambers early in the 19th Century. Similarly, after the "loss" of China, the Truman administration became overly concerned with demonstrating its anticommunism. This, and the governmental loyalty oath, established the climate for the witch-hunting of Senator Joseph McCarthy.

When the Inquisition was first organized at Verona, the stated purpose was to combine propaganda (the spreading of the true faith) with an ostensible judicial procedure. Selecting a heretic for persecution should thus have some publicity value. It is useful to find victims among deviants and those unable to defend themselves, especially if they are imagined to represent a social or economic threat.

With the Catholic Inquisition, there was often a three way split of an accused person's wealth among the informer, the Church and the Crown. In 1233, Orthodox Jews used the Inquisition to denounce other Jews, the followers of Maimonides. Also, weak personalities receive an ego boost and feeling of power if they are able to denounce others to the authorities.

The Nazi Adolf Eichmann explained his task as fighting "opponents hostile to the state". Such opponents were reportedly grouped into two categories: (1) those suspected of assassinations, sabotage, communism and liberalism and (2) sects, including Jews and Freemasons. In a civil religion, sedition takes the place of heresy.

It becomes necessary to inform upon and denounce. At the Lateran Council of 1215, Pope Innocent III made it a legal requirement for every Christian to seek out and exterminate heretics. The "guilt by association" principle forces friends of the accused to denounce him quickly in order to save themselves. Informing is a necessary element of the inquisitorial process. "Every Bolshevik under present conditions should be able to recognize an enemy of the Party, no matter how well he may be masked", said Stalin in 1936.

Torture was officially introduced into the procedures of the Inquisition by Pope Clement IV (1268). The standard practice of the Inquisition included preparatory torture to extract confessions and "previous" torture prior to killing the victim. Initially, priests and monks performed all tortures. The tortured person feels debased and may thus be psychologically as well as physically broken. In 2004, American military personnel were found to be widely using forms of torture, emphasizing debasement, to extract information from foreigners.

Public confession is useful. The victim of the Inquisition could usually save his life by confessing to whatever was asked and promising to sin no more. At Salem this was also true. Confession before a group dramatizes values and enhances social solidarity. It also turns the one who confesses into an apparent supporter of the social order.

Secrecy of police procedure increases terror. In Venice (1454) no open arrests were made, the proceedings of the Tribunal were secret and the condemned were drowned at night in the canal. Where the protection of law does not exist, secret procedures increase terror and make opposition impossible. People feel isolated and helpless. In Argentina (1982), plain clothed military police caused tens of thousands to "disappear". One observer has suggested that in Argentina, rather than to effect terror, the fundamental objective was to remove elements that did not conform to the rightist and religious worldview.

The European witch craze lasted for centuries. Witches and witchcraft became the principal focus of Inquisitorial attention in certain parts of Europe from about 1250 to 1648. Ben-Yehuda has attempted to analyze this craze in terms of timing, content and target.

By 1250, there were very few "heretics" left, and the Dominicans needed something to do. Jews and witches then became the principal target. By the end of the 13th Century, the Church had passed the peak of its power and times were changing. People wanted someone to blame for their anxieties. This atmosphere would be receptive to a witch craze.

Were women targets as witches because they were defenseless, an economic threat and expendable? (It may also be that that were demonized by churchmen because of their sex). Even the media were a factor in the witch craze. The Dominicans Sprenger and Kramer published a witch-finding manual, the *Malleus Maleficarum*. With the new technology of the printing press, it went through twenty editions and reached great numbers of people.

Times of change bring on witch-hunts. Witch-hunting was most pronounced in those areas where change was most rapid and/or the Church felt weak and threatened. The alleged conduct of the witch could be contrasted with the ideal conduct. Where times are changing, such witch trials help to test and define the new boundaries of conduct, to redraw the "cognitive map".

Swanson, from aboriginal studies, suggests that witches appear at times of weak and decentralized societal control. This would seem to apply to the American experience at the time of the Salem witch trials and with McCarthy during the early Eisenhower years.

When the Pilgrim Fathers went to America, they signed a "covenant", constituting a clerical state. When word arrived of a governor bringing a new Charter from England that would grant religious freedom and allow non-Puritans to vote, a frenzy of witch-finding began. The mood had been prepared in Massachusetts by a series of disasters. There had been an Indian war, smallpox, and fires. In 1679, Increase Mather convoked a meeting of the clergy to consider "what had provoked the Lord".

In 1691, nineteen residents of Salem were hanged for witchcraft. In late 1692, Cotton Mather published his *Wonders of the Invisible World*, explaining " I have indeed set myself to countermine the whole plot of the Devil against New England". Lieutenant Governor William Staunton enthusiastically endorsed Mather's book. Staunton was of the theocratic party and sought to have as many potential opponents as possible killed.

The Governor, Sir William Phips, came back from fighting the French and Indians to find the colony in an uproar. The jails were filling and accusations were spreading in ever-widening circles. "I have put a stop to the printing of any discourse one way or the other, that may increase the needless disputes of people upon this occasion", he wrote. When his own wife was accused, the whole witch-hunting process came to a halt.

Witches are often neighbors. Robin Briggs' research (1997) suggests a more local aspect to witch-hunting. The witches are denounced by hostile long-term neighbors and the denunciations come in times of especial difficulty. About a fourth of the accused were men. Briggs also reports that the belief in witches still persists in parts of France.

Senator Joe McCarthy brought modern witch-hunting to America. "The art is concentrating always on a single adversary. The more concentrated the object of the people's hatred, the greater will be the attraction of the movement. Recognizing many enemies would mark the beginning of doubt among the weak and indecisive" (Adolf Hitler). As the Cold War intensified in the late 1940's, a conservative mood developed. Preservation of the status quo and absolute security became the primary goals of America.

Two priests from Georgetown had dinner with Senator McCarthy and suggested the anti-communist crusade as a possible election campaign issue. Father John Cronin, of the Social Action Department of the National Catholic Welfare Conference, gave McCarthy dossiers about people in government whom the Catholics felt should be investigated, reports Father Crosby. Further details are expounded in Father D. F. Crosby's book: *God, Church & Flag: McCarthy and the Catholic Church*.

Both McCarthy and the Department of Justice thought that different legal rights should apply to citizens who were thought to be disloyal and those who were believed loyal. This followed the Inquisitorial precedent of Innocent III. In 2004, the Bush administration in America advocated similar dual standards for those suspected of terrorism and certain other crimes.

Witches serve a community purpose. Witches may be said to be within the community or to be strangers to it. As a stranger, the witch is useful as an aid to boundary definition and to preservation of the status quo. The internal witch is accused of violating a social norm. Being different makes one a target. It is safer to blame a witch, rather than someone with many friends.

Witch hunts seem to arise in response to a perceived threat. The threat is internalized within the community and the community seeks to redefine and renew itself. This may be considered "purification". Denunciation proceeds by degrees from gossip to execution.

Today, subversives, are the "witches". Today, the Church and the Faith and the Devil have yielded place to other symbols of the collectivity: the "American Way", the Nation, the People, Democracy, the Revolution, the War Effort, etc. Sinners against these symbols are denounced as subversives, rather than as heretics or witches.

Petty acts are symbolic. Bergensen (1978) suggests that where the ruling power seeks to create "new man", the moral order seems immanent in daily life and little things can assume great symbolic importance. This could explain how a ritual trial can focus on the symbolic subversion of a petty act. For example, sweeping the sidewalk in front of one's house became a symbolic way of demonstrating one's Christian faith among the converted Jews in Spain. Failure to do so invited Inquisitorial attention. The same concern with symbolic acts is evidenced in today's secular political religions.

Psychiatrists can be used as inquisitors. In his *Manufacture of Madness*, Thomas S. Szasz has drawn many explicit parallels between the Inquisition and the Mental Health Movement. It is his thesis that the psychiatric hospital has replaced the inquisitorial prison. In 1970, the KGB created the Fifth Chief Directorate with the mission of destroying intellectual, religious and ethnic dissent. The use of psychiatry for political purposes was included among its techniques.

Recantation shows unity. The charge of heresy is invented to foster the appearance of unanimity. Without obvious dissent, it can be claimed that such unity exists. "Suffer not a witch to live". Public recantation is a humiliation which serves to diminish the heretic in his own and in public opinion. (In July of 1983, the government of Poland offered to release certain dissident leaders from prison provided that (1) they publicly admitted their offenses and (2) they promised to sin no more).

The show trial allows public recantation and serves to humiliate heretics. Those being tried by the Inquisition were often invited to plead insanity. A show trial is conducted to achieve the humiliation and recantation of the heretic, to publicly proclaim the established doctrine, and to instill fear of non-conformity among the people. Given these purposes, acquittal cannot be permitted. Pope Innocent III announced the principle that suspicion of heresy would remove all a subject's rights, including the right to defend himself. Under the rules of the Inquisition, even the attorney who defends an accused heretic is guilty of "constructive heresy", or "fautorship".

Loyalty oaths debase. Requiring oaths to abjure heresy or to affirm loyalty serves to break the spirit of those so coerced and make them more cooperative. The Nazis used the loyalty oath to humiliate their opponents. Both in Nazi Germany and on the Berkeley faculty in California, only thirteen percent of the professors refused to take the loyalty oath.

Heresy is overt deviation from the official creed. It is only noted when an official chooses to call attention to it. Then, its purpose is to focus public attention and to impose public conformity through fear and ridicule. The publicity of the inquisitorial process may induce a mass behavior wherein nearly the whole society becomes suspect. During the terror of the French Revolution, one leader announced that "everyone is suspect" and "so, you did nothing against the Revolution, but what did you do for it?"

Witch-hunting arises when there is a felt need for action. The period around 1600 saw many witch trials in Germany, Switzerland, France, and Scotland, as well as some in America. The reasons assigned by historians have changed with historiographic fashion. If we include the activities of the Holy Inquisition, the Soviets and Senator Joseph McCarthy, a broader perspective may emerge. Things must be explained in terms of what people believe at the time. A need for action must be felt-priests, agitators and media can work up and manipulate masses of people quickly, so that they feel the need for action and get some strong hints as to what action to take.

Individual psychology requires an explanation and a scapegoat. When something goes wrong, there must be a reason found. A simplistic mind will blame it on God or the Devil. A conspiratorial mind will imagine malevolent human intervention. In any case, psychology requires that the fault must be sought outside the individual complainant.

If the individual has been made to feel guilty or inadequate in any respect, the mainspring for his projection of guilt has been wound. The inquisitor usually suggests motives and explanations. If the interrogation is backed by the threat or techniques of torture, the subject will quickly respond with what he thinks the interrogator wants to hear and produces a confession closely responding to the suggestions.

Catholic and Protestant witch trials differed. Humiliation and confession were the usual objectives of the Inquisition. More generally, it was a form of terror to assure overt conformity. Except in Italy and in Spain and its colonies, the Inquisition ended with the Middle Ages. The 17th Century Protestant witch trials were done within the worldview of Calvinism. The Devil was, for most people, real, as were demons. The elect would be few and most people, as sinners, would be received by the Devil. An individual witch trial could allow the community to define the "other" and thereby draw itself closer to the circle of the elect.

The Protestant trials were essentially a local phenomenon that higher authorities usually sought repress. Agitation, mimicry, and hysteria, could cause trials to spread, and communities could disintegrate. The mass in motion could become too wild a beast to control.

The Soviet trials sought to install a feeling of terror. Torture was not needed. A faithful Party member would do what the Party wanted, even if it involved confession and self-sacrifice. Reluctant participants disappeared.

The McCarthy phenomenon in America might have been very different had torture been employed. The sanctions involved loss of employment and reputation. Americans had seen China taken over by the Communists and the European land mass a potential victim of Soviet divisions. Who was to blame for this situation? The answer had to be "traitors and Communist spies". The Junior Senator from Wisconsin needed a campaign issue and discussed the matter with two priests from Georgetown University- he came out with a list of "communist agents in the State Department". Hollywood and government agencies were thoroughly intimidated and a great hunt for Communists ensued (but almost none were actually found).

Witch-hunts started and ended for various reasons. A spiteful neighbor could become a target for revenge (this was a factor as late as the 1980s in the Argentinean "disappearances"). Terror could be sought as a way to preserve the status quo in the face of impeding political or social change. The Inquisition in northern Europe gave way to the Counter-Reformation. The Protestant trials tended to a contagious hysteria and the wives of influential people were eventually charged. At that point, the authorities stopped the trials. In 1736, the ordinance of James I permitting witch trials was repealed. Lynching of individual witches continued into the 19th Century in both America and in England. Around 1840, the Spanish Inquisition was repealed.

Indoctrination

Indoctrination is done to have people see the world only as the organized ideology wishes it to be seen. Indoctrinators try to provide canned answers for all foreseeable questions. The myth promoted is a special version of history. In joining the elect, one gets the "true" explanation of events. Indoctrination must convey this sense of revelation and must keep things simple.

Symbol and ritual effect indoctrination. Indoctrination makes much use of the "association of ideas". Complex mental phenomena are seen as made up of many small parts, and of connections of these parts. Each sensation is a part, and these parts form patterns and connections through being repeatedly sensed together. Such schemata are networks of strongly connected "concepts" in the brain.

Indoctrination includes a repetition and juxtaposition of symbols in space and time. Indoctrination helps form mental patterns. For groups, this is done with symbol and ritual. "Culture" could be thought of as shared schemata. Interestingly, ritual can continue the culture even when the symbols change. For example, rows of marchers in Red Square parades may be interpreted as a continuation of the banners and icons long carried by Russian Orthodox Church faithful.

Ritual ingrains symbols. A symbol focuses emotions. To begin with, it is only the indoctrinator who decides what the symbol is to represent. Manipulating the symbol conveys the magic of communion with the thing represented. Putting two symbols together suggests a connection. Ritual ingrains in the mind the symbolic representations portrayed.

Attitudes are conditioned with oaths, pledges, credos and hymns, etc. Consider the dress and clothing of authority figures. Advertising, symbol and ritual are employed to condition attitudes. To increase the appeal to the senses, mass meetings can employ singing, chants, fireworks, flags, etc.

Symbols, reasoning and belief sets go through developmental changes. Piagetians claim that the earliest reasoning is done with mental images. As the use of symbols begins, a child cannot hold both symbol and referent (mental image) in mind at the same time. Thus, the child may not be able to distinguish between a symbol and the object that the symbol represents. The name can thus become the object.

Somewhat later in his development, says Piaget, the child does not distinguish between assumption and fact. Already using symbols for reality, the child is blending in assumptions about the world. New experiences and facts are made to fit with the worldview he has formed.

Ideas not formed by the self, but accepted from authority, are quite easy to change by substituting new ideas, if these come from authority as a complete set. On the other hand, information that has been integrated (put together in the mind of the child) tends to be permanent. One ideology may thus replace another if the individual has not thought things through.

Inconsistencies may not be perceived when belief systems are accepted whole from authority or from the cultural environment, because no individual thinking was involved in their adoption. Similarly, long habit may result in reflex ("heuristic") responses wherein the individual does not use other parts of his brain and memory to reflect. Regular participation in rituals, especially among the young, fosters such dissociation (Dorahy & Lewis 2001). What is called "mentalizing" (interpreting events in an empathetic way) also represents an important mechanism through which the individual can live with inconsistencies.

When symbols are employed, it becomes easy to create an unreal story. In religions, many of the stories involve actions and intentions of imaginary agents. Thus, explanations are invented concerning unreal and imagined situations. This process may be called "mentalizing", "theory of mind", etc. Importantly, this imaginary world and the real world can coexist and be mixed up in the individual's mind at the same time (Gallagher & Frith 2003).

Stereotyping is natural. Perception depends partly on internal and partly on external factors. For example, when we see a dog, we associate a whole set of "dog-like" attributes with the animal. Stereotyping is thus natural and necessary. Perception is thus not totally reversible. What of myth or an extreme worldview that education or indoctrination has caused the mind to integrate? Perception has become an idea and cannot then easily be altered.

Should the dopaminergic system (Kapur, 2003) or other psychic messengers cause certain schemata to become salient in the mind, what some call "psychosis" may ensue. One should remember that both the left and right brains can process symbols, but the associations formed by the right hemisphere are far less controlled.

Restructuring the world with words. "Men imagine that their reason governs words, whilst, in fact, words react upon the understanding and this has rendered philosophy sophistical. The idols imposed upon the understanding are of two kinds: names for things which have no existence or are created by unskillful abstraction" said Francis Bacon .

The culture's language itself, conveys ideology. Hanna Arendt noted that the symbolism and mental abstractions of theory are strictly the conscious mental constructions of men, while language is natural, absorbed from the culture. This implies that some ideology is absorbed with the language itself.

Redefine and rename to create "truth". Scholastics taught that symbolic truth was higher than literal truth, there being a "moral sense", an "analogical sense" and a "mystical sense" to words. Euphemisms are pleasant. The Nazi gas chambers were called "Charitable Foundations for Institutional Care". Special meanings offer a shorthand code and the chance for a free ride on the favorable connotation of a split referent.

A better identity can be taken from a group. An adolescent will become aware of the discrepancy between what he is and what he wishes to be. For Piaget, this is the source of "critical consciousness", idealism and the projection of self onto the movement or leader. Feeling inadequate, the recruit will exalt the virtues of the group and the leader.

The primary belief system is unconscious. As language, symbolism, ritual, and repetition form the mental connections, some assumptions get into our worldview without our realizing it. Some call such unconscious assumptions our "primary belief system". Coercion is important: "coercion... paves the way for persuasion, because habitual automation turns to voluntariness", explained a Catholic educator.

Peripheral beliefs that are accepted from authority without much development or integration need not be consistent. Similarly, it is easier to accept a complete value system rather than to attempt to integrate separate ideas. Thus, it is easiest to accept a complete worldview from authority without personal effort.

Monastic training may call white black. "We must learn the absolute annihilation of our own judgment. If anything appears to our eyes white, and the Church declares it black, we, also, must declare it black", said Ignatius Loyola, Founder of the Jesuits. "A true Bolshevik has submerged his personality in the collectivity, the Party.... I shall consider black something I felt and considered to be white, since outside the party, outside accord with it, there in no life for me," said Grigori Pyatakov, Soviet Publicist.

Monastic training and conditioning furnish an example of indoctrination. Like close-order drill, steady and uniform repetition of the same rites removes personal identity and instills attitudes. St. Benedict believed that the average man was weak. He needed to be supported by rules and routines sanctioned and maintained by authority. Private property was seen as militating against a truly common life and as encouraging too much independence.

Perspective is removed to make it easier to restructure reality. Psychologically, the religious recruit is separated from his old frames of reference and uncontrolled stimuli are reduced to a minimum so he will focus only on the indoctrinator. Avoidance of small talk further reduces perspective.

Hypnotic practice shows that when the field of attention field has been constricted it is easier to switch the person away from his usual reference sets. The latter state may be called "dissociation". Subtle suggestions can then help to restructure his reality. Repeated confession and correction causes the recruit to integrate new views. The dissociative effect of repeated ritual, especially among the young, has been noted.

Sex and aggression can be channeled to serve the cause. Christian monasticism emphasizes chastity and the love of Christ and Mary. Having narrowed sensory input, the next step is to block sexual and aggressive drives. These unsatisfied drives need a focus and the indoctrinator will offer one. The system seeks to channel all energy into the emotional outlets of prayer, confession and singing. One Palestinian organization sought to better control the militancy of its younger members by marrying them off.

Making a new man is a goal of all totalitarian systems. "We must create a new kind of human being. For our people, this will be the deed of the century", said Adolf Hitler. "Latin American socialism will promote the advent of the new man." *Priests for the Third World,* Buenos Aires, 1970. Claims about developing a new man are a distinguishing characteristic of totalitarians. Authoritarians seem interested only in outward behavior, rather than inner feelings. Conservatives, generally, have no illusions about being able to change human nature.

Latin American "liberation theologians" continually talked about forming a "new man". The Jesuit and liberation theologian, Jon Sobrino, put it: "Moral activity is aimed at turning a person into the new person... who stands in opposition to the old person".

The Chinese made intensive efforts to form a "new man" in their society. Their behavioral modification efforts included the use of informers, public denunciations, public confession, self-criticism, group study, control over communications, redefinition of language and "thought reform" in school and prison settings.

The Prior explained to the monk Luther: "once you have committed yourself, you are not free to throw off the yoke of obedience, for you had accepted it voluntarily while still free to discard it". As the Prior undressed him, he said: "Lord divest you of the former man and all his works... the Lord invest you with the new man.."

Personality is modifiable through indoctrination, but may begin reverting toward its original nature as soon as the manipulation is removed. One Sandanista in Nicaragua confided : "only Christ can make a new man".

How much can human nature be changed? How much is human conduct influenced by nurture, rather than by nature? Has man changed? Can he change? What, then, shall be his relation to the collectivity? (Even arch-conservatives will call for value indoctrination and behavior training in schools). How much should we try to shape our basic human material? The social implications of the response are enormous.

Thought Reform

Priests who had undergone Chinese Communist thought reform were intensively studied by the psychiatrist R. J. Lifton (*Thought Reform and the Psychology of Totalitarianism*) and his observations for some of the following. Although we have already discussed "brainwashing" as a technique of mental domination, it may prove worthwhile to look again at the subject from the standpoint of religious psychology.

Symbol substitution is a basic technique of thought reform. One Catholic bishop claimed to have resisted thought reform. He found "the identical methods, the identical terminology", in the Communist conversion techniques and in those of his own Church. Part of the bishop's resistance technique was simply to replace the Communist symbols with Christian symbols: "for the 'State', I substitute 'God'; for the 'people' , I use 'Christians'; for 'imperialist evils', I use 'self love' and 'love of pleasure'... I could agree to personal shortcomings because I had many shortcomings regarding God".

Another Jesuit saw these similarities to Christianity in the goals of Communist thought reform:

(*a*) The concept of love (of the people, etc.).
(*b*) The concept of hope in the future.
(*c*) Having faith in the ideology.
(*d*) A deity (the Communist movement).
(*e*) Sacrifice, of martyrdom and sainthood.
(*f*) Stress on humility and selflessness.
(*g*) Stress on applying theory to life.

Some Jesuits explicitly likened the Chinese program to their own Jesuit training. A Protestant missionary thought it resembled the Moral Rearmament movement. Fundamental to the religious analogy is some revealed higher purpose. The elect (priests, monks, party members) articulate the dogma and form the vanguard of the movement toward this higher purpose. All means necessary to achieve the purpose may be acceptable.

Exploiting the sense of guilt is the primary step in thought reform. Most people, and especially adolescents, feel a sense of guilt because they realize that they are less than they could be. Since all humans have greed and certain selfish concerns even when they perform altruistic actions, all may be said to be "guilty".

The first step in Chinese thought reform is to have the victim "confess" such general sin or guilt. "Struggle meetings" are held to obtain such a confession. A protestation of innocence is considered but psychological resistance. Even those who cooperate may be but "radishes" (red on the outside, white on the inside).

Authorities manipulate the criteria for achieving the goal. As with the Jesuit Spiritual Exercises, the natural feeling of guilt is potentiated with an induced artificial guilt. Non-specific feelings of guilt are channeled. Instead of merely feeling guilty, the individual is made to feel guilty about specific things. Everyone, of course, has good and bad aspects. Often, there are dominant and repressed aspects to the same trait. Guilt must be developed concerning those aspects the mentor considers undesirable. Reform consists in replacing selected dominant aspects with repressed aspects, says Lifton.

Contact deprivation is always practiced. As in the Jesuit *General Examen*, contacts with family, friends and the outside world are broken. The individual must feel alone in a controlled milieu with his trainer and his guilt. The mounting pressure of repressed guilt provides the psychic energy for change. This is similar to the acute confusional state preceding religious conversion. Said one subject: "I developed a terrible fear that these thoughts would come out and be known to all".

Never-ending guilt intensifies efforts at reform. Guilt and self-deprecation can produce great dedication. One who distrusts himself will not allow not allow freedom to others. Loathing himself and projecting this feeling on the outside world, the fanatic can never cease in his efforts to reform himself and the world.

In psychological terms, the thought reform process involves:

(*a*) Removal of perceptual and social support structures.
(*b*) Weakening the ego.
(*c*) Inducing feelings of guilt, introspection, self-criticism.
(*d*) Destruction of self-image.
(*e*) Rationalization of guilt feelings.
(*f*) Creating a new self-image.
(*g*) Deprivation shock.
(*h*) Encouragement.
(*i*) Assuming new support structures.

Isolating the belief system keeps away competing versions of reality. It is easiest to accept a complete belief system from authority, without trying to evaluate and fit together the individual ideas. Isolating the belief system facilitates the co-existence of inconsistent beliefs (compartmentalization); the claim of great difference from similar competing systems; and the explaining or denying of inconsistent facts.

Lifton's *Thought Reform and the Psychology of Totalitarianism* (1961) describes the main themes of the brain washing process:

(*a*) Milieu control.
(*b*) Mystical showing of a revealed law
(*c*) The demand for purity.
(*d*) Required confession, privacy traded for unity.
(*e*) Sacred revelation as orthodoxy.
(*f*) Language loaded with clichés and epithets.
(*g*) Doctrine is more important than the individual.
(*h*) Only the collectivity exists, not the individual.

The general steps in brainwashing are: (a) Cut off old links by controlling and isolating the physical and social environment. (b) Show the person that his old beliefs are wrong.

(c) Foster a new allegiance.

Specific techniques of the brainwashing process include: (a) isolation- from former daily routines, associates, family and sources of information. (b) regimen- requiring absolute obedience and humility. (c) social pressure- in group meetings and in interrogations bolstered by a lack of privacy and emphasized brotherhood. (d) study groups- self-criticism, application of principles, joint worship of leaders. e) redemption- salvation depends on succeeding in the reformation process.

Paulo Freire's "pedagogy of the oppressed" explains how to produce revolutionary thought: the objective is to make people dissatisfied ("reject the oppressive consciousness") and to then adopt the new ideology ("conscientization"). The steps: (a) "The oppressed person perceives and modifies his relationship with the world." (b) He gives up "over valuing the past". (c) He gives up "mythical explanations". (d) He stops "debating" and "engages in dialogue". He then develops "critical awareness" because: (1) "Real causes" replace "magical explanations" (2) The dialogue becomes dialectic (3) He adopts new words to describe reality.

There is some consistency in the steps followed by various thought reform operations, but our knowledge of the mental mechanism upon which these operations work is slight. Human perception uses the right and left hemispheres of the brain. The right hemisphere is especially concerned with non-verbal symbolic and spatial perception, but we know little about its use in thought. The left hemisphere is predominant in language and reasoning. We know only a little about how it operates.

For humans, words can become reality. Chimpanzees can learn symbols for concepts, but they do not seem to do so in natural situations. Human intelligence is special because of language.

Training the young is considered necessary. At the SS and Comintern training centers, the development of complete loyalty was the primary objective. A second purpose seemed to be the redefinition of external reality, so that inconsistencies would not be perceived.

"The Church wanted to cure souls; the humanism of the Renaissance sought to develop the spirit; Marxist materialism is preoccupied with the body and with material well-being. We want to make a synthesis of this and to form complete men who will be at once disinterested idealists, fighters, vigorous athletes and cultivated beings", said the Director of an SS school. (Quoted in John Hellman's *Emmanuel Mounier and the New Catholic Left*, Toronto, 1981.)

At the college for Chinese Communist cadres, it took a year to wash out the old ideas and "remold the brain. Theodore White recalls that it was he who persuaded Mao to call this process "consciousness raising".

"Give me a child until the age of seven, and I shall have him for life", is reportedly a Jesuit adage. Until 1982, Cannon law 1374 made it a mortal sin for a Catholic child to attend a neutral public school unless a priest had given special permission. The dissent of U.S. Supreme Court Justice Jackson in *Everson v. Board of Education*, sought to demonstrate that the parish school was the most vital part of the Church itself

Prison indoctrination uses similar principles. Zimbardo (1973) began an interesting experiment by assessing normal young men for authoritarianism, before randomly assigning them as guards or as prisoners in a prison. He found that those who were authoritarian made the best prisoners.

Zimbardo found that the following reactions developed in less than two weeks even though the men knew that they were participating in a simulation experiment:

(*a*) Using numbers, rather than names, diminished identity.
(*b*) Asking for permission induced childish dependency.
(*c*) Guards, without design, created an arbitrary environment.
(*d*) As guards became more aggressive, prisoners became more

passive.

(*e*) Officials quickly began to sacrifice principle situationally.

(*f*) Internal withdrawal offered prisoners the best defense.

(*g*) Power defined all relationships and identities.

(*h*) Half the prisoners showed no loyalty to other prisoners.

Technology requires increased repression. Although technology makes it easy to convey a message, it makes it more difficult to isolate a population from competing views. Two contrary sets of propaganda may thus reach the individual. If people start to be skeptical about the news, then it becomes harder to engineer a social consensus. Government in the face of a dissolving consensus must use increasing force to maintain its hold.

It is the purpose of indoctrination to condition a person for a predetermined role in society. Myth and fantasy can create a world in the mind of the believer. As ritual and rote form the mental connections, some assumptions become so ingrained that we incorporate them into our worldview as truth without realizing it. Some call such unconscious assumptions our "primary belief system". Unintegrated views, accepted from authority, can rapidly be replaced by other views provided by authority. Censorship seeks to keep the worldview undisturbed and the ideology pure.

Intolerance is endemic. We all try to conserve our worldviews. Since most of us are, it would seem, authoritarians, the prescriptions of evangelicals and/or intolerant institutions and movements affect a broad audience. The authoritarian mentality seems fundamental. Although the educated may lip service to tolerance, people are not tolerant.

17

CONVERTS AND FANATICS

The group offers a place to be safer. There may be a basic psychological need, akin to the herd instinct and the pecking order, for an individual to identify himself with a community and to find a position in society. Individuals want to conform and to believe what the group believes.

The person with a weak personality is most susceptible to outside influence. With initiation and conditioning, such persons can rapidly take on the ostensible values and attitudes of the group. When committed to a group, the individual leaves behind his own personal ethics. Marx himself felt strongly the urge to join a group. "I could not rest", he said, "until I had purchased modernity by joining an avant-guard group." Even a minority group is better than no group at all.

Ascetics, instruments and vessels act differently. The independent ascetic has no need to be concerned with how his vocation fits the world. His values are relatively intrinsic. Similarly, the contemplative mystic renounces action. However, if an individual considers himself as God's instrument, he may seek salvation in action. Revolution is justified by "obeying God rather than men". When an "instrument" starts seeking "vessels", beware, for he is becoming a prophet.

Priests and monastics were often misfits. Monastic asceticism seeks to foster the individual's search for salvation and, also, to work well for the institution. For a long time, religious groups offered the only hope of higher education for those without means. The poor, the misfit and the dissatisfied are often attracted by monasticism. The monastery offers a refuge for those who have trouble fitting in with the outside world. For the dissatisfied seeking purpose and meaning, a guided spiritual quest is available.

One abbot recently noted these reasons for joining his religious order: (a) A Christian family often provides the seed. (b) There is the attraction of the group and of the movement (c) One seeks an "encounter with Christ". (d) There is the "critical conscience". As awareness of one's imperfections (guilt) increases, the search for perfection creates an uneasy "critical conscience". (e) Life is made easier by the organization.

Is the monastery also a way dissolving self in the collective psyche, of achieving the unity and peace of womb return? One author claims that the prime psychological characteristics of monastic Christianity were:

(1) self-surrender to God's will and (2) chastity to obtain divine love. Seminarians (Coates, 1973) showed deference, order, affiliation, self-focus, succor and self-abasement. They were neither autonomous nor well able to accommodate change.

(2) **The cult offers a place and a role to the convert.** The ancient Greek city-state constituted a spiritual community, a *polis*, for its members. When that community disappeared in the second century B.C., so did the sense of the world as a cooperative effort. Men felt much more alone. The mystery religions waxed.

The sense of being alone and afraid encourages the search for an ideology. A fear of responsibility also predisposes a person to accept an ideology, for the lack of an essential psychological element usually results in the quest for a substitute. As an isolated individual, the ideologue seeks to join a group.

The weak imagine the group to have what they lack. This union with the "select", or the "chosen", makes the convert feel more whole, more useful and stronger. Psychologically weak to begin with, the prejudiced person feels that his belonging to the elect is tenuous. He needs to keep asserting his membership and his distinction from the non-elect. Thus, he begins to denigrate targets outside the group.

The desire of the convert or recruit to show others that he "belongs" is often dangerous. In order to show his commitment, he may perform illegal, extreme and violent acts. Such acts may also be performed when there is a loss of individual identity, a "deindividuation", as within a mob. Here, individual principles are sacrificed in favor of conduct normative to the specific situation (Portmes and Spears, 1998). The group behavior at the time becomes the rule.

The mere fact of being designated as "in" a particular group generates bias in favor of that group and against outgroups. If outgroup members are easily identifiable, then they serve as clear exemplars for the mental schema of prejudice (Markus 1977). Such schema are retained in a more permanent part of the memory and are resistant to change. Edwards and Smith (1996) have explained this principle of "disconfirmation bias".

The obedient are legalistic. Denial of moral responsibility is possible for someone who has surrendered his judgment to "orders". Reliance on regulations and absolution both tend to focus on specific individual acts rather than on total conduct. This induces legalistic, rather than ethical, behavior.

Ideologies are interchangeable. Since all articulated ideologies offer similar emotional satisfactions, the ideologue can accept almost any ideology and may shift from one to another. In the final elections of the Weimar Republic, voters easily switched from the Communists to the Nazis. After the Nazi takeover, the Black shirts were happy to absorb into their organization the former Communist cadres. Joseph Goebbels himself was interested in both communism and Catholicism, finally declaring that National Socialism was his religion. If morality is thought to consist of following orders and adhering to group standards, then it does not seem to matter much which group one joins or what the standards are. If the belief system or ideology is received whole from authority without personal integration, then the change may be easily effected.

People joining a cult tend to have similar characteristics. Lofland, in his *Doomsday Cult*, discussed converts to a small cult. Converts typically came from lower middle class rural backgrounds. To solve a problem, they were familiar with a religious framework, but understood nothing of psychiatry or political action.

They all believed in the intervention of spirits in daily events and in the existence of a purpose and individual mission in life. Conditions which predisposed such people to join the cult included: a personal feeling of great tension, the alienation of being in a new environment away from close friends, and arrival at a turning point where it was possible or necessary to begin a new course in life.

A close relation with others in the cult seemed crucial for total membership. Some friendship with cult members was necessary to joining. Becoming a "total" convert then seemed to hinge on living closely together. Former Catholics who converted to Pentacostalism in three Latin American communities (Maldonado 1992) were more influenced by friends and relatives than by preachers or TV evangelists. They gave "seeking a relationship with the living God" and a search for "meaning in life" as their primary motivations. In communities of the dislocated and disoriented, they wanted to rebuild their lives.

Harrison examined recruits to the less extreme Catholic Pentecostalism and found them to be middle class, lonely, preconditioned to accept the approach of the cult, without great prior commitments, and as having social relations with members. Social factors can bring a person into such a cult, but belief retains him, says Harrison.

In Lifton's experience, those converted had: (a) a strong, accessible, suppressed identity. (b) unusual susceptibility to guilt. (c) a tendency toward cultural identity confusion. (d) a profound sense of involvement. (e) an authoritarian/totalitarian character.

The young and the marginal are especially susceptible to cults. Man seeks a transcendent sense of purpose, unity and hope. If he does not find himself in a culture that seems to provide such consolation, then he may join or form a culture that promises to do so. Those not admitted to a society may sympathize with an ideology that rejects that society. The marginals need a restorative sense of mission, of identity and importance. If it downgrades authority and offers youth a chance to lead, then youth are likely to support the ideology. Said Hitler: "The Youth Movement is not meant to constitute an organization of the contented and satisfied, but to embrace those tormented by suffering, those without peace, the unhappy and the discontented."

The leader is the focal point of the cult. In a cult, as distinguished from a sect or a monastic institution, the leader is the principal or exclusive focus. Rather than exercise independent moral judgment, a member may externalize this onto the leader. There is often a feeling of imminent Armageddon. The cult may collapse with the disappearance of the leader. Whereas religion and sect are connected with the tradition, the cult may claim to make a great new beginning.

Group think may lead to group hysteria. Fundamentalists often have a rural background and feel marginalized in contemporary society. They thus cherish the feeling of togetherness that a group with like attitudes may foster. Thus, apocalyptic fantasy may easily be transformed into a false of perception of current reality and individuals may see "End Times", "The Rapture", "Tribulation", etc., in current events. The Armageddon scenario also allows for the release of pent-up frustration. One subject claimed that "burning will cleanse the Earth" (Strozier 1996). This is reminiscent of the German ideology that preceded the Nazi era.

"The mass meeting is necessary for the individual who feels lonely and who easily succumbs to the fear of being alone. In the meeting, he starts to feel part of a larger community. Most find this encourages and strengthens them." "The key to mass appeal is not objectivity, but will and power", said Hitler.

Guilt, dissatisfaction and frustration can all evoke a desire for change. Tension can come from "frustration" of desires, such as for: prestige, explanation, sexual satisfaction, for relief from guilt or fear, or for a desire to communicate with God or the spirit of the universe.

Induced guilt is a psychological mainspring. Once the person recognizes his guilt and makes a full confession, then the authorities hold a trial and award a light sentence. Thought has been reformed and public redemption has been achieved.

The confused are ideal subjects. Arendt suggests that the ideal subject for an ideology is one for whom true and false do not exist. The confused are ideal subjects. The person who has difficulty thinking for himself will readily accept the clichés of an ideology. Indoctrination seeks to have the believer primed with canned answers to key questions, to have him see the world as the ideology sees it, and to react in a predictable way.

The fervent embracing of a religion (the "conversion") is analogous to the embracing of an ideology. Both adopt an external system to reintegrate a disordered ego. The "confusional reaction" provides a psychological model for the conversion experience. The overall acute confusional reaction pattern includes: a predisposing psychological environment; conditions of frustration which produce great pressure; a pre-confusional state of angst; feelings of worthlessness and listless conformity; a confusional phase of helpless loneliness followed by a desperate search for a love object to adore and from which to secure succor; a reaction formation of affect reversal wherein one seeks to serve a cause or loved one; reintegration by "going home" to an authoritarian womb-substitute.

Certain psychological circumstances predispose to ego disintegration. The confusional state may include: a new, unfriendly environment; external pressure to conform; stress from severe infantile trauma; or an internal urge for self realization. Infantile trauma may be caused by such poor parenting as constriction, irrational punishment, or abandonment. In general, one looks for experience which prevents normal ego development and tends to produce a surrender to authority as a sort of return to the womb.

The rage reaction to pressure can vary in intensity from mere frustration to homicidal fantasies or the wish to destroy all society (Armageddon). The similar idea of apocalypse has been associated (Deutsch, 1980) with paranoid megalomania. Catastrophe dreams are typical of this phase.

During the confusional stage, the individual finds himself easily distracted by trivia, feeling worthless, lonely and helpless, seeking an object to adore that will give him succor. (This resembles the alienation of the mass man.

During the reintegration phase, the subject may have various dreams relating to the theme of "going home". This may represent a mental reversion to childhood in order to begin again to orient himself to the world.

Those with closed minds do not seem to independently evaluate and incorporate ideas. Since the ideas are assumed from authority without a personal integration, this type of convert finds it easier to accept a new system of belief in a package. Doubt about one's own abilities may cause one to try and suppress such doubts by compulsive serving behavior. This enhances compliance in the resolution phase.

In the successful resolution phase, the individual has found something to love and a purpose in life. He may wish to serve mankind or an institution. Dissolving in something outside himself has brought relief. He now has a place and an identity. Eric C. Lincoln *The Black Muslim in America* [Quoted in Yinger (1976)] speaks of the convert taking on an entirely new identity and entering a life requiring faith, self-control and total hatred.

William James long ago described the psychology of religious conversion: to be regenerated, to receive grace, to gain an assurance whereby a self hitherto divided, and consciously wrong, inferior and unhappy, becomes unified and consciously right, superior and happy, as a result of achieving true understanding.

"Cults" are treated as "new religions" by Richardson (1995) in a sympathetic review that sees them as therapeutic and benign. It appears that the ethos of these groups appeals to the set of psychological needs of a prospective member. Jesus Movement members showed a "dependency-prone" syndrome that was nonetheless functional within their commune. The Rajneesh in Oregon knew what they wanted and went for it, although what they wanted was not altogether conventional (Latkin, 1990). The Hare Krishna (ISKON) group had a rather homogeneous set of personality characteristics and background and seemed to be content with their organization (Poling & Kenny, 1986; Weiss & Comprey, 1987).

The ISKON's were said to be motivated (as are many monastics) by a striving for transcendence. Desires for sex and sensual gratification are redirected toward devotional services. The California Personality Inventory identified obsession and compulsion as their most salient characteristic. Many members tended toward the feminine and were more defensive than trusting. In general, they showed conformity, and emotional stability (Weiss & Comprey, 1987).

Mystics are uncontrolled. For the Jivaro of Ecuador, daily life is said to be only an illusion, for reality is personal and may only discovered in an hallucinogenic state. Mystics generally think in an analogous uncontrolled way. William James said the mystic experience was difficult to express, highly personal, episodic, and as felt in the grip of an external power.

A contemplative hermit, retreating within himself, may find revelation and inspiration, producing a call to action. Mystics may become prophets and thus represent the threat of schism and polytheism. D'Aquili and Newberg (1999) attempt to find physical correlates for mystical experiences.

In his Psychology of Religious Mysticism, Leuba found the following common characteristics of mystics (a) A tendency to self-affirmation and a need for self-esteem. (b) The need to devote oneself to a cause. (c) A need for affection and moral support. (d) A need for peace, singlemindedness, unity. (e) A need for sensuous satisfaction. (f) A tendency toward exaggeration, hortatory and abstraction. (g) Insistency and imperativeness. Said St. Francis: "you will see that one day I shall be adored by the whole world."

The mystical experience and the convert: According to R. W. Hood (1975), the mystical experience included: (1) a sensed loss of identity (2) dissolving self in something greater. (3) a personal, internal and subjective discovery. (4) feeling disconnected in space and time. (5) sensing charisma. (6) experiencing a valid revelation. (7) ineffability. Could most of these also characterize the convert to a movement?

18

TERRORISM

A century ago, Anarchists were blowing themselves and others up. Two thousand years ago, the Sicarii fanatics were doing large scale political murder. Almost three thousand years ago, the Hindu Thugi were murdering. This sort of thing is not new. (See, for example, Berkman's *Prison Memoirs of an Anarchist*). Guerrilla warfare has been called the "weapon of the weak" and terrorism as the "weapon of the weakest".

One's opinion of terrorism depends on how he sees it. Clausewitz said that war was "a continuation of politics by other means". Terrorism can be said to be a form of warfare and terrorists often call themselves "warriors". Also, terrorists may consider themselves as the instruments of a higher power or principle.

There is no generally agreed definition of terrorism. The creation of fear is a common objective and the purpose is to effect political, social or religious change. Revolutionary terrorism aims to overthrow and replace the whole system. Violent and/or unlawful means are employed, often when there is thought to be no real chance of effecting change through legal means.

Terrorism may be the resort when no other way is apparent. R. E. Rubenstein's *Alchemists of Revolution* (1987) observes that in Italy, Uruguay, Argentina, Brazil and (possibly) Germany, terrorists groups emerged under poor economic conditions when educated youth saw no possibility of change through the existing political structures.

Terrorists may seek to speak for a constituency. Rubenstein makes several additional points: (1) ethnic or nationalist ideologies override social programs (2) social grievances having broad-based social support are more important than international terrorist networks (3) "there is no force more terroristic than a nation-state at war" (4) those planning terror may be "ambitious idealists without a creative ruling class to follow or a rebellious lower class to lead".

When dissatisfaction can be subsumed by religious, ethnic or nationalist identities, the potential for mass action exists. (Since Islam is defined as the body of the faithful, *umma*, radical clerics already have a large potential base). Bringing young adults into large political movements with a realistic potential for effecting change could be one response to terrorism.

The motive for the action, the target of the action, the means employed, whether the action is international or indigenous and who does it are all criteria to be considered. Government policy strongly influences the definition of terrorism. Our friends are "legitimate governments" and "freedom fighters"- the others are "dictator/tyrants" and "terrorists".

Propaganda, colonialism and drugs are considered terrorism. The 1987 Islamic Summit in Geneva sought to define terrorism as the use of weapons to intimidate the general public. They considered colonialism and the narcotics trade as inhuman acts with a corrupt purpose creating insecurity and thus as forms of terrorism. "Pollution of information" they thought potentially one of the most dangerous forms (http://al-islam.org/ al-tawhid/definition-terrorism.htm).

Aerial bombing is terrorism. Bombs dropped from airplanes often destroy innocent families in their homes, so such "collateral damage" can be thought to be inhuman and terrorist. Those ordering such bombing may claim that the primary objective or intention, in distinction to the act of a terrorist, was not to harm innocents. Such "collateral damage" may be hundreds of times greater than the willful acts of terrorists.

Some think that state terrorism may include torture, death squads, disappearances and concentration camps. Specious attempts may claim (see the U. S. Code) that states cannot commit terrorism themselves, but can sponsor non-governmental international terrorism. In reality, state sponsored terrorism is usually clandestine, except when the objective is to terrorize the home population.

The lack of affect, of general human empathy, is thought to be a characteristic of some Western urban societies. The remoteness brought about by television and aerial views allows those who cause or foster the harm to become psychologically numb to their human responsibility. They consider themselves as observers or technicians rather than as terrorists.

Shame may reduce the guilt felt over terrorist action. Very authoritarian fathers can cause a child to feel inadequate and shamed. Gilligan notes that pain and punishment increase feelings of shame but reduce feelings of guilt. By shaming others, one diminishes one's own feelings of shame. Similarly, failure to identify with the same sex parent can result in a lack of feeling toward self. Thus can an authoritarian father contribute to the terrorist mentality.

Terrorists may seek to come alive and gain respect. In four decades of studying murderers, Gilligan found that many of them felt "dead inside" and unable to feel empathy. He suggests that one part of their motivation was to seek some response or feeling. Another aspect is to obtain recognition or "respect".

Obtaining such "respect" is a counter to the great sense of humiliation felt by most terrorists. In a speech on retiring in 2003, Malaysia's Prime Minister five times referred to Muslims as "humiliated". Western military imperialism and economic exploitation, oppressive and exploitive local regimes, lack of educational and economic opportunity all contribute to the sense of humiliation felt by young Muslims.

High profile, violent acts, such as the beheading on video tape of a journalist, will obtain the most publicity. The purpose is to embarrass the authorities and destroy the sense of security among the public. They consider such means acceptable to achieve politico/religious ends. Since terrorist violence is usually done for the effect on the public, rather than the victims, it requires an audience and publicity.

Are small groups really representative? Are they not likely to be carried away by their own ideology? Only when it is part of a broader program, such as a revolutionary mass movement or a state-sponsored program, (as in China or Vietnam) has terrorism shown results.

Atran suggests a distinction between ideologically-driven terrorist groups and groups responding to particular local grievances. Both will have ideologies, but the latter would appear less neurotic.

The terrorist himself usually sees no hope for change through conventional methods. He may be an intelligent idealist who sees the existing system as hopelessly corrupt and in need of purification.

C. N. Edwards saw terrorists as feeling that they were denied something that they were entitled to and as being unable to balance their ideals with reality. Edwards feels that the individual terrorist seeks a group to confirm his view of reality. But, most observers suggest that the group or leader forms the ideas of the terrorist. It is also possible that some terrorists, like some serial rapists, obtain psychological satisfaction from causing terror itself.

Apart from youth, there does not appear to be any common psychological characteristic among terrorists.

Purification is a recurring theme. The Old Testament talks of wars for "righteousness", the 16th Century saw the Revolutionary of the Upper Rhine, Savonarola and Machiavelli. The latter called for the simple killing of political opponents, the others called it seeking "purification". Frustration leads to a lack of discrimination and a rage for fundamentalist purism.

Impotence and the desire to be heard characterize terrorists. One month after the attack on New York's World Trade Towers, Orhan Pamuk wrote in the *New York Review of Books* describing the resentment he witnessed in the Mid-East of America's political and economic power by people "living in conditions that give rise to feelings of humiliation and inferiority", that TV and films were daily bringing the lives of the rich to the attention of the poor and that there was an overwhelming feeling of humiliation. "It is the feeling of impotence deriving from degradation, of the failure to be understood, and the inability of such people to make their voices heard".

Tarik Karim sees motivations akin to those that cause inner-city terrorism and envisions similar solutions: education outreach, job creation, health care, housing, and recreation. Importantly, he suggests that activities of non-governmental organizations may offset the influence of the religious madrassaha schools.

Juergensmeyer sees terrorism as a way of symbolically expressing power toward oppressing forces and of regaining some personal dignity. This would represent the fourth stage in the progression: (1) perception of a world gone awry. (2) the foreclosure of opportunity to better the situation. (3) identification and demonization of the oppressors. (4) symbolic acts of power.

The suicidal terrorist may be driven by shame. Revenge, humiliation, frustration and hopelessness are often mentioned as motives for suicidal terrorists. Those who seek to repress such individuals with harsh measures appear to be aggravating the situation, for pain and punishment increase feelings of shame while decreasing feelings of guilt. Guilt is then less likely to restrain the terrorist.

Attempts at repression of terrorism are usually counter-productive. Repression is often designed to decrease the sense of self and beat-down pride. Absent other ego boosters, a repressed desire for revenge may induce masochistic or suicidal behavior. The narcissistic individual is often hypersensitive to shame. Thus, repression appears quite counterproductive.

Hezbollah is a popular religious party. Adam Shatz's study of Hezbollah illustrates the apparent development from the raw armed struggle of an underclass to a successful and moderated participation in the political process. The Hezbollah leader, Nasrallah, studied in seminaries at Qom and Najaf and wears Shiia clerical robes. Upon coming to power in 1992, he had Hezbollah participate fully in the Lebanese political process. Said a local observer: “For the first time, the Shiites here feel they have some power we used to laugh at them as riff-raff.”

Nasrallah is analytical and appreciates Western science and technology. He separates his program into (very successful) community services and “resistance”. His resistance to the Israeli Occupation is very calculated and limited to the minimum necessary use of force. He praises Palestinian suicide martyrs. He has no program to ban books or to impose sharia law and sees no likelihood that Lebanon could become an Islamic state. Pro-Likud officials in the U.S. State and Defense Departments brand him a dangerous terrorist and promise to “go after” him.

Israeli terrorism is mostly state-sponsored. Defined as the threat or use of violence in a systematic way to create fear among a population and thereby influence political action, Israel gives us an example of successful revolutionary terrorism eventually becoming rightist.

Terrorism often arises when some people become convinced that their cause is just, but that normal political processes seem to offer little hope. (Paradoxically, terrorism has been successful only when used as an arm of a larger political movement). Religious commitment is a great help to the conviction that one’s cause is just, for who would challenge God’s command?

Zionist Terrorism

In the First Century (A.D.), the Zealots were a Jewish sect that opposed Rome and its polytheism. Their Sicarii knife men would frequent public places and stab in the back Jews thought to favor Rome. This was to terrorize the population into the Zealot political policy toward Rome. At Masada, in 75 A.D., the Zealots forced a mass suicide ten times greater than that at Jonestown. Masada is admired and celebrated by some Jewish groups.

The Messianic, fundamentalist and Orthodox elements of Judaism may be manifest in withdrawal as with the Haredi, or by universal activism, as with the Gush Emunim. There are many branches of Judaism with many different views and one cannot generalize either about Jews or about Israelis. The Revisionist Zionists were active in terrorism at the time of the founding of Israel.

To try and change the policy of the legally established British government, the terrorist Stern gang (Lehi) made many attacks against the British, even attempted to obtain aid from the Axis, and murdered a British Minister (1944) and Count Bernadotte (1948) of Sweden in Cairo. Yitzhak Shamir was a Lehi leader who decided on these assassinations. Shamir was a Revisionist Zionist who later three times became Prime Minister of Israel.

The Irgun Zvai Leumi was led by Menachem Begin, who later became Prime Minister of Israel. The Irgun was active in indiscriminate terror. They hung British soldiers, etc., and on July 22, 1946, blew up the King David Hotel, killing 91 people, including Arabs, Britons and Jews. On January 4, 1948 the Irgun drove a truck filled with explosives into the center of Arab Jaffa, killing some 100 men, women and children.

The illegal Jewish Hagana militia was largely defensive until the end of World War II. They initially sought to curb the terrorism of the Irgun and Stern gang, but, by July of 1945, decided on a policy of terrorism. To try and force the British authority to allow more Jewish immigration, they began bombing bridges, rail lines and ships. Shortly before the departure of the British, the Hagana began its attacks on Arab cities, such as Acre and Jaffa.

The Irgun and the Stern gang (both Revisionist Zionist), on April 9, 1948, collaborated in massacring 254 Palestinian men, women and children at Deir Yassin. The purpose of such terrorism was to eliminate gentiles from Palestine by killing, by threats, or by forcible expulsion. Similar activity against civilians occurred at Lydda, Ramleh, Dawimyya, Sa'sa, Ein Zietun, Quibya, Kafa Kassem, etc. More than half of the terrorized

Palestinian population was forced to leave Palestine.

David Ben-Gurion, the first leader of Israel, detested the Revisionist Zionists and referred to Begin as a Hitler-like Nazi. Alberta Einstein likened Begin and his party to "a Fascist party for whom terrorism (against Jews, Arabs, and British alike) and misrepresentations are means and a 'fuehrer state' is the goal".

The terrorism that Jewish immigrants engaged in was to drive out the legal British administration and to eliminate gentiles. Since any irredentist claim would be based on events two thousand years in the past, a new ideology had to be fashioned. That ideology was Zionism, supplemented by religious teachings and anti-gentilism. Herzl had called for a "return to Judaism even before a return to the Land of Israel".

Cultural apartness has been characteristic of Jewish culture. For example, except among certain Reform groups, intermarriage with gentiles is viewed with abhorrence. As Christianity arose, the writings of the Talmud (Oral Torah) produced instructions likening gentiles to animals, authorized cheating and deceiving them, calling for their killing, etc. In the Torah itself, Deuteronomy 20 calls for the genocide of gentiles within Israel.

Around 1890, Theodor Herzl began actively seeking to obtain a homeland for the Jews. He had initially favored the idea of assimilation in the Christian community, but, after the Dreyfus case, decided that anti-Semitism made assimilation impossible. After the 1905 revolution in Russia failed, pogroms caused many Jews to immigrate to Palestine. They were there supported by a French philanthropist. In 1917, the British politician Balfour advocated a Jewish national home within a Palestinian state.

Zionist leaders continually acquired land and strove to prepare for an ethnically clean "Land of Israel". The Zionists operated in a well-organized way, in accordance with a long-term political plan and with extensive foreign funding. Their vision was essentially one of a secular, Jewish, socialist state.

The Nazi experience and the reluctance of many nations to accept large-scale Jewish immigration after World War II caused many Jews to see an independent homeland as a necessity. This was supported by a religious teaching that, outside of Israel, Jews were forever in exile (*Galut*). Today, the Likud government of Israel magnifies any incident, anywhere, in order to urge Jews to immigrate to Israel, "where they can be safe".

Immigrants did not move into vacant land. Some 800,000 Palestinians were driven out in the initial ethnic cleansing that accompanied the establishment of the state of Israel. The insistence is now on taking all of Biblical Israel (including the West Bank of the Jordan). Naturally, the present Palestinian inhabitants must be eliminated.

Within Israel, the prevailing ideology has changed from secular Zionism to a religious-based Messianism that embraces such ideas as redemption through the "New Zion", the universal "Kingdom of Israel", the "Third Jewish Commonwealth", and the "End of Days".

Kevin Avruch suggests that the major factors contributing to this new ideology were: (1) success in the 1967 War considered a messianic sign; (2) the ideological vacuum and "crisis of identity" created by the waning of secular labor Zionism; (3) the linking of the idea of maximum territory with a particular Jewish messianic idea. (In a crisis of identity, people are very receptive to a new ideology). Avruch sees the creation and special schooling of the middle-class, Talmud-oriented, "knitted skullcap" (*kipa srugah*) Orthodox schools as a key element in this transformation.

A messianic paramilitary settlement organization, the Gush Emunim, became active under the patronage of Likud government leaders. They decided to illegally occupy as much of Greater Israel as they could. Most of the violence engaged in by Gush-Emunim involved attacks of revenge and intimidation against Palestinians. The Camp David peace talks, however, involved the evacuation of the Sinai. Some members then decided that the peace accord was a sign of divine displeasure requiring atonement by faithful Jews.

One Gush Emunim devotee, Amir, assassinated Israel's Premier, Rabin, later explaining that he, Amir, was acting "on the orders of God". Of course, if one is responding to such a higher law, the judgments and laws of men are irrelevant.

Atonement was to be achieved by killing the guards and blowing up the Dome of the Rock Muslim mosque on Temple Mount. This was said to be pleasing to the God of Israel and leading to a religious revival within the Nation. They also planned to do it in time to wreck the peace accord before the Sinai could be evacuated.

Rabbis had approved all previous terrorist operations, but they would not approve this one. Lesser terrorist acts continued until April 27, 1984, when they planted explosives on five Arab busses. At that point, the principal Gush Emunim terrorists were arrested.

In his study of the Gush Emunim underground, Ehud Sprinzak found no sign of insanity or remorse. There was an extraordinary religious component. In selecting individuals for a terror mission, the community leader sought "pure people, highly observant and sinless, people with no shred of violence within them and who are disinclined to reckless action". Their religious purity would qualify them as God's emissaries. The *vigilante mentality* was evident. The vigilante feels that his action is wholly proper, but that, for some reason, the appropriate government agency cannot act.

David Rapoport says that the Semitic revealed religions have a messianic component that is normally latent but that may become imminent. He thinks that the Return to the Promised Land and/or the 1967 war success might have triggered the messianic reaction. He sees the Christian eschatology of the Second Coming as thought related to the return of the Jews and notes the Muslim tradition that the Mahdi will follow the return of Christ. Thus, events in Israel could have unleashed messianism in Christianity and Islam.

Terrorism could arise in a democracy, Rappoport suggests, because the factionalism of democracy encourages conflict, elections are described with the images of war, and the legacy of the French revolution is the promise of perfection. The search for perfection will imply the use of terrorism.

Recent political terrorism has featured suicide bombings. The use of suicide bombers to cause terror has been very cost-effective and the practice is likely to continue as long as the conditions that cause and facilitate it continue to exist. Those who have interviewed would be bombers are unanimous in saying that psychological pathology is not a factor.

Feelings of humiliation, of repression and of hopelessness do promote terrorism. A State Department study found that poverty was not related to terrorism but that perceived denial of civil liberties was related (Kruger & Malekova 2003). A canned ideology can offer a cognitive order, explaining what is wrong and how to fix it. A terrorist organization will supply the brotherhood and indoctrination necessary to make the commitment of the volunteer irrevocable.

To have enough volunteers and to succeed, a terrorist organization must have community support. United States governmental studies have shown a strong correlation between US involvement in international affairs and terrorist incidents. Policies aiming to repress may have the opposite effect. In 1999, Palestinian support for suicide bombing was 26%. By 2002, such support was at 70%.

19

SUMMING UP

Institutions develop and endure in meeting human needs. So it is with religion and with government. Inertia and force can perpetuate an institution even when it no longer well serves human needs. Nourishment and protection are fundamental requirements. An institution, to survive, must assure protection and nourishment. Beyond this, all is psychology and opinion, structured by ideology.

As the shaman molds the clay to make the image of a god, he gives symbolic form to the thoughts of the people. The basic wish is to feel whole and to feel secure in one's place in the universe. Society and aspects of the personality may be abstracted and projected as gods. The priest, the ruler, and the tradition define the framework of belief to which the individual must conform if he is to feel secure.

What of the human psyche to which such spiritual attention is directed? The human psyche is inconsistent and changeable. Collectively, humans unconsciously seek to alternate philosophies and styles of government. These changing fashions give vent to aspects of the psyche that were suppressed in the previous fashion.

The authoritarian or totalitarian personality has predominated throughout history. The studies of Lawrence Kohlberg indicate that more than eighty percent of people remain at the authoritarian, childhood, level of ethical development. Stanley Milgram's careful experiments at Yale showed that 93 per cent of normal people were willing to participate in the torture of a fellow human when ordered to do so by someone in authority. In both Nazi Germany and at Berkeley in California, 87 per cent of faculty members were willing to sign loyalty oaths. In Communist China, only 15 per cent were not fully conforming.

Early childhood circumstances can produce attitudes of self-hate, shame and doubt, lack of trust in others, and dependence- all of which tend to develop the authoritarian mind-set. Contrary values, such as autonomy and initiative, can also be formed very early in childhood. Such formation depends on the attitudes of the parents and upon the attitudes of the community. Thus, environment, rather than anything innate, could be responsible for the preponderance of the authoritarian personality. If more than eighty percent of people are essentially authoritarians, the perpetuation of liberalism and civil liberties must depend on a minority leadership group and the ideals it articulates for society.

The totalitarian personality seems only to be an extreme form of the authoritarian personality. The closed nature of the totalitarian system induces an excess that may approach psychosis. Totalitarian systems, seeking total control of man and society, seek to regress individuals to a childlike status prior to forming the "new man". As we have seen, certain religious orders and Communist thought reform programs seek to form the new man, whereas the general laity are conditioned to be obedient authoritarians who project their superego onto the priesthood.

Conditions of fear and alienation can also produce the disintegration of personality and the regression to infantile status that welcome totalitarianism. If the early training of the child conditions him to feelings of guilt and shame, then future manipulators will have a ready-made "handle" with which to control the adult. Some organizations and institutions do inculcate feelings of guilt and produce other attitudes that result in the authoritarian personality. Groups making violent demonstrations over "moral" issues are perhaps illustrating this guilt and its projection.

What of today's secular priests, the media? Media operate on children and on adults. It is in the early childhood stage, however, that the authoritarian mind-set is established. Before the age of six, a North American child will have watched television over 5,000 hours. Between the ages of six and eighteen, a child will spend 18,000 hours looking at television available to the general public. The effect of such television watching is probably to induce anxiety, a short attention span, unrealistic expectations, feelings of alienation, and a tendency to accept ready-made images, rather than to integrate facts and to form personal views.

In forming and expressing the values and hopes of the populace, TV has already become the popular religion. Politicians and evangelicals are moving into the medium in recognition of that fact. The structure of modern life dissolves families and classes, producing isolated, non-communicating urban couples. For such alienated and anxious people, television reception replaces interaction and defines reality, the norms and the culture. Thus, the religion and the culture become powerfully coincident in the tube. The feeling of alienation from self and from society is a key psychological factor setting up the individual's conversion to a true-believing, totalitarian fanatic. It is this that totalitarian leaders seek and it is this that television is unwittingly creating.

20

BIBLIOGRAPHY

Abernathy, G. L. (ed.). *The idea of equality; an anthology*. Richmond 1959

Abos, Alvaro *El Poder carnivoro* Legasa, Buenos Aires, 1986.

Adorno, Theodor (ed.) *The Authoritarian Personality* Harper & Row, 1950.

al-Turabi, Hassan "The Islamic Awakening's Second Wave" *New Perspectives Quarterly* 9:52 1992.

Almond, G.A. and Verba, S. *The Civic Culture* Princeton, 1963.

Almond, P.C. *Rudolf Otto, an introduction to his philosophical theology*. Chapel Hill,1984.

D'Aquili, Eugene G. "The Biopsychological Determinants of Culture" in *Current Topics in Anthropology* 1972.

D'Aquili, E., Newberg A. *The Mystical Mind: Probing the Biology of Religious Experience* Minneapolis, 1999.

Allen, V. L. and Levine, J. M. "Social support, dissent and conformity" *Sociometry* 31(2):138-149 1968.

Allport, G. W. et al. *Manual for Study of Values Boston, 1951*. Addison-Wesley Modular Publications #13.

Althusser, Louis *Essays on ideology* London, 1984.

Altemeyer, B. "Why Do Religious Fundamentalists Tend to be Prejudiced?" *Int J. Psychology of Religion* 13(1): 17-28 2003

Alves, Rubem A. *Protestantism and Repression* Maryknoll, N.Y. Orbis Books c1985.

Altemeyer, B. "Highly Dominating, Highly Authoritarian Personalities" *J. Social Psychology* 144(4): 421-447 2004. Altemeyer, Altemeyer, B., & Hunsberger, B. "Authoritarianism, religious fundamentalism, quest and prejudice". *Int J. Psychology of Religion* 2:113-133 1992.

Althusser, Louis *Essays on ideology* London, 1984.

Alves, Rubem A Protestantism and Repression Maryknoll, N.Y. Orbis Books c1985.

Arendt, Hanna, *Eichmann in Jerusalem: the Banality of Evil* Viking, N.Y. 1963.

Asad, T. *Formations of the Secular: Christianity, Islam modernity* Stanford 2003.

Avruch, Kevin "Gush Emunim: The 'Iceberg Model' of Extremism Reconsidered" *Middle East Review* 21(1):27-33 1988.

Badcock, C. R. *Psychoanalysis of Culture* Blackwell, Oxford, 1980.

Bateson, C., Raynor-Prince, L. "Religious orientation and complexity of thought about existential concerns". *JSSR* 22:38-50 1983.

Bateson, C., Schoenrade, P., Ventis, W. *Religion and the individual: A social-psychological perspective* NY 1993.

Bateson, Gregory, *Steps to an ecology of mind* University of Chicago, 2000.

Bauer, Wolfgang *China and the search for happiness : Recurring themes in four thousand years of Chinese cultural history* 1976

Ben-Yehuda, N. "European Witch Craze" 86 *Am. J. Sociology* 1.
Bellah, Robert *Tokugawa Religion*, Free Press, N.Y. 1957.

Ben-Dor G, Pedahzur A. "The Uniqueness of Islamic Fundamentalism and the Fourth Wave of International Terrorism" *Totalitarian Movements and Political Religions* 4(3):71-90 2003.

Ben-Yehuda, N. "European Witch Craze" 86 *Am. J. Sociology* 1.
Benedict, R. *The chrysanthemum and the sword : patterns of Japanese culture.* Boston, Mass., Houghton Mifflin, 1989.
Berelson, B. R., Steiner, GK. *Human Behavior: Inventory of Scientific Findings*, Harcourt Brace, N.Y. 1964.

Bergesen, A. J. "Witch-hunts & China" 17 *JSSR* 19, 1978.
Berry, TD "Personality Correlates of Religious Fundamentalism" dissertation, Wright Institute, Berkeley 1989

Berkman, Alexander Prison Memoirs of an Anarchist: Studies in the Libertarian and Utopian Tradition c. 1970.

Besnard, Philippe *L'anomie.:* (Durkheim, Merton, Srole) Paris, 1987.
Bettleheim, Bruno (1943) "Individual and Mass Behaviour in Extreme Situations" *J. Abnormal and Social Psychology* 38:417-452.

Birdsall, Peter Mind War: Book Censorship in English Canada Canlit, Victoria, 1978.

Bonin, G. and P. Bailey *The Neocortex of Macaca Mulatta* Urbana 1947.
Borkenau, P et al. "Genetic and environmental influences on observed personality." *J Pers Psychol* 80(4) :655-68 2001.

Bourricaud, Francois *Le retour de la droite* Paris, c. 1986. Bracher, Karl D. *The Age of Ideologies* N. Y. 1982.

Briggs, Robin *Witches and Neighbors: the Social and Cultural Content of European Witchcraft* Viking 1997.
Broen, Wm. E. "A factor-analytic study of Religious Attitudes" *J. Abnormal Psychol.* 54(2):176-179 1956.
Brook-Shepherd, Gordon *Prelude to Infamy: the Story of Chancellor Dollfuss* N.Y., 1962.
Brown, D.G.; Lowe, W.L. "Religious Beliefs & Personality Characteristics" 33 *J. Social Psychol.* 103, 1951.

Brook-Shepherd, Gordon, *Prelude to Infamy: The Story of Chancellor Dollfuss* N.Y., 1962.

Brown, L. B. "A Study of Religious Belief" 53 *Brit. J. Psychol.* 259, 1962.
Butler, C. Callahan, L.J. "Personality and Emotional Correlates of Right Wing Authoritarianism" *Social Behavior and Personality* 28(1): 1-14 2000.

Byrne, Richard W. "Evolution of Primate cognition". *Cognitive Science*; 24(3): 543 2000.
Callahan, L. J. ; Wauch, L. A. "Characteristics of a Minor Seminary Population" 13 *Natl. Cath. Guid. Co.* 30, 1969.

Campbell, Joseph, *The Hero with a Thousand Faces*. Princeton, 2004.
Cardno, A. G., Marshall, E. J., Coid, B., et al."Heritability estimates for psychotic disorders." *Arch. Gen. Psychiatry* 56:162– 168 1999.
Carlson, Helen B. "Relationship of the Acute Confusional State to Ego Development" 42 *J. Psychoanal* 517, 1961.
Cattell, Raymond B. *Handbook of Modern Personality Theory* N.Y. 1977.
Christensen, Carl W. "Religious Conversion" 9 *Ann. of Gen. Psych*., 1963.
Castro, Fidel *El processo revolucionario* 1973.
Cheung, F. M., & Leung, K. (1998). Indigenous personality measures: Chinese examples. *Journal of Cross-Cultural Psychology*, 29,: 233-248.
Civardi, Luigi, *The Catholic Action Manual* N.Y. Sheed & Ward, 1943.
Clark, D. A. et al. "Scalable architecture in mammalian brains" 2000 *Nature* 411:189-193.
Clark, S. *Thinking with demons : the idea of witchcraft in early modern Europe*. Oxford UP.1997.
Clark, S. *Languages of witchcraft : narrative, ideology, and meaning in early modern culture*. New York, 2001.
Cline, V. R.; Richards, JM. "Factor-Analysis. of Religious Belief & Behavior" 1 *J. Pers. & Soc. Psychol.* 569, 1965.
Cohen, Lizabeth, *A Consumer Republic* 2003.
Cohen, Sheldon, "The Ontogenesis of Prophetic Behavior" 49 *Psychoanal. & Psy. R.* 100, 1962.
Cohn, Norman, *The Pursuit of the Millenium* London, 1957.
Costa, P. T., Jr., and Widiger, T. A. (eds.) *Personality Disorders and the Five-Factor Model of Personality*, American Psychological Association, Washington, DC 1994.
Cox, R. H. F., *Pan-Africanism in practice.* N.Y. Oxford University Press, 1964.
Crassweller, R. D., *Peron & the Enigmas of Argentina* N.Y. Norton, 1987.
Crowson HM, Thoma SJ, Hestevold N, "Is Political conservatism Synonymous with Authoritarianism?" *J. Social Psychology* 145(5): 571-592 2005.
Davis, John D. *The Moral Obligations of Catholic Civil Judges* Catholic Univ. Press, Washington 1953.
Deutsch, A. "Tenacity of Attachment to a cult leader" *Am. J. Psychi* 137(12):68591 1980.
Diamond, Stanley, *In Search of the Primitive* New Brunswick, N.J. (1974)
Dorahy, MJ & Lewis, AL "Dissociation and Religiosity" *JSSR* 40(2): 315-322 2001.
Douglas, D. C., *The Norman achievement,* 1050-1100. UC Berkeley 1969.
Duijker, H. C. and Frijda, N. H. *National Character* Amsterdam 1960. Durant, Will, *The Story of Civilization* N.Y., 1935.
Durkheim, Emile, *Emile Durkheim on institutional analysis* Chicago, 1978.
Durkheim, E. Cosman, C. et al *The elementary forms of religious life* Oxford, N. Y. 2001.
Edwards, A. L. *Manual: Edwards Personal Preference Schedule* N.Y., 1954.

Emmons, RA & Paloutzian, RF., "The Psychology of Religion" *Ann Revue of Psychol* 54:379-402 2003.
Erdmann, C. *The origin of the idea of crusade*. Princeton 1977
Erickson, E. H. *Childhood and Society* New York, 1950.
Evans-Pritchard, E. *Theories of Primitive Religion* Westport, Greenwood Press 1985.
Faber, Heije, *Psychology of Religion* (1972) Phila. 1975.
Ferracuti, Franco, ''Psychological Aspects of Italian Left and Right Wing Terrorism" *Seventh World Congress of Psychiatry*, Vienna 1983.
Ferre, F. *Language, Logic, and God* London,
Festinger, Leon et al. *When Prophesy Fails* N.Y. 1956.
Festinger, Leon, *A theory of cognitive dissonance* Evanston, Ill., 1957.
Feuer, Lewis S. *Ideology and the Ideologists* Oxford, 1975.
Feuerbach, Ludwig, *The Essence of Christianity* (1841) London, 1854.
Fitz Gerald, Frances *Cities on a Hill* N.Y. c.1986
Fowler, J. W. *Stages of faith: the psychology of human development and the quest for meaning*. San Francisco, Harper & Row (1981).
Fowler, J. W., K. E. Nipkow, et al. *Stages of faith and religious development: implications for church, education, and society*. New York, Crossroad. (1991).
Freire, Paulo, *Pedagogy of Hope* N.Y. 1994
Frey, Northrup, *The Great Code: the Bible as Literature* Academic Press, 1982.
Friedman, Thomas L. "The Humiliation Factor" *New York Times* 5 Nov 2003.
Fromm, Eric, *Psychoanalysis & Religion* London, 1951.
Fromm, Eric, *Socialist Humanism: An International Symposium* N.Y., 1965.
Frossard, Andre, *Be Not Afraid* N.Y., 1984.
Frey, Northrup, *The Great Code: the Bible as Literature* Academic Press, 1982.
Gabbard, CE et al. "Assessing locus of control with religious populations" *J Res in Personality* 20:292-308 1986.
Gardiner, Harold C. *Catholic Viewpoint on Censorship* Hanover House N.Y., 1958.
Gentile, Emilio, "The Sacrilization of Politics" *Totalitarian Movements & Political Religions* 1(1):18-55 2000.
Geertz, Clifford *Islam Observed: Religious Development in Morocco and Indonesia* Yale, New Haven, 1968.
Geertz, Clifford, "Religion as a Cultural System" in *The Interpretation of Cultures* N.Y. Basic Books 1973.
Gilligan, J. *Preventing violence*. New York , 2001.
Gilligan, James, "Shame, Guilt and Violence" *Social Research* 70:1149 2003.
Gimello, R. "Mysticism and Meditation" in *Mysticism and Philosophical Analysis* ed. S. Katz OUP NY 1978.
Glock, Charles Y. *Beyond the classics?*. N.Y., 1973.
Golde, Peggy (c.1967) "Human Nature: The Anthropological Perspective"

Goodenough, W. H. (1963) *Cooperation in Change* New York. Gordon, L. V. *Manual for the Study of Interpersonal Values* Chicago, 1960.

Gorsuch, RL, "Psychology of Religion" *Ann Rev of Psychology* 39:201-221 1988.

Gosling, S. D. "From mice to men: What can we learn about personality from animal research?" *Psychol. Bull.* 127:45–86 2001

Greenough, Paul R. "Indulgence and abundance as Asian peasant values, a Bengali case in point" *J. Asian Studies* 42(4): 831-850.

Greven, Philip, *The Protestant temperament : patterns of child-rearing* Chicago, 1977.

Grosbard, O., *Israel on the couch : the psychology of the peace process.* Albany, New York. 2003

Guthrie, G. M., & Bennett, A. B., "Cultural differences in implicit personality theory" *International Journal of Psychology* 6:305-312 -(1971).

Haddad, S, "A Comparative Study of Lebanese and Palestinian perceptions of suicide bombings and the role of militant Islam and socio-economic status." *Int Journal of Comparative Sociology* 45: 337 2004

Habermass, Jurgen, *Philosophical Discourses on Modernity* Oxford 1987.

Hadden J. and Shupe, A. *Televangelism: Power and Politics on God's Frontier* c. 1987 http://extext.libe.virginia.edu

Halliday, W. R. The Pagan Background of Early Christianity London, 1925.

Hall, John A. (ed.) *The State of the Nation: Ernest Gellner and the Theory of Nationalism* NY, Oxford UP, 1998.

Halperin, David A. (Ed) *Psychodynamic Perspectives on Religion, Sect & Cult* 1983.

Harrington, Evan R. "Social Psychology of Hatred" paper Conference to Establish the Field of Hate Studies, Spokane March 20, 2004.

Hamilton, R. F. *Who Voted for Hitler?* Princeton 1983.

Harrison, Jane Ellen, Prolegomena to the Study of the Greek Religion (1921) N.Y., 1957.

Harris, J. R. "Socialization, personality development, and the child's environments: Comment on Vandell" *Dev. Psychol.* 36:711–723 2000.

Hassan, R. *Faithlines: Muslim conceptions of Islam and society.* Karachi, Oxford University Press 2002.

Herberg, Will, *Protestant, Catholic, Jew* N.Y., 1960.

Heimpert, Allan, *Religion and the American Mind* 1720-1830 Harvard, 1966.

Heinan, John C. Fr., *Priest and Penitent.* Sheed and Ward, 1938.

Hill, P. & Hood, R, *Measures of Religiosity.* Birmingham, Alabama, 1999.

Herberg, Will, *Protestant, Catholic, Jew.* N.Y., 1960.

Hertel, BR & Donahue, MJ "Parental Influences on God Images Among Children: Testing Durkheim's Metaphoric Parallelism" *JSSR* 34(2):186-199 1995.

Hoffer, Eric, *The Ordeal of Change* Harper & Row, 1963. Hoffer, Eric, *The Temper of Our Time* Harper & Row N.Y., 1964. Hoffman, Bruno, *Inside Terrorism* 1999. Hsu, Francis L. (ed.) *Psychological Anthropology* Homewood,

Ill.1961 Hudziak, J. J. et al. "Genetic and environmental contributions to the Child Behavior Checklist Obsessive-Compulsive Scale: a cross-cultural twin study" *Arch Gen Psychiatry* 61(8): 608-16 2004.

Huizinga, J. *The Waning of the Middle Ages* London, 1948.

Hunsberger B, Pratt M, Pancer S.M. "Religious Fundamentalism and Integrative Complexity of Thought: A Relationship for Existential Content Only?" *JSSR* 33(4):335-346 1994.

Irwing P and Lynn R, "Sex differences in means and variability on the progressive matrices in university students: a meta-analysis" *British journal of psychology* 96(Pt 4):505-24 2005.

Kahn, N., "Profiling the Politically Violent in Pakistan" *Peace and Conflict* 9(3):277-295

Inglehart, R. *Islam, gender, culture, and democracy : findings from the World Values Survey and the European Values Survey.* Willowdale, ON, De Sitter Publications. 2003.

Kampen D and Sherwin B., "Estradiol is related to visual memory in healthy young men" *Behavioral neuroscience* 110(3):613-7 1996.

Kirkpatrick L, Hood R, Hartz G, "Fundamentalist Religion conceptualized in terms of Rokeach's theory of the open and closed mind" *Research in the Social Scientific Study of Religion* 3:157-179.

Inglehart, Ronald, "The Worldview of Islamic Publics in Perspective" in Mansoor, M (ed.) *Worldview of Islamic Publics in Global Perspective,* Palgrave, New York, 2005.

Inglehart, Ronald, "How Solid is Mass Support for Democracy and How Can We Measure It" *Political Science and Politics* Jan:51-57 2003).

Inkeles, Alex, *Social change in Soviet Russia* Cambridge, Harvard University Press. 1968.

Inkeles, Alex, *National Character* 1997.

Jaffrelot, C., *The Hindu nationalist movement in India.* New York, Columbia University Press. 1996 .

James, William, *The Varieties of Religious Experience* 1902.

Jantzen, G., *Becoming divine: Towards a feminist philosophy of religion* Bloomington, 1999.

Jaspers, Karl, *The Great Philosophers* (ed. Hanna Arendt) London 1966.

Juergensmeyer, Mark, *Terror in the Mind of God: the Global Rise of Religious Violence* 2000.

Kay, AW., *Moral Development* N.Y., 1969.

Kepel, G. (2002). *Jihad: The trail political Islam. Cambridge, Mass.*, Harvard,

Kepal, Gilles *Christianity and Judaism in the Modern World* University of Pennsylvania, 1995.

Kernberg, Otto F. *Borderline Conditions and Pathological Narcissism* Aronson Northvale 2002.

Kinzer, Stephen *Overthrow: America's Century of Regime Change from*

Hawaii to Iraq Times Books, 2006.

Kirkpatrick, L. A.''Toward an evolutionary psychology of religion and personality" *J. Personal.* 67:921–952 1999.

Kohlberg, L. *The psychology of moral development: the nature and validity of moral stages.* San Francisco, Harper & Row 1984.

Kohlberg, L. *Child psychology and childhood education : A cognitive-developmental view.* New York, Longman. (1987).

Kilbourne, Broc, "Religious Cults" 22 *JSSR* 19, 1978.

King, M. B., & Hunt, R.A. (1975). Measuring the religious variable: national replication. *Journal for the Scientific Study of Religion,* 14, 13-22.

King, M. B., Dein, S. (1998). "The spiritual variable in psychiatric research'' *Psychological Medicine*, 28, 1259-1262.

Kirkpatrick, L. A. "God as a substitute attachment figure: a longitudinal study of adult attachment style and religious change in college students" *Pers. Soc. Psychol. Bull.* 24:961-73.

Kline, P. & Cooper, C. "A factor analysis of the authoritarian personality" *Brit J. Psychol* 75:171-176 1984.

Kluckhohn, C., "Universal categories of culture" *Anthropology Today* A. L. Kroeber (ed.) Chicago 1953.

Kluckholm F. R. & Strodtbeck, F. L., *Variations in Value Orientations* Evanston, Ill., 1961.

Knudsen, E. "Sensitive periods in the development of the brain and behavior" *J Cogn Neurosci* 16(8):1412-25 2004.

Kohlberg, Lawrence, *The Philosophy of Moral Development* N.Y., 1981. Kohn, Hans, *The Mind of Germany*. Scribner's, N.Y., 1960.

Kosofsky, E. S. and F. Adam, *Shame in the cybernetic fold: reading Silvan Tomkins*, University of Chicago Press, 1995.

Krueger, A. B. M., Jitka "Seeking the Roots of Terrorism." *Chronicle of Higher Education* 2003.

Krubitzer, L. & Huffman, K. J. "A realization of the neocortex in mammals" *Brain, Behavior and Evolution* 55:322-335 2000.

Kubizek, August, *Young Hitler* Wingate, 1954.

Kunze, Michael *Highroad to the stake*. Chicago, 1987.

Lamberth, D. C. *William James and the metaphysics of experience* N.Y. Cambridge University Press 1999.

Langer, Walter C. *The Mind of Adolf Hitler* New York, 1973.

Larsen, S. U. et al. (eds.) *Who Were the Fascists: Social Roots of European Fascism.* Columbia, 1983.

LeBon, Gustave, *The Crowd* (1910) N.Y., 1960.

Leighton, Alexander H. and Opler, M. E. *Am. J. of Psychoanalysis* 6:20-27 1946.

Lester, D et al "Suicide Bombers.." *Studies in Conflict and Terrorism* 27:283295 2004

Lewis, Bernard, "Islamic Revolution" and "Islamic Revolution: an Exchange" *NYRB* 1988.

Libeman, CS, "Extremism as a Religious Norm" 22 *JSSR* 75, 1978.

Lifton, R. J., *Thought Reform and the Psychology of Totalism* London, 1961.

Loehlin, J. C., *Genes and Environment in Personality Development* 1992

Lofland, John, *Doomsday Cult* N.Y., 1977.

Lofland, J. & Stark, R. "Becoming a World Saver" 30 *Am.Soc.Rev.* 862, 1965.

Lukacs, Georg *History and Class Consciousness* Cambridge, Mass., 1971.

Mabubani, Kishore, "Asia and a United States in Decline" *Washington Quarterly* 7:5-23 1994.

MacGaffey, Wyatt, "African Ideology and Belief " *African-Stud. Rev.* 24(3): 226274 1981.

Maguire, E. A. "Navigation related structural changes in the hippocampi of taxi drivers" 2000 *PNAS-USA* 97:4398- 4403.

Mannheim, Karl *Ideology and Utopia* London, 1936, 1991.

March, AF "State ideology and the legitimization of authoritarianism: the case of post-Soviet Uzbekistan" *J of Political Ideologies* 8(2):209-232 2003.

Matthews, R., *English Messiahs*, London, 1936.

Maranell, GM, "Dimensions of Religious Attitude" *J. of Soc. & Soc. Res.* 52:430 1968.

McCloskey, Herbert "Conservatism and Personality" *Am. Pol. Sci. Rev.* 52:2745 1953.

McCrae, R. R., & Allik, J. (Eds.). *The Five-Factor Model across cultures.* New York: Kluwer Academic/Plenum 2002.

McKendrick, Neil et al., *The Birth of the Consumer Society* 1982.

McWilliams, Carey, *Witch Hunt: The Revival of Heresy* Boston, 1950.

Mealey, L. "The sociobiology of sociopathy: An integrated evolutionary model". *Behav. Brain Sci.* 18:523–599 1995.

Meisenberg, Gerhard "IQ Population Genetics- It's Not as Simple as You Think" *Mankind Quarterly* 44(2):185-210 2003.

Mellersh, C. S., Hitte, C., Richman, M., et al. "An integrated linkage-radiation hybrid map of the canine genome". *Mammal.Genome* 11:120–130 2000.

Maranell, GM Responses to Religion U Kansas Press 1974.

Meloy, JR "..Violent True Believer" *J. Personality Assessment* 82(2):138-146 2004.

Mehran, Golnar, "Socialization of Schoolchildren.." *Iranian Studies* 12(1):37 1989.

Milgram, Stanley, *Obedience to Authority* Harper & Row, 1974.

Monaghan, RR. "Motivations for Attending a Fundamentalist Church" *J. Scientific Study of Religion*. 6:236- 1968.

Moore, CA., *The Chinese Mind* Honolulu, 1967.

Monaghan, RR., "Three Faces of the True Believer" 7 *J.Sci.Stud.Rel.* 241- 1968.

Mosse, George L. *The Nationalization of the Masses*, New York, 1975.

Murdock, GP. "The Common Denominator of Culture" in R. Linton (ed.) *The Science of Man in World Crisis*. 1945

Nhu-Ngoc T. Ong. And Dalton, Russell J. "Authority Orientations and Democratic Attitudes in East Asia: A Test of the Asian Values"

''Hypothesis.'' *Japanese Journal of Political Science.* June 2005.

Nilsson, M. P. *A history of Greek religion.* 1980.

Nigg, J. T., and Goldsmith, H. H. "Developmental psychopathology, personality, and temperament: Reflections on recent behavioral genetics research." *Hum. Biol.* 70:387– 412 1998.

Nisbett, R. & Ross, L. *Human Inference* Prentice-Hall, 1980.

Nishitani, K. *Religion and nothingness* Berkeley 1982.

Novak, Michael, *Will It Liberate* Paulist, N.Y. 1986.

Nakamaura, H. *Ways of Thinking of Eastern Peoples.* 1968.

Oakeshott, M., *Rationalism in Politics* 1991.

Ohnuki-Tierney, Emiko., *Kamikaze Diaries: Reflections of Japanese Student Soldiers* University of Chicago Press 2006.

Ortega y Gasset, J. *Obras Completas* Madrid, 1964.

Pals, D., *Seven theories of religion* N.Y. Oxford 1996.

Pancer S, Jackson L., Hunsberger B, Pratt M.W. "Religious orthodoxy and the complexity of thought about religious and non-religious issues." *Journal of Personality* 1995

Paxton, Robert O., *The Anatomy of Fascism*, 2004.

Peabody, Dean *National Characteristics* Cambridge, 1985.

Peyrefitte, Alain *The Chinese* N.Y., 1977.

Piedmont, R & Leach, M. "Cross Cultural generalizability of the spiritual transcendence scale in India: spirituality as a universal aspect of human experience" *American. Behaioral. Scentist.* 45(12):1888-2001 2002.

Pfferbaum, A. et al. "Morphological changes in brain structures are differentially affected by time-linked environmental influences despite strong genetic stability" *Neurobiology of Aging* 25:175-183 2004.

Plack, Arno, *Hitlers langer Schatten* Munchen, 1993.

Posthuma, D. et al. "Genetic Correlations between Brain Volumes and the WAISIII Dimensions of Verbal Comprehension, Working Memory, Perceptual Organization, and Processing Speed" *Twin Research* 6(2): 131-139 2003.

Reader S and Laland K "Social intelligence, innovation, and enhanced brain size in primates" *PNAS* 99(7):4436-41 2002.

Redfield, Robert, *Papers* Chicago, 1962-1963.

Plomin, R. & DeFries, J. C. "Genetics and Intelligence: Recent Data" *Intelligence* 4:15-24. (1980)

Poling, T., & Kenny, J. *The Hare Krishna character type: A study in sensate personality* Lewiston, NY 1986.

Portmes, T. & Spears, R. "Deindividuation and antinormative behavior: a metaanalysis" *Psychological Bulletin* 123:238-59 (1998).

Post, Sprinzak & Denny "The Terrorists in their Own Words" *Terrorism and Political Violence* 15(1):171-184 2003.

Poythress, N. G. "Literal, Antiliteral and Mythological Religious Orientations" *Journal for the Scientific Study of Religion* 14(3):271-284 1975.

Quinn P, Westerlund, and Nelson C. "Neural markers of categorization in 6 month-old infants" *Psychological Science* 17(1):59-66 2006.

Reischauer, E. O. *The United States and Japan.* Cambridge, Harvard University Press. (1965).

Proudfoot, W. *William James and a science of religions* New York, Columbia University Press 2004.

Reed, Phillip *Active Faith: How Christians are Changing the Soul of American Politics* Free Press 1996.

Reisman, D. *The Lonely Crowd* New Haven, 1964.

Renan, Ernst *History of the People of Israel* London, 1896.

Rhee, S.H. "Genetic and environmental influcnces on anti-social behavior" *Psychol Bull* 128(3):490-529 2002.

Richardson, J.T. "Clinical and Personality Assessments of Participants in New Religions" *Int. J. for the Psychology of Religion* 5(3):145-170 199.

Riemann, R. et al. "Personality and attitudes towards current political topics" *Personality and Individual Differences* 15:313-321 1993.

Rokeach, Milton *The Open and Closed* Mind N.Y., 1960.

Rokeach, Milton *Nature of Human Values* NY, 1973.

Roper, L. *Oedipus and the Devil : witchcraft, sexuality, and religion in early modern Europe*. NY 1994.

Rose, R. J. ''Genetic and environmental variance in content dimensions of the MMPI" *J. Pers Soc Psychol* 55(2): 302-311 1988.

Rougement, Denis de *Vivre en amerique* Paris, 1947.

Rushton, J. P. "Race, IQ, and the APA report on *The Bell Curve*" *The American Psychologist* 52(1):69-81 1997.

Rubenstein, R. E. *Alchemists of revolution : Terrorism in the modern world.* New York, Basic Books 1987.

Runciman, S. *A history of the Crusades*. Cambridge [Engg.], University Press. (1951).

Rushton, J. P. et al. "Altruism and genetics" *Acta Genet Med Gemballol (Roma)* 33(2): 265-71 1984.

Ryan, John A. & Boland, Francis J. *Catholic Principles of Politics* MacMillan, 1950.

Sageman, Marc, *Understanding Terror Networks* U Penna 2005.

Saler, B. *Conceptualizing religion: Immanent anthropologists, transcendent natives and unbounded categories* N. Y. 1993.

Santayana, George, *The Interpretation of Poetry and Religion* Scribner's, 1900.

Sebreli, Juan Jose *Los deseos imaginarios del peronismo* Legasa 1985.

Shaban, Fuad "Millenialist Discourses.." *Arab Studies Quarterly* 25(1-2):13-2003

Shatz, Adam "Hezbollah" *New York Review of Books* March 31, 2004.

Sherwin B. "Hormones, mood, and cognitive functioning in postmenopausal women" *Obstetrics and gynecology* 87(2 Suppl):20S-26S 1996.

Shuttleworth, F.K. ''The nature versus nurture problem. Part II." *Journal of Educational Psychology*, Vol. 26, pp. 655-681 1935.

Shostrum, E. *Manual for Personal Orientation Inventory* San Diego, 1963.

Skinner, B. F. *Beyond freedom and dignity Indianapolis*, Hackett Publishing,

2002.
Smith, Hedrick *The Russians* New York, 1981.
Sorel, Georges *The Illusion of Progress* Paris, 1908.
Spengler, Oswald *The Decline of the West* (1918) London, 1922.
Stellmacher and Petzel "Authoritarianism as a Group Phenomenon" Political Psychology 26(2): 1 2005.
Sprinzak, Ehud "Fundamentalism, Terrorism, and Democracy: The Case of the Gush Emunim Underground" Wilson Center, Smithsonian, Washington Sept. 16, 1986.
Stern, J. *In the Name of God* Harper/Collins 2003.
Stewart, RA & Webster, AC. "Theological Conservatism and Personality Correlates" *Perceptual and Motor Skills* 30:867-879~~.~~ 1970.
Sprenger, J. and Kramer, H. *Malleus maleficarum* (1495) London, Folio Society~~,~~ 1968.
Strozier, C. B. Apocalypse: On the Psychology of Religious Fundamentalism in America Beacon 1996.
Swanson, G. E. *Birth of the Gods* Ann Arbor, 1964.
Srole, L., Langner, T., Michael, S.T., Opler, M.K., & Rennie, T. *Mental Health in the Metropolis: Midtown Manhattan Study (Vol. 1)*, NY: McGraw-Hill 1962.
Stillman, E. O. and W. Pfaff *The politics of hysteria : The sources of twentieth-century conflict.* Greenwood Press (1981).
Szasz, Thomas S. *The Manufacture of Madness: Inquisition and Mental Health Movement* Harper & Row, 1970.
Szulc, Ted *Fidel: A Critical Portrait* N.Y.: Morrow 1987.
Tawney, R., Equality. London, 1994.
Tang, Y.-A., Shimizu, E., Dube, G. et al.. "Genetic enhancement of learning and memory in mice". *Nature* 401:63–69 1999
Thompson, P. M, et al. "Genetic influences on brain structure"*Nature Neuroscience* 4(12): 1-6 2001.
Timmerman, Jacobo, *Prisoner Without a Name, Cell Without a Number* Knopf, New York 1981.
Tomkins, Silvan, *Critical Inquiry* 21(2):496 1995.
Tyerman, C. *God's War : A new history of the Crusades*. HUP Cambridge 2006
Tooly, J. and Cosmides, L. "The Psychological Foundations of Culture" in Barkow, J. (ed.) *The Adapted Mind: Evolutionary Psychology and the Generation of Culture* Oxford 1992.
Troldahl V. & Powell, F. "A short-form dogmatism scale for use in field studies". *Social Forces* 44:211-214 1965.
Vilas, Carlos M. *Perfiles de la revolucion* ~~*Sandanista*~~ Legasa, Buenos Aires, 1984.
Wakefield, W. L. and A.P. Evans *Heresies of the high middle ages*. Cambridge University Press New York 1991.
Wallace, A. F. (1961) "The Psychic Unity of Human Groups" in *Studying Personality Cross Culturally* B. Kaplan (ed.) New York.
Walzer, Michael *The Revolution of the Saints: A Study of the Origins of Radical Politics* Harvard, 1965.

Warner, Marina *Alone of All Her Sex* Knopf, 1976.

Weber, Max, *The Sociology of religion* Boston, 1993.

Weber, Max, *The Protestant ethic and the spirit of capitalism* Roxbury Pub., Los Angeles, c2002.

Weiss, & Comprey, A. "Personality characteristics Hare Krishna" *J. Personality Assessment* 51:399-413 1987.

Weissbrod, *Lilly "From Labor Zionism"* Theory and Society 10:777-803 1981.

White, Theodore H. *In Search of History* Harper, 1978.

Whiting, B.B. and Whiting, J.W.M. *Children of Six Cultures: A psycho-cultural analysis* Harvard 1975

Wilke, M, et al. "Bright spots: Correlations of gray matter volume with IQ in a normal pediatric population" *Neuro Image* 20: 202-215 2003.

Wilson, D. S. *Darwin's Cathedral: Evolution, Religion and the Nature of Society* Chicago 2002.

Wilson, Edward O. *On human nature* Cambridge, Mass., Harvard University Press, c2004.

Wilson, Glen D. *The Psychology of Conservatism* N.Y., 1973.

Withington, A. F., *Towards a More Perfect Union: Virtue and the Foundation of the American Republic* Oxford 1991.

Yinger, J. Milton, *Sociology Looks at Religion* Macmillan N.Y. 1966.

Yinger, J. Milton, *Scientific Study of Religion* MacMillan, 1970.

Zaman. Q. *The ulama in contemporary Islam: custodians of change.* Princeton, NJ, Princeton University Press 2002.

Zinnbauer, B & Pargament, K. "Spiritual conversion: A study of religious change among college students" *JSSR* 37:161-80.

INDEX